TRAIN THE WOLF IN YOUR DOG

Genetic Clues to Solving Behavior Problems

by Diane Morgan

DORAL
PUBLISHING, INC.

An Imprint of BowTie Press®
A Division of BowTie, Inc.

Published by Doral Publishing, Phoenix, Arizona
An Imprint of BowTie Press®
A Division of BowTie, Inc.
3 Burroughs
Irvine, CA 92618
Printed in the United States of America.

Edited by MaryEllen Smith
Interior Design by The Printed Page

Library of Congress Card Number: 2004101444
ISBN: 0-9745407-2-2

10 9 8 7 6 5 4 3 2 1

To Laura Hussey,
whose wisdom is matched only by her compassion.

Contents

Introduction:
The Shapeshifter Makes Himself Known

"All knowledge,
the totality of all questions and all answers,
is contained in the dog."
—Franz Kafka

You think you know me. After all, we've been together for 100,000 years, more or less. I've guarded your sheep, driven your cattle, found your supper, protected your children, led your blind, comforted your sick, fought your wars, and provided you with entertainment and companionship. I am your best friend—at least sometimes. You think you know me. But do you? Do you even know my name?

I am *Canis lupus familiaris*—the familiar wolf. My old name, *Canis familiaris*, did not perfectly reflect my wolf identity and heritage, so it was changed in 1993. This new designation marks an ancient fact: the wolf (*Canis lupus*) and I, taxonomically and genetically speaking, are pretty much one and the same. The mitochondrial DNA (mtDNA—more on that later) differences between the wolf and me are fewer than those among many human ethnic groups—say, Finns and Swedes or Poles and Albanians. Dogs and wolves can crossbreed and produce fertile young, and that makes us one species.

When you take me into your home, you are harboring a wolf. Remember that.

Having said that, however, I must acknowledge another truth. I am much more than a wolf; I am a dog. You may consider a dog an advanced wolf, an example of some horrible degeneration, or something in between; I don't care. What's important is that in many critical areas, I am really not as wolf-like as I may have given you reason to believe in the last paragraph. Apparently, I have contradicted myself. That's fine. I shall do so again and again. I am, above all, a paradox.

I have made a morphological leap unmatched by any other species—from wolf to Chihuahua to Newfoundland to Poodle to Beagle to Afghan to Pekinese to Puli to Collie to Basset Hound. I can weigh 2 pounds or 200. I can fly like a Greyhound or toddle like a **Bulldog**. (The technical name for this peculiar state of affairs is pleomorphism; I call it shapeshifting. I myself am the Shapeshifter).

My complexity is not limited to my looks; it extends to how I behave. I can be Snoopy and I can be Cujo. I can save your life or I can kill you; I've done both. None of this is my responsibility, however. You made me what I am to suit your needs or whims. This doesn't bother me either. If you let dogs breed randomly for two generations, the Pekinese and Great Dane will disappear. Five or six more generations free of human meddling will result in and all of us dogs looking pretty much alike: mid-sized feral scavengers with upright ears and coat lengths to suit the climate. Take away our scavenging opportunities and most of us will die; those who don't will revert to something very close to wolf-type (it's been there all along). Then your former best friend will become your newest nightmare. It should shock you to realize that after thousands of companionable, domestic generations—generations that have seen the blossoming of so many human-imposed dog-shapes—my mind is still my own and my bloodlines are essentially those of the wolf. I can go home again. Eventually.

Don't be afraid. As much as I resemble a wolf, I am like you as well. I am not a wild animal—not now, anyway. Despite my heritage, I am the most thoroughly domesticated creature in the world. I depend on you for my physical and spiritual well-being. (A Shih Tzu-Pekinese mix recently managed to survive for 5 weeks in the wilds of Canada, but I have no idea how. It's out of the ordinary, believe me.)

> While the wolf is indeed the mother lode of all dog breeds, the same analogy cannot be made for domestic cats. While there are no completely wild house cats, neither are there any completely tame ones. And they all look pretty much alike, despite the desperate and misguided efforts of some to alter an already perfect (but highly annoying) animal.

I don't share your DNA (at least not all of it), but I share your life. Dogs and people even get some of the same diseases—arthritis, obesity, diabetes, epilepsy, glaucoma, cancer, and psychiatric problems—most of which are the result of old age and the settled life. (In the case of obesity and diabetes, it appears we are both victims of the "thrifty gene" which compels our bodies to store fat during lean times. Of course, there haven't been any lean times for those of us in developed countries, so we're penalized for our gene-driven passion to eat.) We can and do infect each other with a plethora of zoonotic ailments. I have my share of obsessive-compulsive disorders, just as you do. I have my moods and I am sensitive to yours. I get depressed, angry, jealous, scared, bored, and frustrated. I love devotedly. I'm sad when you're sick. I will bite your enemies.

I have adapted myself to your world and your life. Some of my kind will herd sheep or chase rabbits all day long, others will guard your house or pull a sled across the frozen tundra, and yet others are content to just lie by your fire on a long winter's night and snooze next to the bag of Doritos. This is what being a wolf—or a dog—means, after all.

You and I are an unlikely couple, are we not? At one time or another, you have been all things to me—my enemy, my competitor, my victim, my master, my best friend. It's a complex relationship. Together we've hunted, scavenged, and scrounged our way across the face of the earth. We have found each other when one of us lost his way (although we've gotten lost together more often). We have come to rely on each other, at least for companionship. I must admit, though, that both of us have occasionally reneged on the implicit contract we have made; our strange partnership has produced its fair share of difficulties. You've neglected, abused, and hurt me. For my part, I've wrecked your house, killed your cat, and bitten your kids.

None of this is really necessary, of course. It never has been, even though the kids and the cat had it coming. Perhaps it's time we came to an understanding. And perhaps it will help if I tell you a little of my history—which is your history, too.

I was once one sort of animal and ended up as quite another. Much the same sort of thing happened to you, whether you want to admit it or not. (Think "ape.") In order to understand what I am now, we must return to the beginning. Let's hark back to the time when I was a wolf, pure and unadulterated. Let me assume my wolf persona (I don't get a chance to do this every day, so cut me some slack).

I live on every continent (except the one with the penguins, whatever that is) and in almost every habitat—mountains, tundra, plains, and valleys. I am almost as comfortable wading across rivers as I am galloping across dry land. I can cope with any climate and compete with any predator. Because I learned the immensely useful skill of cooperation, I am a fearsome and effective killer. When I can't kill, I scavenge; when I can't scavenge, I'll eat berries. I will do whatever I need to do to survive. If that means that I must make friends with my sworn enemy, I will do it. I have done it. You are living proof.

And that's how we came together. You didn't tame me, you know. You didn't "domesticate" me. No, it was I who watched you, tracked you, followed you, and evaluated your potential as a provider—and perhaps something more. I saw how you struck fire from rock and made heat from wood. I saw how careless you were with the food you left around your campsite.

I must tell you, however, the smell of you sickened some of my brethren who slunk away, preferring the cold and dark and freedom to a fat life with you. I made a different bargain, one never made before or since in the history of the world—a bargain between two species. I gave myself heart and soul into your hands—a fearful risk. Even now, I wonder how I found the courage to do it. It has left me, in some sense, a very lonely creature. I stand between two worlds—yours and theirs. If I were to meet a wolf now, he would kill me. Or I would kill him. We are no longer at home together.

Nor am I completely at home with you—not yet. Even after thousands upon thousands of years, I can still feel the wolf stir uneasily within me. It is I, not you, who am the true werewolf, that compelling but unsatisfied creature who shifts shape and psyche and who is, simultaneously, all too human and all too much a wolf.

I inhabit a twilight land, a place of fluid boundaries. I long for the wild yet yearn for the fireside. So do you, my friend. And that's ultimately what draws us together in spite of ourselves—the passion for liberty and the longing for home. We travel together. We are perhaps still lonely, but I must confess, a little less so now that we have each other, the night, and the fireplace.

Chapter 1

The Beginning: The Wolf

"Animals are not brethren,
they are not underlings;
they are other nations,
caught with ourselves in the net of life and time."
—Henry Beston

Everything that you see in your pet dog has its origins in the wild blood of the wolf. More than any other extant creature, the wolf is a true treasure-trove of genetic variation—and the dog is his heir. At one time, people thought that perhaps several species of canids (carnivorous mammals of the family *Canidae*) engendered the dog; however, it is now almost universally acknowledged that the sole progenitor of the domestic dog is the gray wolf—one among several species of extant wolves.[1] In fact, biologists are still arguing about how many subspecies of wolves currently exist, or even what attributes constitute a subspecies. Morphologically and neurologically, the wolf can produce incredibly diverse descendants—jackals, coyotes, dogs, and even foxes are all descended from the wolf. The whole matter is complicated by the fact that over the thousands of years during which dogs were developed, there have been repeated crossings back to the wolf.

The Ancestry of Dogs

Ancient as the wolf is, he has ancestors, as do we all. One of the first recognizable canid forebears is Miacis, a small tree-dwelling mammal that flourished 54 to 38 million years ago.[2] Bears, raccoons, weasels, hyenas, civets, and cats are also (more distant) descendents of Miacis, who was quite a prolific fellow! For the nomenclaturally-minded reader, our friends the wolf and dog belong to the *Canidae* family. The bears are *Urdiae*, cats *Felidae*, weasels *Mustelidae*, raccoons *Procyonidae*, civets *Viverridae*, and hyenas *Hyaenidae*. Before I started working on this book, I thought that hyenas were a branch of the wolf/dog family. Just goes to show you.

From Miacis arose Hesperocyon, the "Western Dog" (38 to 26 million years ago), whose remains have been discovered in the upper-plains states. In fact, evidence suggests that the dog's ancestors evolved in this hemisphere and then migrated to Asia, just the ancestors of the horse did. (No one knows what drove the migration eastward.) The next forebear, Leptocyon, appeared about 23 million years ago, and this animal is considered the most recent common ancestor of all the canids. (Some paleontologists, however, consider the 19-million-year-old Tomarctus a better candidate for this honor.)

These progenitors gave rise not only to the wolf, but also to the jackal, fox, and coyote. Jackals live exclusively in the Old World and coyotes in the New, but they occupy nearly identical ecological niches.

Wolf Species and Subspecies

You would think it a relatively simple task to count up the species of wolves, past and present; alas, it is not. Wolves, inconveniently (for these purposes, anyway), move around, crossbreed with other wolves (as well as on occasion coyotes or even dogs), become extinct, reappear and disappear with little notice, and so on. The number of wolf varieties (and their relatives) that exists depends on who's counting and by what criteria.

For example, using the taxonomy of Juliet Clutton-Brock, as well as the more recent formulations of Ginsberg and Macdonald, most authorities recognize approximately 38 species within the family Canidiae.[3] Besides the gray wolf, other species of lupines include the red wolf (*C. rufus*), which is now found to be a hybrid between a gray wolf and a coyote; Ethiopian wolf (*C. simensis*); maned wolf (*Chrysocyon brachyusus*); and others.[4] Wolves still roam the earth in varying numbers in Russia, Canada, the United States, Scandinavia, Iraq, Iran, China, and India; they even inhabit such unlikely places as Greece, Egypt, Israel, Lebanon, Jordan, and Syria. However, most wolf populations are so isolated from each other that an inevitable reduction in the gene pool may soon render them all extinct. This is because if no crossbreeding is allowed to occur, a natural reduction in the number of animals extant will, in turn, reduce the size of the gene pool. A smaller gene pool results in a greater chance of a "bad gene" taking over and ultimately weakening the population.

Formerly, many common classifications listed as many as 32 subspecies (varieties) of the gray wolf alone—24 in North America and 8 in Eurasia.[5] Sometimes these varieties are termed "races." (A "race" or "variety" is a natural variation within a species; a "breed" is an artificial development arranged by human beings.) Races are geographically dependent, and there is no vast difference between them. Keeping track of subspecies is also made more difficult by the fact that interbreeding may occur whenever different subspecies meet.

The number of varieties detailed is dependent on the taxonomist. Because some scientists are "splitters," who recognize many subspecies, and others are "lumpers," who prefer to group varieties together and recognize fewer subspecies, lists differ. Many wolf researchers, using DNA evidence, now maintain that that there are only 5 subspecies of wolves in North America, all of which originally hail from Asia. Here is that list, which includes current conservation status[6]:

▼ *C. lupus lycaon* (Eastern Timber Wolf): This group includes the gray-coated southeastern Canadian and northeastern U.S. subspecies, including all such species except *C. lupus lycaon* (of Minnesota), which is now often grouped with the *C. lupus nubilus* subspecies. Endangered.

▼ *C. lupus occidentalis* (Mackenzie Valley Wolf): This group includes most of the large Alaskan and western Canadian wolves, including the following varieties which were formerly listed as separate:

—*alces* (extinct)
—*columbianus* (endangered)
—*griseoalbus* (presumed extinct)
—*mackenzii* (endangered)
—*occidentalis* (true Mackenzie Valley Wolf)
—*pambasileus* (Interior Alaskan Wolf)
—*tundrarum* (Alaskan Tundra Wolf)

▼ *C. lupus arctos* (Arctic Wolf): This group contains the white-coated arctic island and Greenland species, including the following varieties formerly listed as separate:

—*arctos* (Melville Island Wolf or Arctic Wolf—endangered)
—*bernardi* (Banks Island Tundra Wolf—extinct)
—*orion* (Greenland Wolf)

▼ *C. lupus nubilus* (Northern Plains Wolf, also called the Buffalo wolf): This large group includes most of the southeastern Alaskan, central and northeastern Canadian, and western U.S. species, such as the following varieties formerly listed as separate:

—*beothucus* (Newfoundland Wolf—extinct)
—*crassodon* (Vancouver Island Wolf—endangered)
—*fuscus* (Cascade Mountain Wolf—extinct)
—*hudsonicus* (Hudson Bay Wolf—endangered)
—*irremotus* (Northern Rocky Mountain Wolf—extinct)
—*labradorius* (Labrador Wolf—endangered)
—*lycaon* of Minnesota (Eastern Timber Wolf—endangered)
—*ligoni* (Alexander Archipelago Wolf—extinct)
—*manningi* (Baffin Island Tundra Wolf—endangered)
—*youngi* (Southern Rocky Mountain Wolf—extinct)

The buffalo wolf proper became extinct by 1926, but is now believed to be the ancestor to wolves now living in the midwestern United States.

▼ *C. lupus baileyi* (Mexican Wolf): This group includes species from Mexico and the extreme southwestern United States (the smallest of the gray wolves), such as:
> —*baileyi baileyi* (endangered)
> —*mogollonensis* (Mogollon Mountain Wolf—extinct)
> —*monstrabalis* (Texas Gray Wolf—extinct)

These "varieties" of wolves are mostly a result of their geographic environment. There are little or no real differences in looks or behavior among any of them, and it takes a real expert to make a definitive distinction. All can interbreed freely if they should happen to meet and like each other (wolves tend not to like members of other packs, a disinclination which has served, along with geographical separation, to keep subspecies distinct). As noted, many of these species are near extinction, presumed extinct, known to be extinct, or exist only in zoos.

To show how perplexing the classification of wolves really is, allow me to quote Peter Steinhart from his book in *The Company of Wolves*[7]: "The red wolf is the most puzzling of wolves. It was originally described in 1791 by John Bartram, who regarded it a subspecies of the gray wolf and gave it the name *Canis lupus niger*. In 1851, Audubon and John Bachman held there was a gray wolf in the North, a black wolf in Florida and the Southeast, and a red wolf in Texas and Arkansas. In 1898, Outram Bangs designated the Florida wolf a separate species and gave it the name *Canis ater*. In 1905, Vernon Bailey recognized the red wolf of Texas as a separate species and gave it the name *Canis rufus*. But twenty years later, the International Commission on Zoological Nomenclature changed the name [back] to *Canis rufus*. In 1967, Barbara Lawrence and William Bossert of Harvard University argued that the red wolf was a subspecies of the gray wolf. In 1970, David Mech held that the red wolf most likely originated from the crossing of gray wolves and coyotes. In 1972, Ronald Nowak, endangered species coordinator for the U.S. Fish and Wildlife Service, examined historical and fossil specimens and concluded, 'The red wolf is the surviving stock of the basic progenitor of all wolves. And it originated right where it survives today, in the southern United States.'" And all this fuss is about just one variety![8] Some new studies, by the way, suggest that *Canis rufus*, once considered a completely separate species from *C. lupus*, has now been shown to be a *hybrid* of the gray wolf and the coyote. There may, however, have once been a distinct species of wolf inhabiting the southern states of North America, related to the "red wolf"; advanced genetic studies will probably solve this mystery very soon. (The South American Dire Wolf [*Canis dirus*], now extinct, also has a mysterious ancestry which has not yet been fully unraveled.)

A less "scientific" but more practical classification of wolves simply divides them into tundra and timber types. The latter dwell mostly in forested areas and tend to be gray or black; the former are often lighter in color, echoing the snowy environment in which they dwell. Timber wolves have more pointed ears, while those of tundra wolves are more rounded, as is common in arctic animals. (Pointed ears dissipate heat—the last thing you want when it's cold outside is your body heat floating off into the wind.) Timber wolves' fur is sensibly shorter than that of the tundra wolf, while tundra wolves have longer legs and broader feet that can handle deep snow. However, these are only minor differences.

We have already noted that wolves and dogs are essentially one species that crossbreed and produce fertile young. The same is true of coyotes and wolves, although nowadays this happens only rarely in the wild. (Historically, wolves and coyotes parted company about a million years ago.) In Maine, however, where I come from, there are numbers of wolf-coyote-domestic dog mixes running amok, so to speak. And don't forget that "red wolf" mystery.

Life Among Wolves

Wolves lead a rich and complex life, the study of which has engaged the best efforts of numerous researchers over the past century or so. While once considered (by some) mere vermin to be destroyed, the beauty and mystery of the wolf continue to fascinate us, particularly now that we know how close the wolf is to the family dog.

Wolves commonly live in packs, as everyone knows. But what is a pack, and how big is it? The answer, as you might expect, is "it's variable." Most wolf packs range from 2 to 20 individuals, with 8 members about average; however, packs of 40 or more have been recorded. There are indeed such creatures as "lone wolves," but they are usually the overflow of a pack whose food supply has reached its limit. Others may have been "widowed" or thrown out of a pack for disagreeable behavior; some may be solitary by nature. At any rate, about a quarter of all wolves seem to belong to no pack at all.

Such wolves may move into an adjacent empty territory or hang around the boundaries between two rival packs. It's a dangerous lifestyle; lone wolves are often killed by resident pack wolves. If possible, they find a mate among other loners and attempt to start their own pack and establish their own territory. Other wolves will flee an area entirely, traveling as far as 500 miles away.

Wolves usually kill members of rival packs wherever and whenever they can—including cubs. They will urinate on the corpses, too, just to mark them as belonging to the victor. On occasion, however, wolves will accept new pack members. L. David Mech observed several such events;[9] it's not common, but it does happen. The fact that this behavior is natural (although somewhat rare) makes it possible for dogs to take in a new member of either sex and, on occasion, a member of another species.

An average pack consists of a "married alpha pair" (almost always the highest-status male or patriarch, and the highest-status female or matriarch), their young, and perhaps the offspring of previous years. (This is called linear dominance hierarchy, if you have a fondness for terms.) Wolves are indeed hierarchical, meaning that everyone occupies a particular place within the pack. Wolf packs tend to have two separate dominance orders—a male line and a female line. In natural, wild-wolf packs, the term "alpha" usually refers to the parents of the other pack members. Alphas do not struggle to establish their leadership; that is the normal position of the pack parents. I should note that the word "alpha," which properly applies to the lead wolf or wolves, has taken on various and convoluted meanings in modern dog parlance. Much of this usage is simply wrong, at least when applied to dogs. Therefore, "alpha" is probably best applied only to wolf packs, not to a group of dogs living in a home. (It is even less appropriate when applied to canine interactions with human beings, so I'll try to avoid it.) In the wild, alpha status offers both responsibility (leadership) and privilege (the best mating and food opportunities).

> Scientists who have attempted to assess dominance patterns in wolves have struggled to arrive at sensible conclusions. They don't even know what qualities go into making a dominant wolf—speed, strength, resourcefulness, altruism, or a combination of these traits. Simple birthright seems to be a large part of it. At any rate, you can usually spot the dominant wolf not so much by the way he acts around others as the way others act around him, displaying submissive behavior. Humans act the same way; you can often tell who is the leader or dominant personality in a group because of the way people gather around him or her. St. Augustine said, "The wolf hates when it flatters." I am not sure how Augustine knew this, but he was quite right. The fawning, submissive behavior of low-ranking wolves to their superiors is not an expression of deep love; it is how the lower-ranked wolf marks time while waiting for the right moment to take over the pack—or at least get to mate with the alpha female (a decision she alone makes).

Among wolves, the sex-segregated dominance order does not fully emerge until the pups are sexually mature; until then it is mixed up. Both wolves and dogs begin jockeying for top position in the litter while still very young—about 3 weeks of age. In a few cases, it's all set by the time the pups are only a month old.

In larger packs, a more complex "dominance order" does exist. In such groups, mature subordinate males, peripheral wolves, and juveniles (who do not become fully integrated into the pack until their second year) come after the alphas. The relationship between males and females is somewhat complex and while males usually dominate females, they certainly do not always do so.

In the wolf world, bonded pairs leave double urine marks which increase in frequency as the breeding season approaches. The markings made by newlyweds are more numerous than those from longer-married (so to speak) couples.

Years ago, some researchers at the Chicago Zoological Park removed an alpha wolf from the zoo pack; the beta wolf took over as expected. When the original alpha wolf was returned to the pack, he became the lowest-ranking male of five. He remained in that position during the following breeding season, and managed to move up only one place the following year. It's hard to know whether this would occur in a true wild pack.

Wolf packs are territorial, averaging 90 to 100 square miles of terrain. That's a lot of land.

As you might expect, wolves thrive best where there are large numbers of prey animals for each wolf. The pack number thus seems to be dependent upon the size of the pack's habitual prey; bigger prey-items demand larger wolf packs. An 800-pound moose can feed 40 wolves—but not much else can. For this reason, packs of such a large size are extraordinarily rare. (Catching an 800-pound moose is not as easy as it sounds.) A kill that does not provide enough food for all is sure to stir resentment among the lower orders of the pack. This may be one reason why so much splitting up is observed in packs, with various members scattering to the four winds. Interestingly, wolves hunt alone (not in a pack) about 80 percent of the time.

It is estimated that a wolf kills 1 to 1.5 large mammals a month. Wolves aren't limited to taking wild prey, either. They will sometimes attack and kill dogs, cats, sheep, cattle, horses, domestic reindeer, and pigs.

But prey size alone is not the absolute determinant of pack size; great variations in size have been observed among packs in the same area that feed from the same prey. As is true of human beings and dogs, individual tolerance and cooperation play a large role in developing internal social cohesion. In brief, wolves in a pack seem to like each other. It is not only more sensible for them to live together, but they also seem to develop strong affectional ties. In fact, L. David Mech, a premier expert on wolves, considers this "affectional" tie "about the same as a dog's bond to its master."[10]

There is certainly a strong case for the origins of affection in all species to be found in mutual need and practicality. Interestingly, Woolpy and Ginsberg have shown that after the age of 7 months, it becomes practically impossible for a young wolf to form new attachments.[11] Most domestic dogs, which have retained many characteristics of juvenile wolves, are able to make new canine friends throughout their lives, although younger animals are decidedly friendlier. People are pretty much the same way. I recall once watching two 6-year-olds meet and stare at each other for about 5 seconds, after which one asked, "Do you want to be friends?"

"Okay," answered the other, and off they went to play. It's about that simple for most dogs. If only it were so easy for adult humans.

This, of course, is not to say that wolves are always friendly. They show aggression, and that's not a bad thing; in fact, it is normal behavior and critical to keeping a wolf pack strong. One of the purposes of such aggression, especially in a big pack, is to determine who leads and to continually test that leader. Democracy may be fine for human beings, but wolves prefer less chaos. In a perfect democracy, for instance, there would be no real pack leader to make critical snap decision about where to go, when to leave, and what to hunt. And even worse over the long run, the weak and stupid animals would have equal mating opportunities and would thus be equally likely to pass on their inferior genes as do the strong and fit. (Of course this is what has happened to domestic purebred dogs; they don't even have to compete for mates.) The entire tribe would degenerate into a mass of slavering idiots who couldn't find snow in a blizzard.

It has been demonstrated that dominant wolves will gang up and pick on a subordinate; in some cases they wound it so badly that it dies. Pack dogs may behave the same way. I have even noticed such behavior in the normally very well-behaved foxhound (when kenneled). Such behavior, however, is rare in housedogs.

In general, alpha wolves have gotten smart enough over the centuries to know they don't need to start an all-out brawl to maintain order—a curl of the lip and a slight snarl usually do the trick.

L. David Mech observed that wolf leaders tend to combine autocratic and democratic tendencies flexibly and situationally.[12] In some cases, the alpha wolf drives the pack onward no matter how reluctant the members seem to be; at other times, he seems more responsive to their desires. While I can't read a wolf's mind any better than you can, one can only assume that the difference may stem from the alpha himself, the makeup of the pack, and environmental conditions.

Aside from some internecine quarreling over status, aggression in wolves is normally limited to three circumstances: (a) harassing prey, (b) protecting the young, and (c) meeting strange wolves. In nature, the pack has to be kept to a certain size; if it gets too big, the local prey won't support the group. That means that stray wolves must be chased off to find their own territory. As mentioned earlier, a pack will, on rare occasions, take in another wolf. This can result in outcrossing that strengthens the breed's genetic makeup.

It is difficult to translate wolf pack behavior into domestic dog group behavior. As we shall see later, it is unclear if or how much a dog incorporates pack behavior into his relationship with his human family or even with other domestic dogs in the household, despite the insistence of some on either side of this issue. Dogs probably do transplant some (but not all) ancestral pack behavior into their domestic relationships. Studies of feral dogs shed some light on the situation, but since feral dogs are not domestic dogs, the same conclusions would not necessarily apply.

Dogs, of course, are not the only animals to be domesticated, and that domestication has had rather unforeseen effects on human evolutionary development. Jared Diamond, among others, has theorized that animal domestication has resulted in human genetic mutations that help us make the most of the association.[13] Here are a few of them: (1) the evolution of genetic resistance factors (including the ABO blood groups) to the spate of new infectious diseases connected with close living and cattle owning; (2) the evolution of adult-persistent lactase (the ability of adults to continue to digest milk, an ability not widespread in the world) in milk-consuming populations of northern Europe and several parts of Africa; (3) the evolution of allozymes (variants of enzymes) of alcohol metabolism which permit the consumption of large quantities of nutritionally important beer in western Eurasia; (4) and the adaptation to a diet higher in simple carbohydrates, saturated fats, and, more recently, calories and salt, with a lower portion of fiber, complex carbohydrates, calcium, and unsaturated fats than the diet of hunter-gatherer societies.

Life Expectancy among Wolves

Wolves in the wild usually die before the age of 5 years from shooting, trapping, and poisoning by humans; from being kicked by deer, moose, or caribou; or from disease, including distemper, parvovirus, heartworm, and rabies (which is rather rare in wolves). Many of these diseases seem to have been passed from the domestic dog to the wolf. Additionally, a fair number of wolves starve to death or are killed by other wolves every year.

Aside from such "accidental deaths," the natural length of a wolf's life is about 12 years—the same as that of a similarly sized domestic dog. Wolves in captivity have been known to reach 16 years of age—again, an age similar to that of a well-cared-for domestic dog.

Wolves and Dogs Compared

While clearly distinct in some ways, wolves and dogs do share many features. Here are a few areas in which we can compare and contrast the dog and the wolf. Most of these differences are due to specialization in dogs (a process through which an animal becomes suited to a particular task).

It's a mistake to think that wolves are automatons. Each wolf is as much an individual as each human, and there are extraordinary differences in how individuals will behave in similar situations. Dogs show equal diversity. It's really hard to generalize; however, that won't stop me.

Physical Size and Shape:

In many cases, it is impossible to distinguish a wolf from a dog on the basis of bone or organ—especially a single bone or a single organ. A wolf's heart or shoulder blade is just like that of a similarly sized dog. (The head is bigger, though, as we shall see.) Even the whole animal doesn't tell the whole story.

The wolf is the largest "natural canid" and is larger than all but the biggest dogs. That, however, doesn't put wolves anywhere near the top of the size scale as far as predators are concerned; one wolf is insignificant compared to a tiger or a bear. (A pack of wolves is a different story, however, which is one reason why wolves are usually found in packs.)

The average adult wolf weighs between 50 and 125 pounds—about the size of a large domestic dog. (Northern wolves are much larger than the desert varieties because bigger animals can conserve heat better.) Males weigh substantially more than females and are about 20 percent larger, which is also true of many dog breeds. (This is called sexual dimorphism.) The biggest wolf recorded weighed 175 pounds—sizable, but still smaller than the biggest dog, which can top 200 pounds. Wolves average 26 to 32 inches in height at the shoulder, which is about the same as a Great Pyrenees. (Some can be bigger, but 3 feet at the shoulder is about the maximum.) Measured from muzzle to tail tip, wolves average between 5.5 and 6 feet in length, with the tail making up about a foot and half of that. (Dogs, of course, are extremely variable in this regard.)

A great overlap exists between the body type of the wolf and that of the typical dog. Wolves, however, especially immature ones, are lankier and rangier than most dog breeds of similar size. To dog owners, they may even look a bit scrawny. (Some of them *are* scrawny.)

Skull and Teeth:

The major anatomical disparity between a wolf and a dog lies in the shape and characteristics of the skull—a complicated series of differences that include orbital angles, tympanic bullae, and other such esoteric features. In general, the skulls are similarly shaped. (I am talking here about a normally shaped dog skull; those of Chihuahuas, Bulldogs, and the like are instantly recognizable precisely because their skulls are so abnormal.)

The difference in the size of the skull is also a distinguishing characteristic between dogs and wolves. Raymond Coppinger, noted canine researcher, observed that a hundred-pound wolf has a skull about 20 percent larger than that of a hundred-pound dog.[14] (Yep, that's a big head, all right.) Even dogs that outweigh a wolf by 50 percent still have comparatively small skulls—and smaller brains. The size difference doesn't become apparent until the age of 10 or 12 weeks. After that age the size of the wolf cub's head will rapidly increase beyond that of the dog pup.

The wolf's braincase is also larger than that of the average dog, and what is true of the skull and braincase is also true of the brain. The same trend toward smaller brain size has been observed between domestic horses and their wild cousins. That alone doesn't make wolves any smarter than dogs, of course, just as large people are no smarter than small ones, Neanderthals than modern humans, or Mastiffs than Toy Poodles. Although the Neanderthals were blessed with a bigger brain than modern humans, they managed to lose out in the end to the smarter (but smaller-brained) Cro-Magnons. Similarly, in the dog world, a Toy Poodle can often outsmart a much bigger dog. It can also, on occasion, outwit its "masters." Whether or not a poodle is smarter than a wolf, however, is something you don't want to investigate.

A wolf's brain is about 10 to 30 percent larger than that of a dog, although most of the difference in size comes from the wolf's greatly enlarged hippocampus—a part of the brain closely associated with the primitive limbic system. The hippocampus is responsible for much of the eating, breeding, agonistic, and other emotionally derived behavior that all of us exhibit. However (and oddly), dogs seem to have a greater sex drive than wolves. That has to tell you something—I just don't know what.

Dogs, especially early, primitive dogs, didn't need the massive brain of the wolf because a larger brain requires more food (literally). Scavengers don't need to plan complex hunts the way wolves do. However, now that we are asking more of dogs, maybe they are getting smarter than their feral ancestors—but it's hard to tell.

The rest of the skull displays other differences between wolves and dogs. For example, the muzzle of a wolf is longer than that of most dogs, and the lower jaw of the average wolf is longer, broader, and heavier than that of similarly sized dogs, except, according to some sources, the German Shepherd. However, the difference is so variable as to be insignificant.

Curiously, the long jaw of wolves (and of some dogs) tends to make the jaws weaker, not stronger. Among dogs, shorter-muzzled dogs (like bulldogs) have the most powerful bite; long-snouted animals tend to rip and tear rather than bite down (the way a tiger can). Because the short-jawed cat has such a powerful bite, it can kill its prey instantly, carry it off neatly, and eat it in peace. Wolves and dogs cannot do this. Their comparatively weaker jaws make it extremely unlikely that they will kill large prey with one bite, and that makes cooperative hunting even more critical. (It also forces them to wait for the prey to weaken and die, which makes a good sense of smell vital because it allows them to follow the trail.) Since a cooperative kill must be shared, wolves eat as quickly as they can. By the way, this is why your own dog bolts his food; he remembers fighting for his share of the take with 20 other equally hungry wolves.

> Because wolves have to eat so much so fast, they need to produce a whole lot of saliva (or, to put it colloquially, drool). Dogs do, too.

Like dogs, wolves have 42 teeth, but wolves also tend to have larger teeth both absolutely and relative to their larger skull size than do dogs. Wolf fangs can measure over 2 inches in length. Even here, however, there are individual differences. It is certainly possible that over the course of centuries of living with humans, huge teeth were one of the first characteristics to go. Dogs didn't really need them and humans didn't want them.

Haircoat:

Like most breeds of dogs, wolves have two coats of fur—a thick, fine undercoat and an outer guard-hair coat. (Dogs' coats are generally softer than those of wolves.) Each follicle gives rise to one guard hair and several fine hairs. As one might expect, northern wolves have thicker and longer coats than their southerly relatives. Wolves also exhibit distinctive tufts of facial hair that hang down and project outward from below the ears.

> Dog skin seems to be thicker than that of wolves. Eskimos preferred to make pants of dog skin because of its superior non-tearing qualities.

Unlike the comparatively monochromatic shades of other canid predators, wolves come in an astonishing array of colors—from pure white to coal black and everything between, including red, gold, brown, tawny, and buff. (The color genetics of wolves is still not well understood.) Gray, however, is the most common color in all types of wolves, although it rather uncommon in most breeds of dogs (with the notable and beautiful exception of the Weimaraner). Wolves have bequeathed their many gorgeous colors to their Shapeshifter descendants, along with stripes, splotches, masks, patches, and other color accents. Even the "gray" of a wolf is not a monochromatic gray, but rather a dazzling mixture of white, brown, and black. Wolves tend to become increasingly gray as they age, as do dogs and humans. (Differences in coat color and pattern result from allelic differences in the production and distribution of melanin, the substance responsible for the color black. A white dog simply has much less melanin than a black one. There is no white gene.)

Tail:

One fairly obvious physical difference between a wolf and a dog, at least to the casual observer, is the hang of the tail—a wolf tail usually hangs straight down in repose, while a dog's often has a dip, upswing, or curl. Additionally, wolves, like most wild canids, have a cluster of stiff, black-tipped hairs (even in an otherwise all-white animal) around a blue-black scent gland in the tail (the dorsal tail gland). The same gland is present in some dogs, but it is not always marked by the black-tipped hairs; for some reason, many older dogs seem to lose the hair around it. The gland is seasonally dimorphic (growing larger during mating season) in wolves, which suggests that it has a function in reproductive communication. It also discharges pheromone markers that presumably indicate trails. The same gland in a dog can cause what is sometimes called "stud-dog" tail (a noticeable bump or swollen area).

Pheromones are special chemicals present in bodily secretions and anal glands that mediate scent communication. Although pheromones aren't identifiable odors, the body can detect them using the same nasal nerve cells used to detect odor or perhaps by another structure in the nose called the vomeronasal organ. The first pheromone was identified in 1956. It was a powerful sex attractant for silkworm moths, of all things. (It took a team of German researchers 20 years and 500,000 moths to isolate it. This goes to show what you can accomplish when you have a lot of time and moths on your hands.) Humans are also apparently hip to (their own) pheromones, but the phenomenon has not been well studied.

The odiferous stuff issued from the anal glands (which are located beneath the tail at the 10 and 2 o'clock positions) during a bowel movement is also unique to each dog. The anal gland in dogs is pretty in similar in form and function to the ones in skunks, but I don't really want to talk about that much, do you? Dogs also have perianal glands, which form a circle around the anus, but humans do not understand their function very well. (Dogs aren't telling, but they can learn something about a fellow dog's status, and even some information about his health, from a careful investigation of the anal area.)

Movement:

As is true of all canids, wolves are built for running (as are dogs—excepting freakish dogs, like Bulldogs). There's an old Russian proverb that says "Wolves are kept fed by their feet." It's true! While tigers and the other cats prefer to hide and pounce upon their prey, wolves just run it down. (They have been clocked at more than 40 miles an hour and can run close to that speed for a couple of miles at least.)

The legs, however, are not the most important indicator of wolves' running ability—after all, tigers have long legs too. It's the nose. Animals that make a living by running pretty much have to have long noses. An amazing portion of a dog's blood supply runs through the nose to be cooled before reaching the brain (which is not a good thing to overheat). A network of blood vessels at the base of the brain called the *rete mirabile* ("wondrous network") handles blood distribution. Short-snouted dogs like Pugs can't deliver enough cooled blood to the brain to enable the animal to run for any distance; they simply overheat.

Wolves are also quite narrow-chested, which helps them plow through deep snow. This anatomical characteristic gives rise to its distinctive tracking while trotting, which is called single-tracking or perfect stepping. If you watch a wolf at a trot, you will see that the hind feet track in the same line as the forefeet; the rear paw pads step into and partially fill the mark of the front pad. The direction of travel is characteristically straight.

Dogs, on the other hand, with their typically wider chests, generally place their hind feet alongside the track set by the front feet. They also tend to meander more in their tracking. Perhaps they have more leisure.

Besides being excellent runners, wolves can and do swim easily. It's not like them to let their prey escape just by crossing a river. Dogs are variable in their attitude toward water.

Eating Habits:

Anatomically, wolves and dogs are both classified as carnivores. (The designation *carnivore* is based upon tooth type and structure rather than dining style, as you might expect—see Skull and Teeth, above.) In fact, neither wolves nor dogs are solely dependent upon meat. I had an Irish Setter who relished blackberries and could delicately harvest them from the thorniest bush, and a Gordon Setter who preferred dry bread to a hamburger. (He would remove the patty from the roll and eat only the bun.) But these are exceptions. In general, both dogs and wolves prefer meat when they can get it—which is as often as possible.

Wolves prefer to dine on elk, caribou, moose, bison, deer, mountain sheep, mountain goats, or even the very hard-to-handle musk ox. Whatever the biggest, fattest, most delectable treat in the area happens to be is what the wolf wants—but seldom gets. Most wolf chases end in failure, so obesity is not a problem. Prey animals do not allow themselves to be eaten without a fight, and many a wolf has met an untimely demise at the business end of a prey animal's hooves, horns, or antlers. Many wolf skulls have been found with deer-hoof-shaped holes in them.

When wolves bag an elk, the whole pack lands on it. The alphas eat first (which favors survival of the fittest and all that) and go for the belly and entrails (which are rich in fat) while the rest start chomping down on the wounded area, where the meat is most easily available. It's a scary sight, I can tell you that—snapping, snarling, and growling for the best seat at the table. Each wolf tries to get what it can. (A wolf's tummy can hold 18 pounds of food. Isn't that wonderful? A whole Thanksgiving turkey, right down the gullet. Of course, wolves don't get to celebrate Thanksgiving.) Most wolves have a "safe zone" of about 2 feet around their food; alphas get more elbow room. You may or may not have observed similar behavior in the family dog.

All mammals, with their high metabolisms, are programmed to be hungry all the time, even if they have recently eaten. In predators, that's partly because most hunts don't result in a kill. If a wolf waits until he really needs food before he starts hunting again he may be too weak to get it. Besides, one never knows when one's next meal will come along. And while it's true that wolves can live on mice if that's all there is, they prefer to concentrate their attention (and energy) on large game, where the payoff is better and the entire pack can be fed. As mentioned earlier, feeding the whole pack is important both to social bonding and to ensure that enough members survive so they can unite to kill the next big animal, whenever it appears.

The domestic dog, of course, does not have to hunt to survive. He has his dinner served up in a dish, but like his brother wolf he prefers meat to bread (my Gordon Setter notwithstanding). One reason why most dogs have to be coaxed to eat dry commercial foods is that they contain about 40 percent carbohydrates (a cheap source of energy that has no capacity to build muscle). With the possible exception of pregnant and lactating bitches, dogs don't require any carbohydrates at all and so never really developed a taste for them—except for carbohydrate-laden chocolate, which can kill them.

Intelligence:

This is always a controversial topic. Researchers have found that although dogs are undeniably easier to train than wolves (they have a vested, inherited interest in getting along with us and doing our bidding), wolves are better problem solvers. L. David Mech recounts how a wolf in his possession learned to open a door by turning the knob with his teeth simply by watching Mech do it; he family dog never caught on no matter how many times it observed the same behavior.[15] There aren't many domestic dogs that can open doors (although I do know of one—a Basset Hound named Truffles—who had lived a life on the lam).

Based on such observations, it is commonly said that dogs are poor observational learners. However, this platitude has so many exceptions as to be almost untrue. All my own dogs learned to use a doggie door by observing others do the same. My Gordon Setter never ripped up his bed until the Border Collie next door taught him how. Our small mixed-breed dog learned to climb onto the cedar chest by watching our pointer mix do it. And when I was attempting to teach our English Springer Spaniel to roll over, our Irish Setter sat on the sidelines, just observing. All of a sudden she started barking excitedly, rolled over very quickly, and looked expectantly at me for the cheese-bit reward. The Springer Spaniel, on the other hand, never quite caught on. My friend Laura Hussey, who trick-trains dogs, always places all her dogs in crates to observe while she is training one by using rewards. By the time she gets to the fourth dog, it has practically learned the trick already. Even when she switches the order of the dogs, the fourth dog has always caught on to the trick before being formally taught. It is probably safe to assume that both wolves and dogs can learn some things by observation and what they learn is partly dependent upon the individuals involved, as well as the innate difficulty of the task.

We can say with confidence that wolves and dogs are both highly intelligent creatures that can not only plan ahead but also take advantage of the present moment. (Neither probably wastes much time in regret.) Real intelligence means learning, and dogs and wolves have a lifelong ability to learn. And even adult animals like to play (dogs more than wolves), which is another key component to learning.

Breeding Cycle:

Wolves breed only once a year (in late winter); domestic dogs have twice-yearly estrous periods. Obviously it is advantageous for pups to be born in the late spring, when food is most abundant and the weather kind. It appears that in wolves, at least, the increasing hours of daylight stimulate special hormones which in turn prompt the release of a follicle-stimulating hormone, and that triggers ovulation.

Dogs can come into heat at any time, regardless of season; however, "primitive" dogs, like the Australian Dingo and the Basenji, exhibit the seasonal estrus characteristic of wolves. Experiments that compared reproductive parameters in captive male wolves and dogs demonstrated that wolves exhibited maximal hormone levels and testicular weights during winter, which is their normal breeding season.[16] Dogs, however, have relatively high hormonal levels all year, which partially explains why male dogs get along with each other less well than do male wolves. Dogs are also much more promiscuous than are wolves, and they reach sexual maturity earlier. Regarding sex hormones, wolves do not fully mature until they are 5 years old, though they may breed earlier if they can attract a mate. Wolves often bond for life—although if one of the pair dies, the surviving wolf may acquire a new mate. L. David Mech observed several pair bondings that remained intact even though no cubs were produced, and one autopsy revealed that a 32-month-old female had never ovulated.[17]

Interestingly, wolves raised in captivity without parents tend to mature sexually at the age of 9 or 10 months rather than the 2 years customary for wild wolves. This is tricky, however; in one sense, wolves become sexually mature at 2 years of age, but pack pressures operate in such a way as to apparently prevent complete maturity until 5 years of age. It is hypothesized that the presence of adults acts as a check upon the wolves reaching maturity. In the absence of parents, evolutionary pressures force youngsters to become adults and breed quickly in order to protect the lineage. Domestic dogs are like captive wolves in this respect and can breed before they are a year old. This may be a trait chosen by early dog breeders, but it is more likely a consequence of so many generations of dogs having been raised without parents. Whether other dogs in the household (most of whom may be neutered) or household humans count as parents, I couldn't say.

It is unclear why the estrous period changed from once a year in wolves to twice a year in dogs. Suggestions include the following: (1) since humans have protected dogs from environmental hazards and fulfilled their needs, dogs have developed the ability to be more fertile; and (2) human beings purposely selected animals with more frequent estrous periods for breeding. Other factors may be involved as well.

Both dogs and wolves can experience a condition called false pregnancy. In the wolf, either a real or a false pregnancy occurs every year. Scientists believe that the evolutionary function of false pregnancy is to prepare not only the females, but also the whole pack (including males and older cubs), to care for the offspring. (Prolactin, a hormone that stimulates nurturing behavior, surges in both male and female wolves while they care for the young.)[18]

The alpha or leading pair may not be the only breeding pair in a pack. Subordinate males have been observed mounting alpha females, although such activity begins early in the estrous cycle, before the female has ovulated. It is usually the alpha female, by the way, who controls who mates with her—not the alpha male. Heat periods lasting 45 days, an extremely long time, have been observed in wolves; of course, the female is fertile during only a very short portion of that time. Researchers speculate that the long, if largely unproductive, heat periods encourage social cohesion by allowing subordinate males to mate with non-fertile females while preserving the genetic lineage of the alpha or leading male.

The gestation period for both dogs and wolves is about 63 days (the time for dogs is independent of size and breed). The "blind puppy period" (about 10 days) and the order of appearance of milk teeth are identical in both species. Wolf births usually occur in May in the northern areas, and there are usually about 7 puppies per litter. (The mom has 8 teats and the pups generally nurse for 34 to 51 days.) If the dam is killed, the male wolf raises the puppies; subordinate members of the pack may also help. This is not characteristic of dogs, which generally rely on gullible humans to do all the real work anyway. This ability to delegate puppy-raising duties to others at least partially accounts for the successful survival of both wolves and dogs.

Young wolves emerge from the den when they are about 8 weeks old—about the same age at which a puppy is ready to go to a new home. At that point, the wolf parent may move the cubs to a "rendezvous site" where they meet up with other pack members and head off hunting, often leaving the pups with a subordinate member of the pack. When the hunters return, the young will whine and lick their faces. This stimulates the parents or other adults to regurgitate food for them. Interestingly, male wolves will help raise cubs, including regurgitating food for them. Such behavior is unknown in dogs. This is possibly (but not probably) because domestic dog puppies are not usually raised with their dads close at hand. Even most female domestic dogs have lost the ability to regurgitate food for their pups—why should they bother?

Wolves also court each other for an extremely long time. Many choose mates when they are about a year old, although they may not breed for another year. It seems that love—not sex—binds them together during this period. However, sex does seem to play a powerful role in the physical bonding of wolves (and dogs), by which I mean the copulatory "tie." In this situation, the mating pair remains stuck together for as long as a half hour. While no one is really sure what it accomplishes (the pair cannot break the tie even if they both seem to wish it), L. David Mech and others speculate that the tie stimulates stronger psychological bonding.[19]

Both wild and captive wolves show a strong preference for choosing the same mates year after year, although there are exceptions to that rule. Perhaps this accounts for both the dog's capacity for intense loyalty and his malleability in easily adapting himself (in most cases) to new owners. This is a somewhat breed-dependent variable, although there are, of course, individual differences as well. It is also not necessarily true that a "one-man dog" is less likely to adapt himself to a new owner. He will simply switch his allegiance to a new "one man"— although it may take some time.

Critical Periods

All animals go through critical learning periods.[20] (This phenomenon was first studied extensively in canids by John Paul Scott and Mary Vesta Marston in 1950.) Like all other animals, dogs, wolves, jackals, and coyotes go through these critical periods. While all researchers in this topic agree that critical periods exist, the exact time frame for each (and what exactly happens during each) is still under scrutiny and subject to modification. These phases are variously termed sensitive periods, critical moments, optimal periods, vulnerable points, crucial stages, susceptible periods, and so on. No matter what you call it, a critical period is usually defined as a specific span of time during which just a tiny bit of exposure to or experience with something new makes a huge impact on an animal, as well as a great difference later in life. Researchers theorize that during each critical period, the mind is ready to receive certain kinds of information most efficiently and the knowledge gained is more likely to be stored in long-term memory. During such a phase, only a few "determining experiences" have major effects on future behavior; identical stimuli may have an enormous effect at one point in an animal's development and almost none at a different time. The sensitive period is preceded and followed by periods of lower sensitivity, and the transition between stages is not cut-and-dried. During each period, the animal (depending on the information presented to it) either continues along the learning path (habituation, impregnation, or self-limitation), or stops; sometimes a learning window closes when a new point is reached.

We also know that there are some differences between breeds as well as between individual animals. Each behavioral system, such as fear or pack behavior, has its own critical period. For obvious reasons, these periods have been studied more thoroughly in dogs than in wolves. It is generally believed that wolves and dogs go through pretty much the same periods, except that dominance orders, or that way wolves orient themselves in relationship to their littermates, may be established in wolves as early as 30 days of age. Because these periods are somewhat elastic—again, they vary from individual to individual and breed to breed—they should be used only as a general guideline. Some developments that occur during the critical periods are naturally ordered events (such as eye-opening); others must be imprinted.

The critical periods include:

1. *The neonatal period (birth–13 days)*:

This is the "denning" period during which the newborn wolf pups are secreted away in a dark den or similar safe place. Both dog and wolf puppies are extremely immature at birth. The puppy brain can control only heartbeat, breathing, and equilibrium. Puppies are blind, deaf, and practically immobile, so their only ways of learning about the world are through touch, smell, and taste—and even these senses are not well developed, although it is reported that newborn puppies have infrared receptors in their noses that help them navigate toward the mother. There is no control of body temperature yet; however, the facial nerve is already mature, which allows the puppy to seek soft, warm surfaces. The mother helps this process by licking the pups and her own teats, thus laying down a saliva trail for the puppies to follow.

During this period there is almost no myelination (myelin is a fatty substance that eventually covers and protects the nerves) of the nerve cells. An unmyelinated nerve transmits impulses very slowly (about 2 meters per second), which explains the sluggishness of a newborn puppy's response to stimuli. Tails are usually docked during this period because people say that the puppies can't feel pain at this stage. However, it's more correct to say that there is only a delay in pain response. The pain is the same—it is only somewhat postponed and pups can't express it in a way that humans can observe.

> Of course there is a prenatal period, but the best studies on this phase have been conducted in rats, so it's hard to say what carries over to the canine and lupine worlds. However, researchers have noted that stressed pregnant rat moms (especially in certain lines) produce young that are more fearful than those of unstressed mothers. It is not difficult to see how this would not apply to dogs—or humans—as well.

Maternal behavior exhibited during the neonatal period imprints very deeply on the puppies. The Swedish Dog Training Center experimented with this by switching some newborn pups to another mother.[21] They discovered that many behaviors previously thought to be inherited were instead imprinted by the mother. The mothers are physiologically affected by the puppies, too; for example, during the neonatal period, the normal adrenal gland response is suppressed, along with its attendant flight-or-fight response. Mother dogs do not flee when their young are threatened. They fight.

In dogs (as opposed to wolves), the neonatal period is usually filled with human intervention as well. This is not a bad thing for two reasons. First, human interference creates a mild stress that benefits the puppies' mental development. (It should be noted that mild stress from other sources is also a regular occurrence for wolf puppies and serves the same purpose.) Second, such intervention lays the groundwork for puppy-human socialization, although it is very tentative and fragile. At this period in the puppy's life, mom absolutely matters most.

> Wolves raised in captivity accept human handling rather passively until they are about 7 weeks of age (although they prefer their own species). After that point they really want nothing to do with us.

2. *The transitional period (13–20 days):*

During this period (at about 15 days) the pups demonstrate the first signs of learning and become much more mobile. The puppy learns to walk and to lap liquids rather than just nurse. At the end of this period, the ears open and the puppy develops a sense of smell. He also learns to urinate and defecate on his own, without the mother's help.

3. *The socialization period (3–12 weeks):*

As far as humans are concerned, this is the most critical of the critical periods. During this time puppies learn to do something remarkable; they develop relationships with both their conspecifics (their mom and littermates) and human beings. By 3 weeks of age the puppy is able to form its first relationships, which, seemingly paradoxically, are with its littermates more than its mother. This is because the mother begins to wean them and leave them alone for short periods. The littermates begin play-fighting with their little needle-sharp teeth. The only function of puppy teeth, by the way, is to cause pain—they are of no help in capturing game. During play-fighting, they discover that a sharp bite to a mate (even with a puppy's weak jaws) causes the sibling to cry out in pain and stop playing. Thus the well-socialized pup learns early on how to inhibit its bite. Those sharp teeth undoubtedly help in the weaning process, too. Dogs with strong dominant tendencies may become aggressive if not handled properly during this time, just as submissive dogs may become extremely timid. This is your best chance to moderate some inherited characteristics.

It has been shown that the total absence of other dogs between the third and twelfth week of a puppy's life encourages its identification with other species (usually people, but occasionally a cat or another pet—or even a vacuum cleaner). As the dog develops, it may even attempt to copulate with the adopted species and will typically reject its own, including mirror images. Limited contact with other dogs produces no serious behavior changes, especially if it is reintroduced before the age of 9 weeks; however, such a dog will probably never develop a real, positive interest in its own species.

Breeders of gun dogs know that they must expose their puppies to the sound of gunshots by the time they are 6 weeks old, which is when fear responses kick in. If regularly bombarded with such noises, the pups come to consider it normal.

Unless dogs are properly socialized during this time, they will react to all new experiences with a fight-or-flee response. Another phenomenon that occurs during this period is the "flight instinct" phase during which they first feel the call of the wild—or, in other words, they may tend to run off. It is critically important not to allow this to happen; if it does, do not punish the dog on its return. To do so only imprints the value of running away on him. The puppies' learning also progresses very rapidly during this phase, and they are usually completely weaned by the end of this interval. The latter part of this period (7 to 12 weeks) is sometimes called the human socialization period because puppies learn to adapt to a human environment at that time.

It is commonly noted that wolves (and dogs) are pack animals. However, pack behavior is not totally controlled by genetics. Technically, this is an epigenetic ("above" the genes) behavior that is developed during this critical period. If a dog does not learn pack behavior then, he won't ever learn it. This can be an advantage or a disadvantage to a dog's human partner, depending on the dynamics of their environment.

It is important to remember that the dog-human bond is not inborn—it must be imprinted during this critical period. By 5 months of age (and this is slightly variable), the socialization window closes. This means that the dog will tend to react to new experiences with aversion unless his owners constantly provide support and encouragement. This tendency, which is known as xenophobia or neophobia, has obvious survival value for wild animals because new things are more often than not dangerous. Even humans react to something strange with caution. A well-socialized dog, however, will trust his owner when meeting new objects. Usually.

4. *The juvenile period (12 weeks to puberty, which is usually around 16 weeks):*

In this adolescent stage, puppies begin to show a great deal more independence. In dogs, this period marks the time when they begin to think for themselves and are less likely to automatically follow their owners around. Novice owners call this disobedience; it is, rather, natural behavioral development. If you encourage overdependence at this point you could end up with separation anxiety problems later. However, it is very important to teach your puppy to come to you reliably when you call before this period ends—and the earlier the better, because it gets much harder after the dog has developed some independence. This is also the perfect age for puppy kindergarten, particularly since most vets recommend that owners wait until their dog is about 12 weeks of age before allowing him to interact with strange dogs.

A 6-month-old dog has a relative brain development about equal to that of an 18-year-old human, in the physical sense. However, the attainment of puberty doesn't guarantee emotional maturity in dogs or wolves any more than it does in people. Some mature emotionally before they mature physically (and puppies are often awkward and gangly at this stage, like humans), some after. However, by the time a dog is about 16 weeks of age, his personality is pretty much defined for life.

Dogs that are kept in kennels up to the age of 14 weeks and not allowed to bond sufficiently with humans often make difficult pets. This can happen in "show kennels" (where the breeder keeps the dogs long enough to decide which are likely show prospects) just as easily as in puppy mills. Unless the breeder is extremely conscientious about giving each puppy enough petting and bonding time, the result can be disastrous for the unsuspecting pet buyer.

Dogs often show strange patterns of behavior during this period, particularly toward new objects. For example, when we installed central air conditioning in our home, our Gordon Setter stood in the yard and barked furiously at the unit outdoors when the motor began running. When it shut off, he ran over to the unit and urinated triumphantly on it. He behaved in a similar manner toward a bird feeder and some balloons tied to the mailbox.

5. *The adult period (puberty to death):*

Depending on breed and other considerations, puberty can begin anywhere between the ages of 6 and 16 months. At this time, hormones rise to adult levels and the dog is considered mature (at least sexually). Even so, the adult dog retains many behaviors similar to those of the juvenile wolf; in fact, we can say that the dog *is* a juvenile wolf.

Senses

In general, the sensory acuity of dogs and wolves is similar; greater variation is noted among various breeds of dogs than between dogs and wolves.

Hearing:

In most respects, dogs and wolves outperform human beings in the hearing department. Their hearing range runs from about 20 hertz (cycles per second) at the low end up to over 50,000 hertz at the high end; humans can hear only up to about 20,000 hertz, although the lower end of our range is about the same as a dog's (or a wolf's). (Dog whistles take advantage of the dog's ability to sounds inaudible to us.) It is important for dogs to be able hear such high-pitched noises because many rodents squeak in this range, hence their uncanny (to us) ability to suddenly start digging like mad in the ground to capture a mole or small rodent. Their hearing is still pretty pathetic, however, compared to a dolphin's, which can hear noises up to 130,000 hertz.

In addition to being able to hear higher sounds, wolves and dogs can also hear fainter sounds and pinpoint them more accurately. (J.A. Altman at the Pavlov Institute of Physiology found that dogs can accurately locate the source of a sound in six one-hundredths of a second.[22]) Dogs can detect a faint sound at 75 feet; a human must be 58 feet closer to hear the same noise. Wolves can hear howls from other wolves for 6 miles in the forest and 10 miles on the tundra. This ability to pinpoint sounds is partly due to the cup-shape of the dog's ear, which is essentially unaffected by the ear's being erect or floppy.

Dogs can also move one ear at a time. Much of the dog's ear mobility is due to the 16 muscles that control ear movement.

> Pavlov discovered that dogs can tell the difference between pitches one-eighth of a tone apart on the musical scale, which perhaps accounts for their ability to distinguish their owner's voice from others'. It has been clearly demonstrated that sheepdogs respond only their owner's whistle amid the whistles of many others trying to distract the dog. Oddly, Pavlov found that his dogs salivated at chord differences but not in between, which leads some to speculate whether or not dogs have absolute pitch. It is known that there is a "music center" in the dog's brain, just as there is in a human's. Their hearing ranges over about 8.5 octaves, which is the same as that of humans.

Some researchers hypothesize that such extreme acuity makes dogs much more sensitive to noises that we think are reasonable. They have to learn to ignore these sounds in order to be comfortable in our society.

Smell:

Smell is a canid's most refined and highly developed sense. It is a major means of communication and a detector of food and other important information. In fact, it is so vital that many experts recommend a prospective puppy buyer visit a puppy at around 5 weeks of age to imprint the dog with his scent. (I have no information as to whether or not this really works.) Wolves and dogs have an olfactory region about 14 times larger than that of humans, with a corresponding hundreds- or even thousands-fold enhancement of smelling ability. This is no mystery considering that dogs have bigger noses, a much larger area of olfactory mucous membrane, and many more smell receptors. No one is sure how much better a dog's sense of smell is than a human's; estimates vary from 1000 to 100 million times better. The average human being has about 5 million olfactory receptors; a German Shepherd has around 220 million. It is said that if you laid the receptors out flat, they would cover more area than the rest of dog (laid out likewise). Moreover, the turbinal bones (small, curved bones located in the nasal passages) of the wolf and dog are arranged to enhance every passing odor; in humans, those same bones *reduce* and *deflect* airflow. The dog's wet nose helps, too, since the moisture acts like glue to odor particles. The fragrance-charged mucus clings to the microscopic hairs on the sensitive receptor cells where the smell is converted into an electrical signal that travels to the cerebral cortex and limbic system, which mediate emotion and sensation. In humans, this is one reason why smells seem to magically transport us, at least emotionally, back to old times and places. A dog's nose also contains infrared temperature-sensitive receptors (remember the denning period). These receptors can help a dog find a person buried deep in the snow.

> One interesting study done with identical twins found that dogs could distinguish between twins if the scents were given simultaneously—but not otherwise. However, other studies have shown that dogs can distinguish between fraternal but not identical twins, so it seems that current research has not reached a firm conclusion on this supposedly remarkable ability.

A dogs' olfactory sense is so acute that when its owner smells different, the dog may act differently to him or her. Dogs have, on occasion, even exhibited aggressive behavior toward familiar young girls who have begun to menstruate. The smell of alcohol has a bad effect on many dogs, especially since it is often associated with abusive behavior. A rescue dog may start acting oddly around a new owner if the latter has had a beer to relax, and the owner may not understand that the dog is reacting to a smell that has meant pain in the past. And of course people who use alcohol (or drugs) act differently. (Dogs are right to be cautious.) Dogs can also distinguish cows in estrus from others, and differentiate among sweat samples from human armpits, feet, and palms.

One of the great advantages of odors is that they persist for hours or even days, which enables dogs to detect past events. This is one way in which the sense of smell is superior to that of sight, touch or sound, which exist only in the moment.

Taste:

Dogs are able to taste right from birth, although they never develop the complex sense of taste that people do. This is partly because they do not have as many taste buds (humans have about 8,000; dogs, about 1,700) and most of those are concentrated toward the rear of the tongue, so food is almost swallowed before it is tasted. Like us, they can distinguish sweet, sour, bitter, and salty, and they also have some primary taste receptors that respond to water; in fact, dogs may be able to differentiate among different kinds of water better than people can. (No filling the empty Perrier bottle with tap water and claiming it's the real thing for them.)

Dogs do have a sweet tooth, which demonstrates that they have adapted to eating (at least to some extent) simple carbohydrates, such as those found in berries—which probably provided needed energy during hard times. Nowadays they like chocolate, which can kill them. (Dogs also have a particular liking for antifreeze, which is even more lethal than chocolate.)

Interesting studies with pet dogs have shown that dogs' food preferences are grounded in more than anatomy or even habit. Katherine Houpt of Cornell University did some fascinating taste studies with dogs and found that such factors as where the dog slept at night and to whom in the family the dog was most closely bonded influenced its eating preferences.[23] She also found that dogs preferred pork to lamb, beef, or chicken (possibly because of the higher fat content); most weren't crazy about horsemeat either (although it must be said that some dogs really like it). They liked meat rare rather than raw (it would be interesting to try the same test with wolves). Not surprisingly, dogs prefer canned food to dry and like it served at body temperature.

> While some people express surprise at the dog's preference for cooked food, I am not one of them. After all, human beings lived on raw food for millennia before we figured out the fire thing. Cooked food probably tastes better in some aesthetically absolute way, and wolves are probably praying for the day a McDonald's opens up in their neighborhood.

Touch:

Touch is a critical sense for all mammals and is present even in newborn puppies, to whom the touch of the mother provides comfort. And while it's been shown that people benefit from touching dogs, the reverse is also true. Gently caressing a dog that knows and loves you will slow his heart rate, reduce his blood pressure, and even cause his skin temperature to drop. Dogs have special sense organs called vibrissae (whiskers) on their muzzles, beneath their jaws, and above their eyes which help them determine airflow and reveal information about the texture of objects. Touch sensitivity in dogs varies from breed to breed as well as individually. Terriers are less sensitive to touch (and pain) than are most other breeds.

Vision:

People used to believe that dogs (and presumably wolves) could not see in color. Period. We know now that is not true, although they're unable to do it as well as humans can. Dogs can't distinguish among red, orange, yellow, or green, as is true of many colorblind people, but they can differentiate among closely related shades of gray, blue, and violet that are indistinguishable to humans. Humans, however, have the edge when it comes to depth perception and picking out minute details of an object.

The ability to see color depends on the ratio of rods (black-and-white sensitive cells) to cones (color-sensitive cells) in the retina. And if you're wondering if your dog can see images on TV, the answer is…maybe. They probably couldn't in the old days, but with the new, big, high-resolution screens they seem to be able to do so. I know my own dogs have responded to visual images of dogs on television (even when the televised dog was not barking). In fact, our Gordon Setter responded to seeing Gordon Setters on TV (courtesy of an American Kennel Club [AKC] video) even when the televised Gordon was not vocalizing or doing anything other than trot around. He did not respond in any particular way to videos of Basset Hounds. This mirrored his behavior with real-life dogs—ignore Bassets, react to Gordons. I cannot explain this phenomenon, but have observed it repeatedly. This was not an experiment designed to see if the dog would respond—I'd turned on the video for my own edification and the dog happened to be in the room. No one was more surprised than I at his reaction, which included voluble barking and an attempt to climb into the television set. Later, we did turn this episode into an experiment and, sure enough, the dog reacted the same way every time the Gordon video (and only the Gordon video) was shown. On a less high-tech note, researchers have found that when dogs were shown life-size paintings of other dogs, they approached areas of higher gland concentration and sniffed them.

Dogs see better in dim light than people can and their eyes are, coincidentally, a darker color than wolves' eyes (as a rule). Dogs are also able to detect motion about ten times more easily than we do. In other words, movement visible to a dog would have to be exaggerated 10 times before we would notice it.

Wolves and dogs (for the most part) have better peripheral vision than humans do, although wolves surpass both humans and dogs in this aspect. Our field of vision is about 180 degrees; sighthounds like Greyhounds have a remarkable 270 degrees of peripheral vision. Even a dog with a pushed-in face, like a Pekinese, has a visual field of about 190 degrees, although their binocular vision doesn't work nearly as well since the eyes are sort of turned to the side. Wolves are even worse off in regard to binocular vision than are most dogs. Apparently you can have good binocular or good peripheral vision, but not both.

Interestingly, the eyes of all dogs, coyotes, jackals, and wolves are about the same size and shape; the radius of the eyeball is about 11 millimeters regardless of body size or breed. The eyeball itself is more "flattened" than that of a human, as is true of most carnivores, but they can alter focal length and change the shape of their lenses just as well as we can.

Despite what you may have heard to the contrary, sight is important to dogs. In fact, there exists a group of dogs called sighthounds (including Salukis, Whippets, and Afghans) who hunt primarily, as you might guess, by sight. However, it's also true that going blind isn't the end of the world for them, while blindness would mean death for a hunting wolf.

In case you're wondering, the yellowish-green eye-shine of a dog or wolf in the night is caused by a membrane that lines the retina called the *tapetum lucidum*, which means "bright carpet" in Latin. (Some individual dogs do not possess a *tapetum lucidum*.) It is a highly reflective layer of cells that works to gather all available light. This structure, together with the high proportion of rods, gives a dog or wolf the ability to see better at night and to detect even slight movement. The wolf's primordial prey is deer, moose, and elk—animals which are most active at twilight (the technical term for this is "crepuscular").

ESP:

Extra sensory perception has long been attributed to dogs, particularly the ability to know when their owners are returning and similar feats. Scientists in Japan have discovered that dogs can predict earthquakes, too. They can also sense the onset of seizures in their owners, and may be able to detect cancer as well. There is a bit more about canine ESP in Chapter 4.

Okay, Here's the Big Difference:

Dogs like us. Wolves don't. Dogs like to be around us so much that many of them suffer separation anxiety when not in our company; wolves prefer their own kind. Their happiness is directly proportional to their distance from us.

Here's another big difference, which is apparently (but not really) at odds with the first: dogs are a lot more dangerous to humans than wolves are. At least they are nowadays, which is what counts. There has never been an authenticated unprovoked attack upon humans by any North American wolf, but dogs kill a dozen or so people every year—and the killers are not limited to Pit Bulls, Huskies, and Rottweilers. Homicidal dogs have included Dachshunds, Brittany Spaniels, Basenjis, West Highland White Terriers, and a Yorkshire Terrier (who, admittedly, had some help from a bigger dog). But still. Just when you though it was safe to go into the kennel…

European wolves have been known to take human life, specifically during the Middle Ages and the Renaissance. During the Hundred Years' War, for instance, wolves fed on the corpses of soldiers, and having apparently gained a taste for human flesh, took to darting into Paris to snatch up children and dogs.[24] In fact, the Louvre (named for the wolf) stands on a spot once frequented by them. In the United States, wolf predation has been pretty much limited to livestock. Early settlers killed off most of the deer (the wolf's natural prey) and put fat, juicy sheep and cows in pens where they couldn't escape. A wolf would have to have been a fool not to take advantage of the situation—and wolves are not foolish. Still, it hurt them in the end since the offended settlers put a bounty on them in both the Jamestown and Massachusetts colonies.

All right, all right. There are a lot more dogs than wolves running around, and if as many wolves as dogs lived in houses with us they'd probably be chowing down on humans with monotonous regularity. But wolves don't live in houses with us. They don't even like us. They like to live in the forest or tundra, as far away as from us as possible. When they see us, they flee. Dogs indeed have become our familiar wolves, and familiarity breeds—well, you know—contempt.

Chapter 2:
Nexus: The Shapeshifter Takes Hold

"And the Woman said, "His name is not Wild Dog
any more, but the First Friend, because he will be
our friend for always and always and always…"
—Rudyard Kipling, *Just So Stories* (1902)

Perhaps the wolf has always fascinated us. After all, early humans must have seen the wolf as a cooperative hunter like ourselves, one who traveled in bands like us, who had families, feuds, and fights over food as we do. We must always have recognized the connection between us; it just took a few thousands years to make it official. But a few questions continue to nag: what happened, how, when, and where? The answers, as one might expect, are interconnected.

What Happened?

Somewhere in Eurasia, a tiny shift took place between 12,000 and 135,000 years ago. Not on the windswept mountains or barren plains, nor in the shadowy valleys or encircling ocean, but rather in the cells of the wolf. The DNA of the wolf subtly changed—a change that (apparently) led to two kinds of wolves: those who were amenable to domestication and those who were not. (The remaining wolves seem to be decidedly in the "not" category.) The great generalist, the wolf, gave way to the great specialist, the dog.

The Shapeshifter was born. And it probably didn't take long (self-selection usually doesn't), although it didn't occur all at once, either. One wonders what would happen if the same experiment were carried out on several generations of wolves today. A few desultory attempts have been made, but the results have been unsatisfying; it was tried with foxes as well. It could be that the "domestication" gene is now extinct from the wild wolf population, for any wolf coming close to human habitation in recent times has almost inevitably been shot.

> Russian biologist Dmitry K. Belyaev spent 26 years domesticating the silver fox (*Vulpes vulpes*) at the Institute of Cytology and Genetics in Novosibirsk, Russia.[25] He used the ability to be "tamed" (domesticated) as his only criterion for selection. Belyaev's colleague, Lyudmila Trut, continued the work after Belyaev's death; she recently reported that after 40 years, 18 generations, and 45,000 foxes (that's a lot of foxes), the institute now has 100 fully "tame" foxes. Consider, though, that "tame" is a relative word; it was reported that even the "tame" foxes would bite when handled. Domesticated dogs who display such behavior would be euthanized. The animals are characterized by floppy ears (almost unheard of in wild animals) and rolled back, white-tipped tails. For some reason, the splashy tails and floppy ears seem to accompany tameness—at least sometimes— although the reasons are not clear. The experiment also has a down side as far practicality is concerned. The silver fox is a staple of the fur industry, which was totally uninterested in the strange colors that kept popping up in the subjects. Even more to the point, foxes are not wolves—they belong to an entirely different genus. Their behavior is also quite different from that of wolves, particularly regarding sociability. Foxes, for instance, do not form packs. Thus, what applies to foxes does not necessarily apply to wolves (or dogs).

DNA

DNA (deoxyribonucleic acid) is the stuff of inheritance and genetics. It consists of long strings of complex chemicals called chromosomes, which are arranged in pairs. The pairs consist of one chromosome inherited from each parent. DNA is the code that provides the information needed to produce a living organism. Dogs have 39 pairs; humans, 43. Each chromosome carries hundreds or perhaps thousands of genes, each of which holds the code for a different protein. The entire collection, totaling 30,000 to 40,000 genes, is called the genotype. (The whole-body characteristics that result from the expression of the genotype are referred to as the "phenotype." What you see in a dog is the phenotype; what you don't see is the genotype.) When the genes are "expressed," the associated proteins are produced and the body is created. Timing, however, is extremely important. Certain genes must be expressed before others, and some may only be active for a short time during development. Dogs and humans share many of the same genes, especially those regulating basic processes such as cellular replication and protein manufacture. Genes may also exist in multiple forms, called "alleles," which produce similar traits in different animals of the same species.

Most of the body's DNA resides in the nucleus, a separate compartment located in the middle of most cells. The nucleus has its own copy of the entire genetic code. Other DNA, however, exists in tiny structures scattered throughout the cell called mitochondria. Their primary function is to produce energy for use by the rest of the cell. This DNA is inherited separately from nuclear DNA and is called mitochondrial DNA (mtDNA for short). mtDNA is a code for those proteins needed by the mitochondria to carry out their task. Unlike nuclear DNA, which is inherited from both parents, mtDNA is inherited only from the mother, so all the mitochondria in the body are descended from mitochondria present in the ovum. (Sperm have no mitochondria of their own, poor things.)

Domestication does not make dogs "better" or "worse" than wolves. It simply makes them different. Just as wolves are not suited for a civilized life with people, dogs are not designed to live in the wild. In the same way, specialized breeds per se are neither an improvement on nor a weakening of the feral dog, or even of the modern mutt. Specialization is supposed to make certain dogs better at certain tasks. Sometimes this works, sometimes it doesn't. Mother Nature has been developing different kinds of animals a lot longer than we have, and sometimes even she makes mistakes. However, Mother Nature kills off her mistakes, while we humans sometimes take pride in ours.

In the beginning, as is still the case today in some places, dogs were used primarily for food, clothing, and perhaps sacrifice. Hunting and herding duties came later. (Hunting dogs were at first a necessity. They did not become a symbol of wealth and status until the Middle Ages.) To what extent dogs were companions in early societies is still something of a mystery, although certain breeds prized for food—such as the aptly name chow chow—remain more remote and less companionable today than breeds developed for work partnerships and, presumably, companionship

> Some researchers hypothesize that the first dogs may be the ancestors (or at least a close relative) of today's Carolina dog—a shy, reddish-yellow dog of remarkably wild and wolflike demeanor. These dogs do not hang around civilization like true feral dogs, but instead inhabit wild and swampy places.

It bears repeating, although it should be obvious, that the most dangerous animals are wild ones kept as "pets." Such animals lose their fear of people but not their basic dislike of them. Familiarity can indeed breed contempt, particularly in this case. If the same number of people kept tigers or wolves as keep dogs, I'd imagine that the annual fatality rate would be rather high.

How Did It Happen?

How the transition from wild to domesticated took place is a matter of controversy, as is everything else in the dog world (from the morality of ear cropping to the best way to housetrain the family pet). At one time it was thought that ancient people stole wolf pups or rescued orphaned puppies to raise themselves. That probably did not happen; the ability to get along with people is not a learned or heavily environmentally-influenced trait (try rescuing a crocodile or great white shark—or even a tiger—and see what happens).

Here are some factors that lead a species to become domesticated (adapted from E.O. Price)[26]:

▼ A social structure organized along a dominance hierarchy

▼ Gregarious social groups

▼ Males affiliated with social groups

▼ Non-aggressive intraspecies behavior

▼ Sexual signals provided by movements or posture (so humans can figure out when to breed them)

▼ Solicitous of attention

▼ Wide environmental tolerance

▼ Capable of ingesting many kinds of foods

In 1963, F. E. Zeuner noted that an almost invariable concomitant of domestication is human persecution and the consequent extinction of the wild ancestors—something we have certainly seen with dogs.[27]

Wolves probably selected themselves for domestication. The best current theory hypothesizes that as wolves followed human hunters to scavenge leftovers, some wolves grew more comfortable around people. Those who remained fearful and suspicious probably either never followed people at all or kept a greater distance. Over time, more and more puppies were born that inherited their parents' bolder, more "domestic" attitude. So far as we know, this very special animal is the only one who domesticated itself.

It is certain that all dogs are descended from the wolf—not the coyote, coyote hybrid, or jackal, as was also proposed at one time. And the wolf from which they are descended is the Old World wolf, not the North American gray wolf (which is now considered only a distant cousin in the lineage of the domestic dog). More will be known when the Dog Genome Project is completed.[28]

At any rate, it should be obvious that since more than one dog had likely become "domesticated" (and was hanging around the camp), those animals would have mated with each other as opposed to the female going off in search of the more skittish wild wolves. Furthermore, as Stephen Budiansky reports in *The Truth About Dogs*, researchers studying feral dogs in Italy have demonstrated that when a group of dogs obtains a valuable resource (like a garbage heap), they tend to hang onto it and keep out all intruders—including local wolves.[29] (I'm not sure how many wolves still roam the hinterlands of Italy, but apparently the feral dogs keep them away.) Thus the tendency of a family group to guard resources from others also ensures that breeding rights remain within the clan. Budiansky further hypothesizes that growing human populations would tend to break up and displace wolf packs, so even attempts at breeding would never get a chance to take place.

We also know that as more human-oriented animals become reproductively isolated from the wild population, they compose an inbred "founder group" or "deme" that, over successive generations, will undergo a genetic drift and multiply its numbers. This genetic drift will respond to changes in environmental and cultural demands. For example, if the human population is looking for a guard dog, territorial animals that are strongly attached to their humans will be selected and allowed to breed, and so on.

One factor that may have played a part in the selection of nearly every breed was what H. Hemmer termed *Merkwelt*, or the perceptual world of the dog.[30] Highly perceptive, quick-reacting, stress-prone wolves gave way through selective breeding to animals with a greater tolerance for stress, weaker perception, and slower reactivity.

Hemmer suggests that this evolution (or devolution) may be the combined result of hormonal change, brain-size reduction, less acute vision and hearing, and the retention of juvenile traits into adulthood—a process called neoteny.

The neotenic theory (and a similar hypothesis called the "mesomorphic remodeling theory") holds that selection for domestication favored dogs who reached reproductive maturity during the adolescent rather than the fully mature period (by which time behavior is fixed). Remember Mech's experiment with wolves removed from their parents? They matured sexually at 9 or 10 months rather than the normal lupine 2 years. The domestic dog exhibits traits characteristic of both juvenile and adult wolves—traits that are inherited but not fixed, which allows for great diversity. Thus the dog is able to draw from a wider variety of behavior packages to become what is required of him by his humans. The first change, Hemmer believes, may have been the coat color. The earliest, most primitive dogs were a solid tawny-yellow color (like that of the present-day dingo or Carolina dog). He believes there may have been, at least at one time, an association between temperament and coat color.

While hardly uniform, this suggestion resonates today. Many experienced Labrador owners note character differences among the yellow, black, and chocolate varieties; in other breeds, however, there seems to be no difference at all. This is a case in which a behavior pattern might accidentally accompany another characteristic, or one characteristic might accompany another whether it was selected for or not. This happens all the time. A related theory is offered by Raymond Coppinger:[31] suppose a villager selects a dog for special care because it has an interesting coat color. A dog given special care is more likely to survive and thus pass on the gene for that color to its offspring. Once humans get involved, we tend to look for weird things.

Whatever domestication means, everyone agrees that dogs have a particular knack for it. Most animals (tigers, rhinos, hyenas, zebras, crocodiles, and the like) aren't very good at it. Certain other animals, like chickens, pigs, and goats, are domestic only in the sense that they put up with humans to a certain extent; horses have become "tame" in that they permit us to ride them, but every new foal has to be "broken," just like his wild forebears. As for cats, the old saying that every alley cat is potentially a house cat—and the opposite—is very true. Even truly wild animals like zebras, crocodiles, (and wolves) can become accustomed to their keepers.

Where Did It Happen?

Evolutionary geneticist Robert Wayne and his fellow researchers believe that the birthplace of the dog was probably East Asia (possibly present-day China) because animals from this region have the most mtDNA variation today.[32] This suggests that those dogs have been around much, much longer than dogs from, say, North America, who undoubtedly crossed the land-bridge from Asia with their human companions—the first "Americans." (It was once suggested that New World dogs developed here and Old World dogs developed in Asia. We now know that is not true—all dogs come from Eurasia.) Additionally, many genetic sequences were found *only* in East Asia, which suggests that dogs existed there for a length of time sufficient to allow that particular population to acquire some unique characteristics.

Biologist Jennifer Leonard from the Smithsonian Museum of Natural History in Washington, D.C., collected the remains of dogs buried in pre-Columbian North, Central, and South America and compared their mtDNA with that of the east Asian dogs (which were dug up from the Alaskan permafrost) to determine the place and time of origin of the modern domestic dog.[33] (It was essential to pick ancient New World dogs, because native American dogs were very likely interbred with European ones soon after the European colonists set foot on the continent, thus making contemporary American dogs useless for the study.) She writes, "Our data strongly support the hypothesis that ancient American and Eurasian domestic dogs share a common origin from Old World gray wolves. This implies that the humans who colonized America 12,000 to 14,000 years B.P. [before present] brought multiple lineages of domesticated dogs with them. The large diversity of mtDNA lineage in the dogs that colonized the New World implies that the ancestral population of dogs in Eurasia was large and well mixed at that time." DNA evidence further suggests that dogs domesticated themselves in more than one place, but probably not in hundreds of places; it was a rare—though not unique—event. Leonard also asserts, based on the collected DNA evidence, that the earliest North American settlers brought 5 separate lineages of dogs along with them.

Leonard's work reinforced that of Peter Savolainen from Stockholm's Royal Institute of Technology, who researched genetic variance within dog populations by examining mtDNA sequence variation among 654 domestic dogs, which represented all major dog populations worldwide.[34] Robert K. Wayne and Carlès Vila, evolutionary geneticists at UCLA, assessed differences in a section of the mitochondrial genomes of hundreds of different breeds as well as those of wolves, coyotes, and jackals. They found that dog and wolf DNA differ from each other by about only 1 percent, while that of wolves and coyotes (which diverged from a common ancestor a million years ago) differed by 7.5 percent. This further proves that only wolves are the ancestors of dogs, and also refutes Charles Darwin's assertion that jackals were somehow involved. Konrad Lorenz, the Nobel-prize winning ethologist who coined the term "imprinting," also thought that some breeds were descended from wolves and others from golden jackals.[35] Jackals are innocent of the charge. (Jackals don't even behave like wolves—they are loners and don't form packs.) All dog DNA sequences differed from the closest jackal sequences by 20 mutations, as opposed to—at most—12 in wolves. In fact, one DNA sequence is identical in both dogs and wolves. It turns out that this dog-family also includes the "primitive" species such as the Australian Dingo, New Guinea singing dog, and the Basenji. So what all this means is that every single breed of dog, from the Australian Dingo to the Chihuahua to the Gordon Setter to the Siberian Husky to the Pharaoh Hound to the Chow Chow, share DNA sequences that are essentially indistinguishable from one another.

This doesn't mean that all dog behavior is identical, however, any more than their physical appearance is. For one thing, there is no "behavior gene." That doesn't mean that some aspects of behavior aren't genetically influenced, or even controlled; it means that there is no "retrieving gene" and no "lead-blind-people" gene. In other words, behavior is a multifactorial phenomenon; genes may control behavior, but only in a complex, integrated fashion.

Scott and Fuller discovered, for example, that primitive breeds like Basenjis (whose name means "wild thing") behaved very differently, particularly as very young puppies, than Cocker Spaniels. In experimental conditions, 62 percent of Cocker Spaniels showed no fearful reactions at all to the normal behavior of handlers; all Basenjis showed at least some fearful behavior.[36] In fact, Basenjis acted very much like wolf cubs until 5 weeks of age—avoiding human contact, vocalizing alarm, running away, snapping when cornered, and exhibiting other sign of wolf-like shyness. Basenjis also struggled much more frequently and forcefully during leash training than Cockers or Beagles, and exhibited more aggression during play. But Basenjis are dogs, not wolves, and were readily tamed through human contact. Such adaptability has great survival value in the semi-feral conditions in which they developed.

The researchers hypothesized that there is a single dominant "wild gene" in the Basenji that accounts for the differences in behavior. Although recent advances in genetics makes this supposition unlikely, it is true that Basenjis have retained more of the "wild" characteristics of their ancestors than have other breeds. Even their physiology is a bit different. For example, unlike most dogs (but like wolves), Basenjis come into heat only once a year. However, while wolves tend to come into heat in late winter, the modal time for Basenjis is September and October. (When researchers crossed Basenjis with Cocker Spaniels, however, the offspring's heat cycles were quite variable.)

When Did It Happen?

Long before sheep, horses, or cows became part of human culture, dogs were with us. The exact date is still uncertain, in part because researchers have not yet decisively concluded if the process began with one wolf family (in which case the earlier time period applies) or with three.

Wayne and company push the wolf domestication date back to about 135,000 years ago, a date that leaves most of their colleagues (like Savolainen, a former colleague of Wayne's) growling.[37] Some opponents object to such an early date on the dubious grounds that primitive humans could not have been "sophisticated enough" to keep the newly domesticated dogs from crossbreeding back to wolves. (After all, these people survived the Ice Age.) Besides, wolves would probably not have accepted the proto-dog into their pack. And the new dogs, as mentioned earlier, would not have welcomed the outsiders.

> One reason that the timing question remains unanswered is a linguistic one—we have no precise definition of "domestication." What qualifies an animal for this designation? Well, a 12,000-year-old grave discovered in Israel contained a woman with a puppy in her hands, while a man was buried nearby with two small canids. Many scientists consider this evidence proof that truly domesticated dogs existed from that time. They're just guessing, however, as they have no way of knowing for sure what the relationship between the woman and the puppy was—or how they both ended up dead.

Those researchers who suggest a later, Mesolithic (when people where settled—about 15,000 years ago) as opposed to Paleolithic (when people were probably somewhat more nomadic—about 750,000 years ago) origin of domestication have a present-day model of how it might have occurred. As Ray and Lorna Coppinger observed on the island of Pemba off the East African coast, the local feral dogs could be approached by human beings but not touched.[38] The dogs roam the village in family groups of two or three and make their living by scavenging from the locals, who live a hunter-gatherer existence. Although the dogs are not helpful to the people (and are in fact considered "unclean"), they are tolerated. Since each home on the island has its own latrine and dumpsite, the dogs have a wealth of resources; each family of dogs tends to "adopt" a certain house. Early domestication may well have proceeded along these lines—although it's hard to say.

Feral dogs were once ubiquitous in every urban area. Most first-world countries have eliminated them through trapping and euthanasia; in developing countries, however, they are still a common sight. Most are shy, gentle creatures (vicious dogs would soon be killed by local human inhabitants) and, although ignored or even despised by villagers, they manage to eke out a living by eating refuse or occasionally the corpses of dead villagers. According to Ray Coppinger, who has studied them for decades, these village dogs are not "strays"; they are the true descendants of the first Mesolithic dogs and carry the world's most ancient and pure canine blood. They are the nexus among wolves and Wolfhounds, Weimaraners and West Highland White Terriers.

Stray and feral dogs have a bad rep, but they are much less likely to attack people than coddled family dogs because they are less territorial (they have no territory to defend) and prefer to stay clear of people.

Feral dogs tend to grow to resemble each other, not just within a particular gene pool as one might expect, but worldwide. Hot-climate feral dogs have short hair, tulip-shaped ears, and tend to be of small-medium size (usually under 30 pounds and 17 to 18 inches at the withers). Such a dog can handle the heat, keep itself clean, and is big enough to find some prey (like mice), yet small enough to feed itself easily. Cold-weather feral dogs have a heavier coat and tend to be a little larger, which helps them to preserve body heat.

Modern village dogs have certainly abandoned the hunting behavior of their ancestors. They also consume a much wider variety of foods than will a wolf, although a wolf will sometimes devour a small amount of plant material even if not forced to it by a lack of game. Feral dogs are too small to be effective killers of big game (even if there were any big game to be had) and they make a much better living as inoffensive scavengers. All canids can survive on a plant-only diet (if the proteins are balanced), but they prefer a meat diet (and thrive better on it as well).

The Beginning of Breeding

The development of breeds began very early in the annals of the dog-human relationships (3,000–5,000 years ago). These original breeds were largely identified by function: sheepdogs, pointers, sighthounds, and so on. Looks didn't much matter. (In fact, several ancient writers describe vastly different looking dogs as belonging to the same "breed.")

For instance, shepherd dogs come in various sizes, shapes, and ear types; however, they were originally considered one breed because of their identical function. Soon, however, breed typing came to be based upon anatomical features rather than function, although such classifications were still largely related to practical use. The Roman writer Columella recommended that sheepdogs be white so they wouldn't be mistaken for wolves by the sheep or the shepherd. (Columella was obviously unfamiliar with the white wolves of the arctic regions.) At any rate, many modern sheepdogs are indeed white or pale, including the Komondor, Kuvasz, and Maremma. Columella also recommended that guard dogs be black with big square heads so they would scare away thieves—and have drooping ears, which were intended to serve the same purpose. I can't figure out what's so scary about drooping ears myself, but that was his opinion.

Many features common in domestic dogs, such as variegated colors (or rich solid colors like the mahogany of the Irish Setter and the steel gray of the Weimaraner), floppy ears, absurdly short legs, and crank tails have no evolutionary advantage—at least not so far as anyone can see. Most of them are maladaptive; in the natural course of things, they would soon have disappeared. Bright colors make a predator too visible, floppy ears are prone to infection, short legs make long-distance running impractical, and crank tails are not able to communicate intentions.

Some of these mutations are advantageous in the service of humans, however. For example, a short-legged Dachshund is able to enter a badger's den and pull out the prey. However, I suspect that most of these traits were allowed to persist for that most human of all reasons—people found them charming. No one yet knows for sure what phenotypical characteristics are linked with which specific genetic mutations, although there are some interesting hypotheses. Most experts believe that many of the odd traits found in dogs but never seen in wolves result from disruption of the timing of the early developmental stages rather than genetic differences. Others, such as the dwarfism of the Basset Hound, are surely the result of a different sort of genetic mutation.

It should be noted that the development of the most extremely weird dogs took place in the imperial palaces of China, where the nobility had the time and leisure to indulge their whims in the pet-production department. As for the hunting usefulness of Dachshunds and other short-legged hounds, it's not clear whether people found them cute first and useful second, or whether they noticed that shorter-legged animals could contribute something valuable to the success of the hunt and were bred selectively.

So far, it is a matter of controversy as to whether the smaller skull (and brain) and less formidable teeth of dogs were selected (as some writers suggest) to reduce the conspicuous ferocity of the animal, or whether (as other writers seem equally sure) these features unintentionally accompanied other desired traits in domesticated dogs. Those like Coppinger and Schneider, who suggest the latter, point out that larger teeth are advantageous in the hunting of dangerous game like bear (or wolves) and hence would have been valuable attributes to Neolithic hunters, who would have preserved them if they could have.[39] They believe that in some way not yet understood, the small brain and small teeth were necessary concomitants of domestication. We may never know the truth. We will (probably) never be sure whether factors like diverse coat colors were selected on purpose or were a side effect of some other mutation or change important for domestication.

Chapter 3:
The Dog Today, or It's the Breeding, Stupid

"Extraordinary creature!
So close a friend, and yet so remote."
—Thomas Mann

About 400 million dogs currently exist on planet Earth (about 55 million in the United States alone), and there are at least 420 known breeds. (Of course, the vast majority of dogs are mixed—often several times over—breeds.) We see dogs everywhere—on farms and city streets, in suburban parks and maybe in your own living room. In contrast, only about 400,000 wolves are left, and they have kept, at least until recently, to the loneliest reaches of the farthest places. Despite their geographical and numerical separation, however, there exists a close psychological and physical kinship between *Canis lupus* and *Canis lupus familiaris*. And paradoxically, despite their many similarities, the rite of passage we call domestication has forged a great gulf between them.

A statistical curiosity: 400,000 wolves, 4 million coyotes, 40 million jackals, and 400 million dogs. Odd. Because they have learned to live in close proximity to people, the coyote population continues to expand while that of the wolf declines. New observations, however, suggest that a few wolves are moving into the suburbs—perhaps taking a page from their descendants' book.

A couple of centuries ago there were only about 15 identifiable dog breeds; now there are at more than 400. (The precise number varies depending on the source and the date from which one is counting.) Most of today's recognized breeds were created during or since the late nineteenth century, and they were developed mostly through hybridization, mongrelization, or crossbreeding—all of which are pretty much synonymous terms. One partial exception seems to be certain Norwegian breeds, which have a highly divergent type of DNA. This is as yet an unexplained anomaly, for even the Xoloitzcuintle (Mexican Hairless) and the Australian Dingo have the same DNA hodgepodge as the rest of dogdom.

The Saluki is considered the oldest commonly recognized dog breed (dating from 329 B.C.E.), although I'm betting the Siberian Husky is even older. The Saluki is pictured in ancient art; the people who developed the Siberian Husky, the Chukchis, left no similar legacy. However, just because the Chukchis didn't draw or sculpt their dogs doesn't mean that the animals didn't exist; the same can be said for many other old breeds. Yet we must not make the opposite mistake—assuming that because a certain breed (like the Siberian Husky) seems to bear closer physical resemblance to the wolf than, say, the Saluki, it must therefore be older.

The newest breeds have emerged within the last few years, and the practice of producing unique breeds will probably continue indefinitely. Stephen Budiansky, in his wonderful book *The Truth About Dogs*, writes that dogs "are a brilliant evolutionary success almost without parallel in the animal world, and they owe that success to their uncanny ability to worm themselves into our homes, and to our relentless anthropomorphic psyche that lets them do it."[40] This wise observation suggests that as we busily examine the dog for the mysterious qualities that so endear them to us, we ought to take a look into our own minds as well. Just as the dog has the genetic capacity to morph itself into the being of our desires, we humans have the ability to imagine an ideal dog—and the skill to create that being out of the raw material the dog offers.

Budiansky follows his remarks about the dog's aptitude for evolutionary success with an observation that I question: "…[W]hen man [or presumably woman] comes face to face with dog, the will to inflict serious bodily harm mysteriously melts away. Dogs, in an evolutionary sense, know this. They cringe, they whine, they look soulfully into our eyes, and we say, 'Aww. The heck with it,' drop the rock and go our way." If only this were true. The reality is that human beings have inflicted incredible pain and suffering on dogs. We do not always drop the rock. The dog's pleading and cringing are evolved behaviors that worked well in the wolf community; with humans, the same behaviors have been successful only on a limited basis. Human beings have neglected dogs, abused them, abandoned them, raced them, raised them to fight each other to the death, willfully tortured them, irradiated them, and vivisected them (the horrendous injuries scientists have inflicted on the gentlest of all dogs, Beagles, are beyond mentioning). Dogs are eaten, beaten, and starved over much of the earth. For centuries, dogs that weren't treated as vermin were working dogs that were considered akin to livestock, not family members. The treasured pets we like to read and write about are distinctly in the minority, even today. Lately there has been a sea change in the attitudes of the more enlightened; thoughtful people are now routinely outraged by cruelty to dogs and any other animals—but apparently not infuriated enough to put an end to it.

Breed and Character

It makes perfect sense to most people that just as various breeds of dogs have developed different body types, head shapes, coat lengths, and working abilities, their temperaments have also become differentiated.

For example, it is easier to train a Labrador than a Bulldog; German Shepherds can be persuaded to bite people more easily than English Setters. It is not sensible to pretend otherwise—and it's dangerous.

Yet, in researching the mysteries of breed and breed characteristics, I have come upon an amazing number of otherwise supposedly knowledgeable people who maintain that their breed (whatever it is) has no particular character or temperament—any differences lie in the individuality of each dog. "Every Wirehaired Bulgarian Windwalking Birdsniffer is different!" they insist. "Just like human beings, they can range from saints to devils." Although it is true that each dog is an individual, this does not mean that there are no common breed temperaments. Chow Chows, as a group, do not have the personality of Border Collies despite the fact that some overlap (at least in individual cases) exists. After all, unlike human beings, dogs have for millennia been bred partly to express a certain kind of temperament—from fierce and independent to sweet and docile.

> I suppose part of the difficulty arises from the fact that we sense—but refuse to recognize—a terrible parallel. If we acknowledge that different breeds have natural temperamental differences, what does that imply about humans? The cases are not analogous. Human beings do not come in "breeds"; we appear in randomly bred bunches across the planet. And because there is no "breeder," we are more like varieties of wolves than breeds of dogs. And just as wolves (as a group) do have a certain temperament, so do people (as a group). As Steven Pinker shows in his masterful *The Blank Slate: The Modern Denial of Human Nature*, the idea that humans are infinitely malleable is unsupported by modern science.[41] We too are "hard-wired" to a degree and so exhibit the same basic characteristics all over the world.

But in dogs, breeding matters—for behavior as much as for looks; a little is in the training and a whole lot is in the genes. Although a significant amount of research has been done concerning genetic patterns of disease inheritance, investigations that use genetics to assess behavioral patterns are just beginning. The first studies, done early in the twentieth century, concentrated on vocal trailing in Foxhounds and gun-shyness in German Shepherd dogs. Early researchers had little to go on but rudimentary Mendelian genetics, and while their conclusions were interesting, they were also probably oversimplified. They suggested, for example, that gun-shyness was controlled by a simple gene series with two alleles—N for undersensitivity and n for oversensitivity. They coupled this idea with a gene for body sensitivity which they labeled S for undersensitivity and s for oversensitivity. Based on these theories, they suggested that breeders of police dogs try to produce dogs that were Nn/Ss—which seems logical but is perhaps impossible. We now know that ear and body sensitivity are not controlled by single genes, although such sensitivities are indeed specific traits important to the breeders of many working dogs. Elaine Ostrander, a molecular geneticist with the Dog Genome Project, worked to isolate the specific genes responsible for herding behavior in Border Collies and the Newfoundlands' passion for swimming.[42] She crossed, recrossed, and crossed again between the breeds, and finally concluded that a number of genes are responsible for each behavior, as one might expect. The multifactorial nature of most behavior makes it difficult to identify, let alone control.

No matter how the balance between nurture and nature finally works out with human beings, we already know the answer with animals: if breeding didn't matter, we wouldn't have breeds. If it were all in the training, we could make Pekinese herd sheep as easily as Border Collies do. Dogs don't have to do everything they can in order to survive as do wolves because we humans support them. Thus we can develop breeds of specialist dogs, choosing traits that relate well to what we want the breed to do. If they lack the ability to make their own living, it doesn't matter; they don't have to. On the other hand, specialization allows them to develop traits that make them superior to their forbears in many ways; that's why some dogs can run faster than wolves, outfight wolves, etc. No one breed of dog can do it all the way a wolf has to; conversely, no wolf is well adapted to the specialized tasks we ask of contemporary dogs.

If the observation that breeding matters needs any more substantiation, one can refer to John Paul Scott and John L. Fuller's classic study *Genetics and the Social Behavior of Dogs*, published in 1965.[43]

(This famous study also established the timing of critical periods in developing puppies and, although it is forty years old, it remains exceedingly timely.) Their research, which examined breeds as temperamentally different as Basenjis and Cocker Spaniels, demonstrated that although the dogs were raised and fed alike, they retained their inherited behavior patterns—although there was variation among individuals as would be expected when dealing with such an adaptable animal.

> When researchers Scott and Fuller crossed Basenjis and Cocker Spaniels, they found that, in general, their scores on obedience, leash fighting, spatial orientation, reactivity (which was tested, unfortunately, by administering mild electrical shocks to the subjects), cue response, and motivation were intermediate to that of the parents. They emphasize, however, that genetic mechanisms alone could not control all types of behavior, and found (apparently to their surprise) that "trait structure was somewhat fluid." Dogs are always surprising people, it seems.

Scott and Fuller also attempted to measure the intelligence of various breeds. (Intelligence should not be confused with trainability, although it usually is; wolves, for example, are intelligent but not trainable.) Using various types of problem-solving tests, Scott and Fuller demonstrated that no single breed they tested consistently came out on top. Hunting dogs (Beagles, Basenjis, Terriers, and Cocker Spaniels) tended to rank highest, probably because the tests were designed to measure independent thinking skills. These are the same breeds, by the way, that sometimes rank lowest on standard "dog intelligence tests." (I'd like to test the intelligence of the human who designed those.) Some of the challenges consisted of putting a towel over a dog's head and timing how long it took the animal to remove the towel. Presumably, the sooner the towel comes off, the smarter the dog. Why this should be so is hard to imagine. Some dogs seem to enjoy having their heads draped with towels.

Beagles did the best of Scott's tested breeds, while Shetland Sheepdogs, which are often considered much smarter, fared much worse. The explanation may lie in the fact that Shelties are oriented to working with people and thus look to them for direction, while hounds are expected to find game independently. Hounds are stubborn, which in the field is called "persistence." (In like manner, hounds are much more motivated by food rewards than are dogs bred to work by human command.)

Of course, every trait that dogs exhibit was mined from the mother lode, the wolf. Herding dogs encircle and pick out their "victims" the same way a wolf circles a herd of deer. The sheepdog guards its flock the way a wolf guards its pack—by using strong protective rather than strong killing instincts. In some cases, we've done such a good job in our selection that we've out-wolved the wolves. Most gazehounds can outrun a wolf; bloodhounds can follow a cold trail (it's not in a wolf's interest to follow an ice-cold game trail); and junkyard dogs are much more aggressive and nasty. These qualities don't make the dog a better animal than the wolf; it just makes them better suited to our needs. Neither a guard dog nor a bloodhound would last a month in the wild without a lot of lucky breaks—and nature is pretty stingy with those.

The Beginning of Breeding

When human beings started breeding domestic dogs, we chose a specific wolf behavioral trait (or, more recently, a look) that we wanted to emphasize in each breed. Originally, nearly all breeding was done to produce certain working abilities; back then, no one cared what a sheepdog looked like as long as it could herd sheep.

The ancient Roman historian Pliny divided dogs into groups according to their function: *villatici* (house dogs, by which he meant guardian types), *pastoralis pecuarii* (sheepherding dogs), *venactici* (sporting dogs), *nares sagaces* ("wise-nosed" or scenthounds), *pugnaces* ("fighting") or *bellicosi* ("war") dogs, and *pedibus celeres* ("fleet-footed" dogs or gazehounds).

During the Renaissance, there was a huge proliferation of breeds. Hunting was a major pastime in those days, and so most breeds were hunting types adapted to different sorts of game: wolfhounds, boarhounds, deerhounds, otterhounds, elkhounds, foxhounds, and the like. If we wanted a dog to hunt independently either in a pack or alone, we chose the traits that gave rise to hounds (pack dogs that often go after larger game like fox, gazelle, or otters) or terriers (lone hunters that tend to pursue smaller game easily handled by one dog). We didn't select for cooperation in terriers because they didn't need it—and, by gosh, they don't have it.

We selected vocal animals for watchdog duty and quiet ones for stealth hunters. Even today we use the silent bloodhound to track criminals whom we don't wish to alert to our presence and the noisy beagle to tell us where the rabbit is headed. In any event, there's no way a pack of beagles can sneak up on the perpetually nervous rabbit. Pack hunters are usually noisy, alerting one another to the presence of prey; lone hunters are quiet.

There is a widespread (and ancient) belief that scenthounds have long ears to "stir up" scent particles and carry them to the nose. There is no evidence to support this frequently repeated allegation, and many tracking dogs do not have especially long ears. German Shepherds and Norwegian Elkhounds are superior trackers, but have erect ears; conversely, other breeds that do not typically hunt by scent (such as Salukis) do have long ears. Breeds like Beagles, Bassets, and Bloodhounds are called "scenthounds" because that's the way they find game; it's a genetic thing. It is usually claimed that these breeds have better smellers than other breeds, but studies have not really confirmed this. Bloodhounds (who do have long ears) seem more adept than other breeds at following smell-trails that are quite old, but this seems to reveal more about their perseverance and single-mindedness than their smelling powers. Scientific tests conducted to find out which breed really has the best nose have had mixed results, although there seems to be a correlation between big noses and keen scenting ability. This seems only logical.

This is not to say that purely aesthetic choices were not involved in early breeding attempts—at least in some cases, Certain breeds, notably toys, were probably selected purely on those grounds. During the latter half of the nineteenth century in Europe, the emphasis in the dog world began to shift from work to looks, even in the so-called working and hunting breeds, which in turn gave rise to the development of nearly half of the world's present breeds. A few of these are refinements of older working breeds, but most of the newest breeds were developed to be companion animals. It was also during this period that "breed standards" were developed—the odd idea that the value of even a working dog was at least partly dependent on its looks rather than its function. Today, however, every breed standard (as we shall see) emphasizes looks, including elements that have no connection with any supposed purpose. In fact, looks became the sine qua non and are now more important to many breeders than either health or temperament. That is not to say, however, that every companion dog has the same kind of temperament; companion means different things to different people, and what one person considers an acceptable temperament may not be welcome to another.

The shift of emphasis from function to looks accompanied the birth of kennel clubs. The first was Great Britain's Kennel Club (1873); the AKC followed shortly thereafter. Prior to that time, dogs were assigned to rather loose, "unofficial" groups, such as terrier, mastiff, pointer, and so forth. The development and naming of specific breeds (such as differentiating a Norfolk from a Norwich terrier) took many, many years. For a long time, some breeds that are now considered separate breeds were shown together in the ring. Today, however, breed clubs are "closed registries" that prohibit crossbreeding, a common practice until recently, and one which served to keep the gene pool larger and breeds strong and healthy. The only thing you have to do to get your dog "registered" with most kennel clubs nowadays (at least in the United States) is to prove that its parents were registered. The dog itself could harbor a host of genetic defects, but the AKC does not require any testing in order to get the dog registered—something that is now readily available for many genetic conditions.

Stephen Budiansky suggests that the obsession with purity of breed in dogs coincided with the Progressive Era obsession with "racial" (read "white Anglo-Saxon") purity in humans.[44] Not entirely by coincidence, one of the best known early writers on dog breeding, Leon Fradley Whitney (1894–1973), also wrote *The Case for Sterilization* (about human beings) in 1934, for which he received a nice congratulatory letter from Adolf Hitler himself. Whitney didn't confine himself to books on eugenics and dogs, either; he is also known for his immortal *Keep Your Pigeons Flying*. You must have read it. At any rate, eugenics became the catchword of the post-Victorian age, with tragic consequences for humans. Dog breeds suffered as well.

The Pitfalls of Breeding

Developing breeds is a risky business, particularly for the objects of the breeding program. More than 100 years ago, Darwin told us that artificial selection serves human whims; it does not inherently benefit either the dog or its breed. Natural selection, on the other hand, does work to enhance the survival of a species, although it doesn't give a hoot about any individual animal. The multitude of dog types now extant are the result of (1) our deliberate selection of traits we find useful to us (the working dog model), and (2) our equally deliberate selection of bizarre or exotic traits that we find "cute." Unfortunately, some negative effects on health and temperament have accompanied both types of selection.

Two related kinds of inherited disorders occur in dogs, both of which are the inadvertent result of deliberate selection. First are the out-and-out disease conditions—those that become increasingly widespread with the overuse of popular sires (especially in breeds with small populations). Von Willebrand's disease, a bleeding disorder once rare but now seen in many breeds, is one example. The second are the result of the unfortunate practice breeding for extreme "type," which distorts the normal wolf phenotype to an unhealthy extent. Dogs can morph only so much before trouble sets in. Almost invariably, the distorted part of the anatomy becomes the focus of disease—the back, the breathing apparatus, or the ears.

Modern selective breeding can produce beautiful, skilled, and sociable animals. But selective breeding has also produced such canine wonders as:

▼ Oversized Great Danes who are potential cases of bloat on four paws.

▼ "Teacup" Chihuahuas so fragile they break if you look at them funny.

▼ Pekes so pop-eyed that their eyes can easily be dislodged from the skull.

▼ Bulldogs with such unnaturally shaped skulls that they are unable to be birthed naturally.

▼ Hairless dogs unable to cope with sun or cold.

▼ Dachshunds so long that ruptured disks are almost a certainty.

▼ German Shepherd dogs whose sloping toplines are so extreme that they seem to be morphing into hyenas.

▼ Cocker Spaniels with ears so long and heavy that they are almost continually infected.

▼ Komondors whose spectacular coat will turn into a giant mat if not laboriously cared for daily.

▼ Bassets and Bloodhounds whose eyes show so much haw that they have a high risk of eye infection and the invasion of foreign bodies.

While earlier breeding strategies seem to have had some objective usefulness, such as propensities for herding, hunting, or guarding, the traits listed above benefit neither the dogs nor ourselves in any practical way and are, in fact, detrimental. The only benefit of such traits is that we think they are charming or cute.

Most bulldogs and other brachycephalic breeds can't breathe very well because they suffer from "airway syndrome," a condition resulting solely from the anatomy of their smashed-in faces. Many toy breeds (which are often considered "babies" by their owners) have the same rounded head type and a skull that is sometimes not even completely closed. One can only conclude that early breeders found it too cute for words and perpetuated the trait—another example of neoteny. The passion for smashed-in faces is apparently linked with the charm of puppies. Puppies, when compared with adults of the same breeds, have larger, rounder heads and shorter muzzles in proportion to their body size. Since human babies share some of these characteristics, perhaps there is a generalized mammalian preference for such a look in our young.

Juliet Clutton-Block presents the Pekinese as the most extreme example of a purely "pet" dog.[45] She writes, "[I]ts soft fur, large eyes, and 'infantile' face must represent the ideal baby substitute and the complete antithesis of the wolf." The evolution of the Pekinese's skull from that of the wolf, she notes, "must rank as one of the most extraordinary examples known of morphological variation within a single species." Morphologically, yes; however, some of the wolf-spirit still remains. The Pekinese is a formidable watchdog for its size, and as Clutton-Brock herself notes, this little "lion-dog" was first bred in the Imperial Palace of Beijing to look like the lion-spirit of the Buddha. How closely the Pekinese resembles a lion, however, is somewhat debatable.

Selecting for anatomically perverse features is only part of the problem, however. Many deleterious traits have crept in as an unintended concomitant of a desirable or at least accepted trait. For example, Bruce Fogle notes that modern dogs are exhibiting an "avalanche of rage syndrome."[46] This condition sometimes appears in Cocker Spaniels, and it occurs most often in buff-colored Cockers, less often in the black variety, and almost never in those of mixed color. Somehow, rage syndrome is genetically connected (at least partially) to coat color. No one bred for rage, presumably, but we've got it now. There are a number of behaviorists who deny that rage syndrome is actually a physical condition, but that's a whole other argument. We also see deafness in white Bull Terriers, but not in the colored variety. Breeders were obviously not breeding for deafness, but for whiteness; they got both. The sudden explosion in anterior cruciate ligament (ACL) problems in many breeds may relate to certain conformation "standards." For instance, ACL rupture in dogs was once primarily a disease of older animals; today we see dogs affected at younger and younger ages. It's not because they're getting injured (in canines this condition is usually a result of abnormal degeneration of the ligament, not sudden stress), although that can occur; and when one knee goes, in about 75 percent of the cases the other knee will too, and usually within a year. (Exceptions ordinarily occur when the rupture was due to injury.) It is unclear whether the blame lies in breeding animals that are prone to the problems or whether the breed standards themselves encourage disease by emphasizing abnormal structure.

As Dr. Vicki Adams of Britain's Animal Health Trust writes, "While some health problems in purebred dogs have been shown to be due to specific genetic mutations, other health problems are thought to result from the selection of animals for breeding *according to* breed standards" (emphasis added).[47]

Most significant, of course, are defects that are literally written into the breed standard. Let's consider one aspect of canine health: the eyes. The "Current Eye Disease Overview," sponsored by the AKC Canine Health Foundation, states that "[s]ome of the ophthalmic conformation standards for certain breeds are unacceptable by today's standards.[48] Eyes excessively deep within the orbit as well as those more prominent than normal predispose a dog to an entire life of ophthalmic disease (persistent ocular discharge; chronic conjunctivitis; corneal ulceration and pigmentation). Medical and surgical treatments of these conditions are of variable success and expensive. Prominent or protruding nictitating membranes or 'haws' are abnormal and should also be addressed. Eyelid disorders are also part of several current breed standards and need to be eliminated."

The good news is that what we've bred in, we can breed out—as long as the gene pool is large enough. We can maintain the looks of a breed we like, at least to some extent, and ameliorate or even dispense with aggressive tendencies or unhealthy sequelae. After all, responsible people no longer raise dogs to fight with each other. For example, the spunkiness of terriers may be genetically linked to intraspecific (dog against dog) aggression, but that's not necessarily so. However, as long as show terriers are rewarded for "sparring" in the ring, breeders won't attempt to ameliorate their pugnacity; as long as breed standards applaud an animal's aggressive nature, it's unlikely that problems with aggression will decrease. And as long as people who have no victories in their own lives take pride in owning a dangerous dog, we'll continue to see attacks upon human beings—usually children.

Another interesting example is bloat. In the past 30 years there has been a 1500 percent increase in this life-threatening condition. Much of it has to do with the popularity of kibble as a dog's sole source of food, but the incidence of bloat is also strongly related to body type. Dogs with a deep, narrow abdomen are at higher risk. (It is a better predictor that the chest measurement, which is also sometimes used.) Researchers believe that that a deeper, narrower abdomen supplies the space needed for the stomach ligament to overstretch during the aging process. (Most bloat occurs in older animals.) If breeders really care about reducing the incidence of bloat in their breed, they should start attempting to restructure the breed into a more normal and healthy configuration. I'm still waiting for a serious dialogue to start on this subject.

Jane Brackman writes in "Working Hard to Hardly Working" that "eliminating spinal degenerative diseases will introduce inconsistency in tail carriage and gait, or that identifying markers for eye disease and eliminating the breed carriers will introduce variation in muzzle-width—looks not in keeping with breed standards.[49] What if we find out that some physical conformation requirements are counter to health in our pedigreed dogs? Will we be able to shake loose our concept of breeds as animals that look identical—the breed ideal the Victorians formulated for us?" Will we, indeed?

Dog Shows

One of the stated purposes of all this breeding, crossbreeding, and inbreeding relate to the infernal world of dog shows, which is as strange and inbred as the animals they feature. The first dog show was a social occasion organized by British aristocrats to raise money for charity; today it has become a deadly serious event centered on money, egos, and delusion. Of course, many fanciers participate in shows "for fun," but big kennels, big prestige (in the dog world), and increasingly big money at the top make it clear that it's not all about fun, much less charity, any more.

In the modern show dog we have arrived at a peculiar state of affairs. The dog is neither a working partner, as the sheepdog or guardian or hunting dog was; nor is he a pet or companion animal. (A show dog may incidentally be a pet or even a working dog, but as a "show dog" he is neither.) In fact, in the show dog we have reached the final objectification of the dog—the canine as a work of art, a commodity. As Oscar Wilde maintained, "all art is quite useless," and what strange works of art we have constructed—in many cases not so much beautiful as ornamental, or interesting so much as bizarre. In show dogs, we see pampered "pets" who all too often are never allowed the joy of running through fields and getting dirty. I know several show beagles that have never seen a rabbit, and show pointers that can't point.

Most of these highly advertised works of art are empty shells of dogs that are seldom asked—and would probably fail—to do what they were bred to do. In fact, they are often required to demonstrate qualities converse to their original function. This doesn't make them bad dogs, but let's not fool ourselves about the purposes that lie behind the breeding of these dogs.

The glory (if it can be called that) of such dogs lies in their ability to approximate a vaguely written breed standard. The goal is to a win a "title" of "champion" for the dog, after which the animal is considered "finished" (which is, to me, a dismissive and almost ominous-sounding term). In order to gain the title, many owners resort to a professional handler who ostensibly possesses some magical ability to "show" the dog (a feat that consists of trotting the animal around the ring and presenting him to a judge in such a way that, at least notionally, emphasizes the dog's good points and disguises the bad ones). However, the handler's real value may lie in his or her skill at exploiting dog-show politics and the good-old-boy network than in showing dogs. (It is perfectly legitimate to hire someone to handle a dog; it is not legitimate to dye your dog's coat, correct its bite with braces, or have its appearance altered and "faults" corrected through cosmetic surgery. These things are done, however—and quite regularly, too.)

To reach the pinnacle of dog show success—an invitation to the Westminster Kennel Club Show—a "campaign" budget of about $100,000 a year is required, which includes "advertising" the dog in breed magazines. (In a real sport, like horseracing or basketball, the participants do not need to advertise themselves. Their performance is all the advertising they need.) Is this really "breeding for the love of the breed"?

One problem—and perhaps the most serious one—with dog shows is that they reward extremes. For example, let's consider the word "long" as it relates to dog anatomy. If a coat is supposed to be long (Maltese), let's see how long it can be made, even until it drags along the ground. If a stride is supposed to be long (German shepherd dog), the longer the better, even to the point where the gait becomes unnatural. Basset ears must be long, and so longer must be better, even though the dog may step on them. It is this kind of thinking that rules the ring, even when it is officially discouraged.

Dr. Irene Stur of the University of Vienna Animals Genetic Institute postulates that when we breed for external traits only (as in breeding show dogs to standards), we also concentrate the genes linked to those that produce the desired overt characteristics.[50] Those linked genes can often produce undesirable traits, including behavioral problems. For example, "depigmented breeds," such as pointers and Dalmatians, have problems with deafness, as do English Setters. Breeders and their clients may like white, but no one likes the deafness that can accompany it in certain breeds. At one time breeders selected for white-coated Bull Terriers—until they found out how closely this color was related to deafness; they now cross back to colored Bull Terriers in order to avoid the problem. The same principle applies to merle, a beautiful color that appears in Australian Shepherds and Dachshunds. It is unfortunately associated with many birth defects, including neurological, eye, and ear abnormalities. (When a genetic expression of one trait like color is connected to another apparently unrelated trait, like deafness, it is called pleiotropism.)

Temperament is also at risk. In the world of dog shows, no standard of performance (other than trotting around the ring), health, or even good temperament (other than not biting the judge) is tested. Field trials require dogs to perform, but even great field trial dogs don't always make great hunting dogs because the conditions are often quite different. As long ago as 1944, when Thorne studied shyness in Basset Hounds, researchers and breeders alike knew that timidity is a heritable characteristic in dogs, as is aggression.[51] But until kennel clubs mandate such tests, show judges start seriously penalizing these traits when they are presented to them in the show ring, and breeders get serious about eliminating such dogs from their breeding programs, we'll continue to see such problems. Conversely, for example, many friendly, good-natured dogs lower their tails when meeting a new person; this is a sign of socially acceptable, submissive behavior and should be rewarded. However, if the breed standard calls for the tail to be carried high (a dominant posture for most breeds), the friendlier, more submissive dogs will be penalized and perhaps denied a championship. And the genes of the "winner" will be passed along to the next generation.

This problem is compounded when breeders mull over litters looking for the most independent, least people-oriented dogs for show (which will also pass those traits on to future generations), selecting pups for their orientation to their environment rather than to their caretakers. True, these animals are less likely to suffer separation anxiety than more dependent, human-oriented puppies and are more likely to accept changing handlers with aplomb in the dazzling world of dog shows, but they are also more likely to be bossy and aggressive.

To be fair, I must say that some working dogs are selected for autonomous behavior; hounds, for example, need to be independent thinkers to do their jobs. And since people aren't home as much as they used to be, we probably need to select dogs who can handle being alone or go without the luxury of having a dog. However, it's also true that the more independent the dog, the more problems there are likely to be with control-complex aggression unless they are matched with equally strong, independent owners—and they usually aren't.

The Inbreeding Controversy

One cannot talk truthfully about contemporary dog breeding without mentioning the dark shadow that is falling over the entire purebred community—and is now encroaching upon crossbreeds and mongrels who have been victimized by the taint of "pure" (read "inbred") bloodlines and their attendant diseases, such as von Willebrand's, progressive retinal atrophy, epilepsy, and other genetic health problems unrelated to anatomical structure but which are clearly inherited.

Unless prompt and drastic steps are taken to stem the tide of genetic disease in dogs, all breeds may implode due to their own genetic weaknesses. Selective breeding is both the hero and the villain here, for while it results in developing animals finely tuned for almost any task, it also produces over-refined, genetically impoverished, immunodeficient monsters.

> Many of the 400 or so inherited disorders reported in canines are also seen in humans. I don't know whether that makes me feel better or not.

No contemporary breed is free of heritable diseases, and they are rampant in most. Even crossbred dogs, once the saviors of dogdom, are now not much better off than purebreds since they've managed to collect many bad "purebred" genes along the way. However, they don't usually pass them along since mutts are more likely to be neutered than purebreds, whose deluded owners think they have something valuable if the family dog has AKC registration papers. Randomly bred mongrels usually manage to weed out the worst diseases over time without "help" from us.

As mentioned earlier, many breeders tend to breed for "show-worthiness" rather than for health (after all, there are no ribbons or trophies for soundness), and since many genetic health problems don't show up for several years (such as a susceptibility to cancer), they get away with it. Breeders don't mean to do this, of course, but that's what happens. Too many people are too impatient to get their kennel off to a good start rather than waiting to see what they really have in their line. If breeders would wait until their dogs were 5 years old or so (or at least until our knowledge of genetics takes some vast leaps forward) to begin breeding them, the dog breeds of this world would be better off. Those who worry about fertility declining with age worry needlessly (at least where dogs are concerned), because sperm count doesn't really drop until a dog is about 10 years old. Females, of course, must be bred earlier—but it is not necessary to start breeding them at 2 or 3, which is the current common practice.

> Crossbreeding is, as implied, the crossing of two different breeds; outcrossing is breeding dogs from different "lines"—in other words, dogs that are not closely related; line breeding is the breeding of closely related animals. Inbreeding is the crossing of first-degree relatives like brother and sister or sire and offspring—a highly concentrated form of line-breeding.

Current AKC rules allow no crossbreeding that would help insure diversity. As a result we have deaf Dalmatians and English setters, endemic heart disease in boxers, collapsed tracheas and luxated patellas in tiny toys, and certain types of cancer in Bernese Mountain Dogs. Bulldogs have to be delivered via Caesarian section because of the size and conformation of their heads. Of course, purebred dogs are truly isolated populations, because, by definition, they have far less genetic diversity than do their free-breeding wild counterparts. However, there are reasonable limits beyond which we ought not go. And as mentioned above, some genetic problems like von Willebrand's are so widespread that even crossbreeding may not entirely solve the problem.

It is true that some inbreeding is a necessary and recognized part of all breeding programs because it helps establish uniformity of type, especially when a breed is being developed. You can't even develop a breed without some inbreeding. It is, however, a tricky balancing act; the practice carries inherent genetic dangers that increase as inbreeding or line-breeding continues within a breed.

It is commonly said that there is nothing inherently wrong with line breeding if you work with clean or completely monitored stock. The idea is that if you start with no genetic diseases there is nothing to pass on, and if you carefully monitor the dogs you have for genetic diseases you will not allow a "bad gene" to escape into the general population. This line of reasoning may be theoretically true—if only there were existed lines of dogs free of all genetic diseases. It is probably impossible to find completely "pure" stock these days, and continued inbreeding concentrates the problems that do exist. Additionally, the damaged stock invariably gets into irresponsible hands sooner or later.

> The United Kingdom is taking a step in the right direction. More than 70,000 members of 180 breed clubs have been issued a Kennel Club questionnaire that seeks to collect information concerning disease, cause of death, birth defects, and other data inform dog owners. The survey will hopefully give the most accurate picture to date of the frequency of breed-specific illnesses, such as deafness in Dalmatians. The next step will be developing breeding and testing programs that will eliminate such conditions.

However, there is another problem with inbreeding, even if one sets aside (as if one could) the problems of deadly genetic diseases. It's called "inbreeding depression," which is defined as a reduction in the fitness of inbred offspring as compared to that of offspring resulting from outcrossing.

> To be fair, there's another kind of genetic deterioration called "outbreeding depression," which occurs when two completely isolated stocks mix. It happens most notably when domestic genes somehow get into a wild population. Genes that are perfectly adapted to domestic life don't do the wild population any good, and vice versa. This is one problem seen in hybrid "wolf-dogs," which will be discussed later, but is pretty irrelevant as far as domestic breeds are concerned.

Inbreeding depression is expressed in lower litter numbers, weaker immune systems, reduced fertility, and lower survival rates. The semen of inbred males contains a higher proportion of malformed sperm with lower motility rates. DNA studies of the famous Isle

Royale wolf pack (located on the Minnesota-Ontario border) have confirmed a high level of inbreeding (the small population is trapped on an island).[52] As a result, there is now great concern as to whether or not this well-studied pack will survive (although, in this case, moose-killing ticks are fellow culprits in decimating the herd).

Peter Steinhart has declared that "[t]he last wolf won't succumb to a bullet.[53] It will weaken from the slow but inexorable loss of genes. It will die from uniformity." The purebred domestic dog is in similar peril. Scott and Fuller write that "[t]he well-known effect of hybrid vigor can be utilitized in dogs as well as corn…breed inter-crosses might be used to produce superior working animals…[i]f there are objections to crossing breeds, separate lines within a large breed might be developed to serve the same purpose…[w]e see no reason for the non-acceptance of planned hybrid matings once their purpose is understood."[54]

Plant and animal breeders have known for centuries that out-breeding results in superior vigor and increased yield of offspring.[55] However, outcrossing is not without its own perils. Random out-crossing may produce very healthy individuals, but outcrossing as it is commonly done today removes the natural biological method (the death or infertility of homozygous individuals) of reducing the number of bad genes, which can either be lethal or capable of crip-pling, blinding, or sickening dogs. What happens instead is that deleterious recessive genes are not even noticed until they become so widespread and recurrent within a population that the carriers them-selves are eventually mated. Thus a popular sire that carries an injurious recessive gene can be bred to literally hundreds of females, resulting in the bad gene's spread throughout the entire gene pool. This is exactly what has happened in dozens of breeds today. The popular sire problem is more pronounced in show lines than in work-ing or performance dogs, because the genetics that control behavior are much more complex than those that determine looks. For exam-ple, it is unclear how successful livestock-guarding dogs are in passing their abilities on to their offspring. Champions in this category seem to have only marginally more luck in producing brilliant shepherd-ing progeny than regular sheepdogs. (The same phenomenon has been noted in gundogs.) Ah, the mysteries of heredity. Interestingly,

Coppinger found that his Maremma/Šarplaninic crosses performed better (meaning were more trustworthy and attentive) than purebred Maremmas, purebred Šarplaninics, purebred Anatolians, or Anatolian/Šarplaninic crosses.[56] Apparently there is room for improvement even in the most selective breeding—and the improvement may be found in outcrossing, which is anathema to conformation breeders.

"Fitness" is an important related concept and one central in evolutionary biology. Fitness is defined as the relative ability of an individual to leave descendants and hence transmit its genes to future generations. A reduction in fitness results from the expression of deleterious recessive alleles (multiple forms of genes that produce similar traits in different animals of the same species). Biologist Christopher Eckert explains it this way:[57] "*Recessive* alleles are expressed in homozygotes but remain unexpressed when they occur with a *dominant* allele in heterozygotes. *Deleterious* alleles originate when the underlying DNA sequence of a functional allele is altered by mutation to code for a gene product which is either harmful or simply doesn't work. Since mutation is a universal feature of DNA, all plant or animal populations contain deleterious recessive alleles. At any given locus, however, deleterious alleles are usually so rare that offspring produced through matings among unrelated individuals are almost never homozygous for harmful alleles. With inbreeding the odds of producing an offspring homozygous for a deleterious allele are much higher. Because rare deleterious mutations are transmitted along family lines, brothers and sisters are much more likely to carry the same deleterious alleles than unrelated individuals."

Dr. John Armstrong, a geneticist with the University of Toronto, explains that all animal populations carry a genetic load of about 3 to 5 lethal equivalents (LEs—lethal mutations that would kill if homozygous).[58] The trouble, however, lies in the equivalents. One LE may actually be 10 genes, each of which reduces genetic (reproductive) fitness by 10 percent. There seems to be a continuous distribution from 100 percent lethality to less than 1 percent lethality in such genes, and maybe 100 or more are involved. Therefore, given that we have 35,000 genes, if even 350 genes were detrimental that would only be 1 percent of the total. When a dog (cat, mouse, human) is bred, the progeny receives, on average, 50 percent of the father's genetic load and 50 percent of the mother's. If two individuals are selected from a fairly large population, few if any of these genes will match up and, even if they do, most will cause only a minor loss of fitness that is not easily noticed.

Close relatives, however, are more likely to have the same set of LEs, which will much more likely be expressed homozygously in some of the offspring. The worst may kill very early and thus tend to eliminate themselves from the gene pool; others that produce obvious defects would be noted by a responsible breeder and eliminated from the line. The most dangerous, however, are those that reduce fitness by "only" 5 to 10 percent. Most of these "underachieving" genes will not be detected, and so we may inadvertently be selecting for some that happen to be linked to traits we like—deafness in white dogs is a good example. In other cases, someone will finally note that bitches are having whelping problems and that litters are becoming smaller; the majority of breeders, however, will attribute the problems to food contaminants, water pollutants, and the like. The latter factors may play a role, but the ills they cause are likely magnified by the reduced fitness of the individuals being bred.

Dog breeds are becoming progressively more inbred. "My observation is that most breeds are on the road to extinction," Armstrong declares. Dogs will remain, of course; the species itself is not endangered. But healthy examples of the breeds we love so much are becoming almost as endangered as wolves.

Time will tell, but we are already seeing the fertility problems Dr. Armstrong has alluded to. And Dr. Helmut Wachtel, in "Breeding Dogs for the Next Millennium," wrote, "The average inbreeding level (inbreeding co-efficient) of dog breeds is…estimated to have reached 14 percent."[59] We already know that harmful health effects in commercial cattle start to be seen at 9 percent. And Dr. Armstrong observed in "Longevity in the Standard Poodle" that standard poodles with a coefficient of inbreeding (COI) of 0.0625 (i.e. 6.25 percent) or less (first cousin pairing or less with no shared ancestry) lived four years longer than those with a COI of 0.25 (25 percent) or higher (the equivalent of brother/sister pairing).[60]

Over a quarter of a century ago, Scott and Fuller wrote, "The breed associations were founded in order to overcome the limitations imposed upon the individual breeders, and it is possible for them to accomplish much more through long-continued selection programs. In the future, the breed associations can accomplish more than they have in the past by modifying their objectives and making use of newer genetic theories and techniques. First of all it should be realized that breed is a *population* of individuals showing a limited but still important degree of genetic variability. If selection is confined to one narrowly defined type, the result will almost inevitably be the accidental selection of various undesirable characteristics. Breed standards should include regulations relating to health, behavior, vigor, and fertility as well as body form."[61] Amen.

Special problems appear in the rare breeds. Some breeders believe that because the gene pool is lost, they need to breed nearly every available dog so genetic diversity will not be compromised. What happens instead is that bad genes spread throughout the entire pool and pollute it completely. The buck stops with the breeders.

At present, DNA tests are available for only about 5 percent of genetic canine diseases. We must do better than this. The Kennel Club of England deserves kudos for its efforts in this direction. Under the leadership of Jeff Sampson, a molecular biologist who heads their genetics program, the Brits are ridding their breeds of progressive retinal atrophy (PRA) and CLAD (an immune-deficiency disease). The AKC, the Canine Health Foundation, and some breed clubs are also working to the same ends in the United States.

The Breed Standard

The stated goal of conformation breeders today is to develop a dog that best exemplifies that fuzzily written document, the "breed standard," which in some cases specifies such minutiae as nail color while ignoring such important considerations as temperament or size. The breed standard bears scant relationship to historical function, but instead increasingly reflects personal and perhaps idiosyncratic preferences derived from heaven-knows-what Freudian or Jungian depths. Although the breed standard was designed to settle arguments about what is or is not a "good example" of the breed, it has caused almost as many problems as it has "solved."

Sometimes breed standards describe temperament; sometimes they do not. (Some do specify that the breed be
"aggressive," which is less than helpful.) Because dogs in the
United States are now mostly companion animals, it seems reasonable that temperament should be included in all breed
standards—and put at the top of the list to indicate its importance, not stuck at the bottom after a section about the presence
or absence of dewclaws and how dark the eyes should be.

Most breed standards are vague enough to accommodate almost
any interpretation, while others are indecipherable. Additionally, the
meaning of words changes over time; for example, what was considered "big" in 1910 may not be "big" by today's standards.
Furthermore, many critically important elements were left out of
some breed standards simply because the writers of the standards
assumed that everyone knew what the ideal bite, gait, size, or temperament of the breed in question was. To be fair, people probably did
know, since the original breed standards were written for those
already expert in the breed. Today, it serves as a kind of vague check-
list for would-be dog-showers.

There is very little connection between phenotype and fitness. One example is the Siberian Husky. Although show
Siberians are undeniably gorgeous (a truly subjective standard),
most of them are not very good at pulling sleds in the Arctic.
Too much hair, for one thing—all that hair collects snow (particularly between the toes), which makes running painful. A
show beagle can't succeed in field trials (no nose), and a field-
trial beagle is just about useless for real-life hunting (too slow).
Conversely, field-trial Gordon Setters are too fast for most hunting situations.

I leave it to the reader to assess the following excerpts from breed
standards, which were chosen almost at random. Again, note that
while many standards make some reference to temperament, judges
do not test for this critical factor in the show ring other than dismiss-
ing dogs that growl at them, bite them, or attempt to flee. Some

standards include details about coat trimming and nail care that may be important to a dog's overall health and conditioning; others are not. After all, a Poodle is a Poodle no matter how you clip his coat. The fact that some breed standards carry on at great length about the type of clip the dog must wear to be shown indicates, to me, an odd set of priorities. And how a dog's coat is trimmed certainly does not relate to either structure (except perhaps to hide its faults) or temperament.

A Breed Standard Potpourri

▼ "In motion all parts blend into a smooth, powerful, harmonious symmetry." (Curly-coated Retriever. The description is obviously the work of a poet manqué)

▼ "Dogs who fail to keep their tails erect when moving should be *severely penalized*." (Soft-coated Wheaten Terrier)

▼ "Nail color may vary from black to transparent." (Belgian Tervuren)

▼ "Nails are short and strong." (Border Collie)

▼ "Nails thick, blunt." (Miniature Pinscher)

▼ "The dew claws, if any, should be removed from the hind feet." (German Shepherd dog)

▼ "Dewclaws may be removed." (Tibetan Terrier)

▼ "The head should be refined in accordance with the sex and substance of the dog." (Cardigan Welsh Corgi)

▼ "A dry head and tight skin are faults." (Basset Hound)

▼ "An almost human expression" (Brussels Griffon)

▼ "Hide very thick and loose fitting." (Border Terrier)

▼ "The shoulders are elastic but never loose with moderate breadth at the withers." (Ibizan Hound)

▼ "Invisible gray undercoat on neck permissible." (Doberman Pinscher)

▼ "Urajiro (cream-to-white ventral color) is required in the following areas on all coat colors: on the sides of the muzzle, on the cheeks, inside the ears, on the underjaw and upper throat, inside of the legs, on the abdomen, around the vent and ventral side of tail." (Shiba Inu)

▼ "An aggressive or belligerent attitude towards other dogs should not be faulted." (Rottweiler)

▼ "Aggressive toward other dogs." (Akita)

▼ "In show trim the body should be well covered but tidy, with the head (except for the whiskers) and the ears and cheeks clear." (Kerry Blue Terrier)

▼ "The Chihuahua should move swiftly with a firm, sturdy action, with good reach in front equal to the drive from the rear."

▼ "Eye color will generally tone with coat color." (Bearded Collie)

▼ "The topline of the muzzle is parallel to the topline of skull, and the junction of the two forms a well-marked stop, which is midway between the occiput and the tip of the nose, and on a level with the eyes." (Briard—in which you can't see the eyes anyway. The standard also says, "The fully coated silhouette gives the impression of two rectangular forms, equal in length but differing in height and width, blending together rather abruptly." I am not picking on Briards, but their standard seems more vague than most)

▼ "A Pug's bite should be very slightly undershot." (This condition is a detriment to proper ingestion of food, but who cares about that? Incidentally, the Bulldog standard is even worse)

▼ "Both sexes are properly balanced between 12 inches and 14 inches at the withers." (Parson Russell Terrier).

▼ The Greyhound standard does not mention gait—and this in a breed whose main claim to fame is its running.

To be fair to contemporary breeders, I must say that the vagaries of breed standards are nothing new. The Roman writer Marcus Terentius Varro, describing sheep guardian dogs, mentioned that their lips were "blackish or ruddy" with a short muzzle showing "two teeth on either side," and legs "bowed rather than knock-kneed."

What Are Breeds For, Anyway?

So we have a most unusual situation in modern dogdom: the average pet owner must not only deal with the wolf in every dog, but also with the manufactured heritage it bears. For example, a Collie has its normal quota of wolf, with its attendant difficulties and joys. However, the Collie has also retained its instinctive heritage of sheepherding. This is not a problem for shepherds, but most modern Collie owners have never even touched a sheep, let alone own a flock of them that requires the services of a sheepdog. Still, the herding component of the dog is there and must be dealt with, as owners discover when they catch the Collie herding the cats or kids. By the way, there is no particular reason why the herding instinct can't be modified in the way that everything else about this breed has been—but then you'll have people having fits about the "original purpose" of the breed.

Let's complicate things still more. The average, modern, run-of-the-mill Collie is a lousy sheepherder because most modern breeders have not selected to produce the best sheepherder, although they have done nothing to discourage (or promote) that instinct. So the dog still has the instinct but without the ability—which may be the worst scenario.

Don't blame the dog; we did it ourselves. For owners and promoters of working dogs, the death knell rang as soon as the AKC registered the breed. Although the AKC has begun to promote sheepherding and other performance events, they are artificial constructs that don't approximate either real conditions or the herding trials developed by the herding breeds themselves very well. Field trials don't make the dogs better pets, either, so what we have done with herding dogs (as we have with field dogs) is create a third class of animal: performance dogs, which are (literally) designed to be neither pets nor working dogs. For example, performance tracking dogs are expected to follow a human scent (smeared on a wallet or something similar); in real-life conditions, dogs will "air-scent"—lift their heads and sniff the air. "Air-scenting" is not allowed in AKC tracking. Similarly, in field trials for scenthounds, it doesn't count if the dog sees the rabbit—he has to smell it. In real hunting conditions, dogs find rabbits any in any way that is convenient.

Incidentally, the Border collie, once a total working dog (but now registered with the AKC), is headed in the same direction as other former working breeds. One can only pray that the few surviving shepherds who use this breed keep the remnants to themselves. Many die-hard shepherds in Scotland and elsewhere kill puppies that have no potential as sheepherders. This seems cruel, but it has served to keep the breed functional. The only humane alternative would be to neuter every animal that does not make the grade and sell it as a pet. Unfortunately, dogs of working Border Collie heritage don't make good pets for most families; all they want to do is herd things. I pet-sit a Border Collie occasionally, and the entire time she is at my house all she wants to do is herd the cats.

A Kaleidoscope of Breeds and Types

Since I have been going on at such length about breed type, I guess I should specifically discuss dog "groups"—a collection of breeds related by function. Some of the earliest work in classifying dogs by type was done in 1570 by one Johannes Caius of Cambridge University (the current College of Caius [pronounced "Keys"] is named after him; he also moonlighted as physician to Queen Elizabeth I). Caius and others like him did not have the advantage of examining DNA or even elaborate paper trails—they simply figured out what dogs did and classified them accordingly. I have attempted to follow his lead, although the classification I use here should be blamed on me, not Caius. My categorization is only loosely related to the AKC classification system, which contains such singularly useless categories as "Non-sporting," "Working," and "Miscellaneous." Before present-day breeds formally emerged, there were "breeds" with such engaging names as lyemmers, tumblers, "thievish" dogs, and lurchers. Those were the good old days.

Even though most dogs no longer perform their historic tasks, they have still inherited the basic temperament appropriate for that job. This is an important consideration when deciding which breed is right for a particular owner. This seems so obvious as to require no further elaboration; however, human nature being what it is, people often seem determined to select the most inappropriate dog possible. It is a strange contrariness that is specific, I think, to *Homo insapiens* (man the unwise).

Husky/Spitz Breeds

At one time this group, which includes Malamutes, Huskies, Chow Chows, Samoyeds, and other spitz-like breeds, was considered so different from "normal" dogs that it was classified as a separate subspecies—*Canis familiaris palustris.* These dogs were believed to be closer to their wolf progenitors than, say, Cocker Spaniels. They are not, but it is easy to see why people would think that. These are ancient breeds and are perhaps, along with the sighthounds, the oldest of all. They were developed in the northern latitudes to work at sledding and drafting. A few had other jobs, though, such as the hunting Elkhound (beloved of the Vikings) and the guarding Chow Chow. The character of these breeds is diverges widely, from the friendly Siberian Husky to the aloof and sometimes dangerous Chow Chow. Sledding dogs, which were bred to work as a team, show little inter-dog aggression (in more technical terms, they show little "hierarchical behavior" towards each other). Most spitz breeds score low-to-moderate on the three important behavior scales of reactivity: excitability and activity level, aggression, and trainability.

Sled Dogs: Sled dogs are an important subclassifiction of spitz breeds which includes Samoyeds, Siberian Huskies, and the Alaskan Husky (which is not an AKC-recognized breed, but an animal selected for its ability to race in events like the Iditarod or Yukon Quest). Despite their diverse backgrounds, all sled dogs share some common features. First, they have the ability to get along with one another, an important trait selected directly from wolf-pack behavior. Dogs that squabble while in harness aren't going to get very far. Overly aggressive or even dominant dogs are selected against by breeders, and sled dogs tend not to develop a strict hierarchy—the lead sled dog is not necessarily the leader of the pack. This is because mushers need flexibility in moving their dogs to different positions in the harness should circumstances demand it. In normal dog relationships, animals of opposite sexes make the best partners. This, however, is not always workable for sled teams because males tend to be larger, and it is critical that partners be approximately the same size so their gaits are balanced.

Overlarge dogs are also selected against. Although bigger dogs are often faster, they have less endurance, radiate too much heat, and use more energy carrying their own weight. (Malamutes, because of their size, are not used for racing; some mushers also think them less favorably inclined toward one other than Siberian Huskies.) Excessively small dogs have too short a stride, are insufficiently strong, and are unable to conserve heat; that's why Pomeranians seldom enter the Iditarod. However, many Iditarod mushers cross their dogs with swift, long-legged hound breeds, such as coonhounds, to get additional speed from them.

And as Raymond Coppinger and Richard Schneider point out, the most successful canine racers produce little to no sweat through the glands in the footpad.[62] (Arctic wolves do not have functional sweat glands at all because they don't need them.) Footpads that sweat heavily tend to make snow clump into ice between the dog's toes, which causes pain and inefficient running.

To my knowledge, why sled dogs like to pull sleds has never been fully explained. Some researchers (Coppinger and others) liken it to a form of play, but this seems a little weak to me. Paulette Jones, a Siberian husky musher, believes that Siberians don't like to pull as much as they like to run; whether or not a sled is attached is of little importance. Some researchers have suggested that hounds don't make good sled dogs because they are too easily distracted by potential prey. My observations are different. All sled dogs can be distracted from the trail if it is crossed by a deer—their strong prey drive simply takes over. I've seen Siberians leave the trail to go crashing into the woods after game.

Hounds

Hounds are defined as hunting dogs that find prey and chase it to its den or tree, which then (usually) allows the hunter to kill or capture the animal. Different types of hounds were developed both to hunt specific species (rabbits, otters, foxes) and to work on different kinds of terrain. They are the earliest hunting dogs and can be subdivided into two groups: gazehounds (or sighthounds), a truly ancient group who rely upon their eyesight; and scenthounds, who depend upon their noses. Hounds, especially scenthounds, exhibit less "agonistic" behavior than most other breeds—a trait that means large numbers of them can be kept together with a minimum of fighting. Interestingly, scenthounds are known for their ability to gorge themselves, consuming enormous amounts of food at one time. Whether this is because they have traditionally been kept in large packs and allowed to compete for food or because they were sometimes allowed to devour the prey (again, competitive eating) is not clear.

> Studies dating back to the 1940s demonstrate that male dogs are better scent trackers than females. Their sense of smell also becomes more acute after they have been given some caffeine. Perhaps the old adage "Wake up and smell the coffee" has more validity than was previously thought.

Scenthounds exhibit a low level of reactivity, low levels of aggression toward people and other dogs, and low-to-moderate trainability. According to Caius, scenthounds are characterized by hanging ears and large, "bagging" lips. These baggy lips may indeed help gather in the in scent, but may also serve to inhibit fighting because of their sensitivity. The same may be true of the floppy ears, although one variety of scenthound (the Elkhound) has erect ears. (However liable to infection floppy ears may be, they apparently do not inhibit a dog's hearing. Experiments that taped the ears up to expose the canals versus letting the ears hang down naturally did not reveal any difference in the dog's ability to hear faint noises.) They are also considerably noisier than sighthounds.

Scenthounds are generally heavy-boned and slower than most gazehounds; however, some members of the family (such as fox-hounds) can be extremely fast. Familiar scenthounds include Beagles and Bloodhounds; the latter, once known as Saint Huber's hound, is the oldest and was developed in Europe. Caius put bloodhounds in a separate category because, unlike all other scenthounds, bloodhounds are used not for hunting game but only for man-trailing—they often assist in capturing criminals and finding lost children. They display no aggression (despite their scary name), and usually announce their success by happily licking their goal. Foxhounds display strong aggression toward foxes, but not chickens. This behavior was developed by careful breeders who put their young dogs out with "puppy-walkers"—farmers who have chickens. Hounds typically do not develop hunting behavior until after the "farm animal socialization period"; thus a Foxhound properly socialized with chickens can be trusted to charge harmlessly through a yard full of them when hunting a fox.

> In the early 1960s, Scott and Fuller placed a single mouse in a one-acre field, then introduced some dogs of different breeds.[63] Beagles found the mouse in one minute; Fox Terriers took 15 minutes; and Scottish Terriers never located the mouse, although one accidentally stepped on it. What is puzzling about these results is that Beagles are bred to hunt rabbits and Terriers to kill vermin. Perhaps another test is needed—or maybe there's not so much to this breeding-for-a-purpose as I thought.

Scenthounds use their eyes and ears as well as their noses, of course, although in artificial, human-contrived events like field trials, sighting a rabbit doesn't "count"—it must be scented out. In real life, hounds use all the faculties at their command to find the rabbit. They certainly don't ignore one that goes hopping past whether they managed to scent it out first or not.

> Hounds and other hunting breeds seem to be more strongly motivated by food than are other kinds of dogs (although, of course, all dogs like food). But when we consider what a dog's

breeding decrees, we understand that food is not the only possible (or even necessarily the best) reward in all cases. Giving a dog a chance to do what it most enjoys—chasing game, herding sheep, interacting with its owner—carries intrinsic rewards; you don't always need to shove a piece of cheese at a dog. My Irish Setter would zip by any treat for a chance to run or chase a ball. Incidentally, human psychologists are beginning to think that overpraising or over-rewarding a child for learning redirects the behavior in an unfortunate way—away from intrinsic satisfaction towards a yearning for parents' praise. Whether this hypothesis can be translated into the dog world is as yet unclear.

Gazehounds were developed to locate and run down game by sight in the open terrain of the Middle East. Most of these breeds run alone and are relatively silent. They are typically aloof, display low levels of aggression, and are excitable only when they see prey. Today, this group includes coursing breeds, such as Greyhounds and Whippets (which can outrun even a Greyhound for short distances; a Borzoi can outrun even a wolf). Other examples include Salukis, Afghans, and Irish Wolfhounds. Gazehounds tend to have long, thin legs and eyes that are more forwardly placed than those of most other dogs. Apparently there were other types of sight-hunters in Caius's time which have since disappeared.

The gazehound is characterized not only by its reliance upon vision, but also how by it relentlessly "hounds" its prey. Gazehounds have a strongly developed chase (predatory) instinct which often causes trouble when they pursue cars and bicycles. They are known for their great gentleness (but aloofness) with human beings.

The premier gazehound sport is lure coursing, although almost every breed of dog enjoys it. In lure coursing, the animals chase a lure (usually a couple of plastic bags that look disconcertingly like fleeing rabbits) on a motorized pulley around a large field. Dogs don't have to be "taught" to lure course they way they need to be taught obedience, agility, schutzhund, or even tracking—they do it by themselves, just for the joy of it. This sport is a favorite not only of dogs, but also of their owners, probably partly because it is the one dog sport in which the owners don't have to do anything but settle back with a beer and watch.

Terriers

Compared to hounds, terriers are comparative newcomers, and most of them hail from the British Isles. They were mentioned in fifteenth-century writings, and by 1677 Nicholas Cox had divided terriers into a short, crook-legged type and a long-legged, shaggy kind. Things have changed since then, but still come in two basic types: short-legged, smaller varieties that work in rocky dens hunting mice and other vermin; and long-legged, larger terriers that go after bigger game. The word *terrier* derives from the French word *terre* (meaning "earth"), and terriers are certainly earth dogs who go after their quarry by digging for it. This is, logically enough, called "going to ground."

Dachshunds, which come from Germany (as do Schnauzers), combine hound and terrier qualities. That makes them unique hunting dogs. They are not usually classified as terriers, but they really are.

Famous terrier breeds include Airedales (largest true terriers), and Scottish Terriers (like Franklin D. Roosevelt's Fala and George W. Bush's Barney). These courageous dogs are known for their thick skins, endurance, and their insensitivity to pain and touch (especially the fighting types). The Cairn Terrier, for instance, lived up to its name by scrambling around piles of rocks after vermin. Most terriers have narrow fronts, straight legs, and somewhat "slanted" eyes (in comparison with other dogs), which allow a greater field of vision that is useful when hunting varmints in holes. Many short-legged terriers have long bodies. Terriers as a group exhibit low-to-medium trainability, very high reactivity, and very high levels of aggression.

Fighting dogs, such as Pit Bull Terriers, were deliberately selected to fight to a degree unknown in other breeds—or, for that matter, in the wolf. It is said that fights between terriers, particularly in days past, sometimes went on until one of the participants was dead. This sad inheritance has destroyed the reputation of these breeds for many people. However, there is no reason why this propensity, intended for the cruel sport of dogfighting, could not be bred out; we bred it in. Dog-fighting dogs were originally placid around people (because those who weren't were killed); that ended, however, when vicious human breeders decided that redirecting terriers' innate dog-dog aggression towards people would be fun. This is the origin and even the raison d'etre of many modern "pit bull" type dogs. On the other hand, well-bred American Staffordshire Terriers that are many generations removed from dog fighting now tend to be somewhat less dog-dog aggressive and are also safe around people.

Guard Dogs

Caius called these dogs "homely" in the old sense that they kept to home and were used to guard the estate. (Some were also used as war or fighting dogs.) They are big, strong dogs with great peripheral vision and high reactivity. In fact, dogs bred to guard are able to activate their guarding instincts much faster, more intensively, and at a much lower stimuli than wolves, who tend to be quite cautious. Guard dogs tend to be one-person or one-family dogs and, as such, are extremely protective and territorial.

Mastiffs and their allies are paramount among guard dogs and are considered to be one of the "foundation breeds" for many modern types, including the Saint Bernard and Boxer. There are images of them dating back to the time of the Pharaohs.

In recent times, the need for vicious guard dogs has decreased—at least among law-abiding people. However, as the general pet market has increased, breeders have softened the tempers of these breeds to the point of great gentleness. Doberman Pinschers are much more suitable family pets than they were in days of yore—or even 30 years ago—because breeders have succeeded in breeding some of the sharpness out of them. (This presents a different conundrum; guard dogs that can no longer perform their historic function of guarding seem to be anomalous, to say the least.) However, other breeds have gone in the opposite direction; many dogs once bred to protect property have become more generally aggressive—even toward their owners. This peculiar characteristic does not seem to have been common in earlier times. No one knows whether the difference lies in the way dogs were treated in times past as compared to today, whether the dogs themselves have changed, or whether there is a genetic component.

In addition to house-guarding dogs, I include livestock guarders like Komondorak in this group. (Don't you like the word *Komondorak*? That's what you have in the rare event you need more than one Komondor.)

Livestock Guard Dogs are among the oldest (and, according to Coppinger, most numerous) of all working dogs. Most sheep-guarding breeds were developed in Europe, where wolves remained a threat longer than they did in England; they include the Komondor, Great Pyrenees, Maremma, and Kuvasz. Livestock-guarding dogs exhibit considerable independence and morphological variation, since uniformity of type (although many of them are white as Columella urged) is not crucial to a guarding dog the way it is to a sled dog (who must match its harness mate) or, to a lesser extent, the herding dogs who need to exhibit precise movements depending on the livestock and terrain involved.

Implacable toward their enemies but tender and attentive to their charges, livestock guard dogs are carefully socialized (imprinted) to sheep (or whatever it is they are supposed to guard)—not humans—between the ages of 4 and 14 weeks. During this period the puppies are handled very little by human beings, sleep in wool-nests, are not given any affection, and (in most cases) are not provided with shelter, although they are kept well fed. They live and sleep among their flock. However, the dogs are not permitted to play with the sheep since play is a form of practice hunting and stalking—behaviors one most certainly does not want directed against the fold. When properly socialized, they show little predatory behavior and, unlike herding dogs, do not stalk in response to motion. Sheep-guarding dogs do not chase and kill predators; they usually just surprise and disrupt them. Sometimes the disrupting behavior works because the invader finds it so odd—it consists of, perhaps, inappropriate tail wagging or even playing. At other times, however, the guardian will ferociously attack the predator.

It has been hypothesized that livestock-guarding dogs display early-juvenile motor patterns well into adulthood, which gives trainers time to inculcate the desired behavior in the potential guardian. It is known that these dogs typically don't display any predatory behavior until they are about six months old. Sheep-guardian dogs also have low levels of dopamine in the basal ganglia of the brain, especially in comparison with sheepherders like Border Collies or sled racers like huskies—another juvenile trait which correlates well with the neotenic theory.

However, unless well-fed *and* well-socialized with the sheep, a few sheep-guarders may decide to eat their charges. (They are still dogs, after all.) In fact, a study by J. Green and R. Woodruff demonstrated that 40 percent of dogs purchased for the experiment and placed with livestock breeders injured the livestock—and 15 percent killed them.[64] These dogs did keep predators away, so I suppose it can all be chalked up to the win-some/lose-some theory of sheep-raising.

There is a great deal of argument about what exactly sheepdogs think they are. Some people believe that the sheep-guarding dog thinks, for all intents and purposes, that he *is* a sheep—until an intruder comes along. Coppinger thinks it's the other way around— the dogs think the *sheep* are dogs. That makes more sense to me (after all, sheep don't protect each other, so far as I know—they just run away), but we will probably never know for sure.

Raymond Coppinger and Richard Schneider tried very hard to teach Border collies to be sheep guardians and sheep guardians to be sheepherders with absolutely no success, despite the fact that the breeds were raised in a controlled environment.[65] Of course, behavior is not passed along precisely the way a physical trait is, but is largely the end result of a constellation of inherited traits that are enhanced or partially suppressed by the environment. And, of course, the target animals must have the genetic predisposition to be imprinted with a specific behavior. Border collies are simply too specialized as sheepherders to be any good at guarding.

Interestingly, although Coppinger had no luck at all trying to imprint sheep-guarding abilities upon a purebred retriever (it still preferred to retrieve), it seems that most mongrels can be imprinted with the proper behavior. Many cultures apparently did just that; they didn't breed for anything special, so all the innate wolf characteristics must still be there. With more specialized dogs, however, we can assume that the appropriate guarding instincts have just been bred out. A successful livestock-guarding dog apparently must have (1) the correct genetic programming and (2) the correct socialization. Any other formula is a disaster for the sheep.

Herding Dogs

We'll include both sheepherding dogs and drover dogs in this category. Herding dogs can be divided into three types: headers, like Collies (who try to move stock from the front); heelers, like Corgis (who are bred to bite and nip at the hoofs of the stock); and catch dogs, like Catahoula Leopard dogs and Brazilian Fila dogs (who grab and hold stock, or at least prevent it from moving). All three types perform their tasks by chasing and biting, which cause fear and flight in the livestock.

Another way to classify herding types includes "driving," in which a dog pushes stock through gates and chutes; "mustering," in which the dog brings stock from far away to the shepherd; and "tending" (performed mostly by German Shepherd dogs), in which the dog acts as a "living fence" to keep the sheep within a certain area. "Tending" partially accounts for the unusual gait of the German Shepherd dog.

Their role vis-à-vis cattle is far more antagonistic than is that of the livestock guardian; in fact, the sheepherding dog demonstrates behavior exactly like that of his forebear, the wolf. The dog eyes, stalks, and chases sheep. It is trained to "get down" before it proceeds with the "grab bite" (in which the dog seizes the prey), which would then give way to the "kill bite" (in which the dog bites to kill) and the dissection/consumption that occurs in the wild. It is presumed that the latter stages (grab and kill) of the typical wolf hunting pattern have been suppressed. The "catch" types of herding dogs, like Pit Bulls (which alternated between herding and fighting duties and used to catch hogs by the ear), must be supervised very closely in this regard; however, such behavior is not so prevalent in Border Collies. Dogs bred to herd cattle as opposed to sheep are most likely to grab-bite—it's the only way to make cattle listen—but it's a fault in sheepherders. The ideal sheepdog is one bold enough to chase and herd the sheep, yet too timid or inhibited to bite them. Coppinger found that predatory behavior in Border Collies begins when they are around 10 weeks of age, when they began to play-stalk. Sheep are highly attuned to stalking behavior and, by nature, avoid dogs who display it. This is what the Border Collie wants—he is not trying to make friends.

Herding dogs in general rank very high in trainability and reactivity, and many have a strong prey drive. Many herding dogs (Shetland Sheepdogs in particular) are highly sensitive to sound. If owners do not understand this, they may end up talking much too loudly to them (screaming, from the Sheltie's point of view) and, instead of emphasizing their point, succeed only in terrifying the dog. Other herding dogs, such as Border Collies, are extremely light-sensitive and react to the slightest movements of the hand, which is why they are so easily trained to follow hand signals. Some trainers, such as John Fisher, suggest that Border Collies are mind-readers; what is really happening, however, is that they are reading their owner's physical pre-signals (such as moving in a certain way before giving a command). Thus the quick-minded Border Collie simultaneously obeys the anticipated signal and builds a reputation for having ESP.

Hunting Breeds

Retrievers, pointers, setters, and spaniels are included in this group. All have a highly developed prey-drive that has been genetically altered to stop before the rip-and-tear phase (which precedes the kill phase—it is meant to bring down the prey animal so it can be killed). The action of setting or pointing is a moment frozen in time; a "natural" dog would continue the attack. For most practical purposes, therefore, they are among the least aggressive of breeds. They are highly trainable for the jobs they were selected to do (meaning don't try herding sheep with them). They are also highly reactive and have a very high activity level.

Pointers and Setters are sometimes also referred to as gundogs—hunting dogs that were developed after the invention of firearms (beginning in the 17th century). These dogs were trained not only to find game like hounds but also to either point it out to hunters or retrieve it. Pointers and setters are used almost exclusively for bird-hunting, and all have excellent peripheral vision. Bird dogs use their eyes as well as their noses; they have to. Birds probably don't leave much of a scent on the ground.

Pointers and setters are extremely fast dogs, bred to hunt well even if their owners are on horseback. When they see a bird, pointers tend to stand with one leg raised; setters, which were originally designed to hunt the low-flying game birds common on the British Isles, tend to drop lower. (Those behaviors are changing in the United States and Canada, where hunters favor a dog who stands tall, "steady to wing and shoot.") Additionally, early single-shot shotguns took a bit of time to reload, so a dog that "set," rather than one that rushed off too quickly in the direction of the bird before the fatal shot was fired, was preferred. There are four commonly recognized setting breeds: the Irish, English, Gordon, and red-and-white Setters. Pointers include the English pointer, the German shorthaired pointer, and the wirehaired pointing Griffon. All of these breeds require enormous amounts of exercise.

> The first really competitive dog show was held in Newcastle, England, in 1859 (despite the fact that the British Kennel Club was not established until 1873). It was for setters and pointers only.

Retrievers are another group of gundogs that were selected for their soft mouths (inhibited bite), which allows them to carry the shot game carefully back to their humans. Scott and Fuller found that there is probably a critical period during which dogs learn to retrieve.[66] Although they didn't have a very large sample to work with, they found that 9-week-old animals learned much better than adults. Unfortunately, however, the natural soft bite of many retrievers is being lost because it is no longer bred for. Trainers who use "force-fetch" training methods simply devise ever more "efficient" ways to produce the desired softness of mouth (it all involves pain to the dog, of course) so breeders don't have to trouble themselves about producing dogs born with the wanted trait. Retrievers are bred to work extremely closely with human beings and are highly trainable. Many of them are also workaholics, rivaling even Border Collies.

> Among retrievers, the Labrador is known for its ability to gorge itself as hounds do.

Spaniels, like pointers, setters, and retrievers, are considered gundogs. Caius described them as gentle, pretty dogs, and indeed the best of them are. They are most famous for springing at and flushing out game. The most famous modern spaniel, the American Cocker, is almost never used for hunting anymore; the instinct has been pretty well bred out. They are now pets only.

Toy Breeds

Toys were the first group of dogs specifically bred for companionship. In some cases, toys are reduced versions of larger dogs (toy Poodles and Pomeranians); in others, they seem unrelated to any larger version (Chihuahuas and Maltese). It seems that the reduced-sized versions often retain the characteristics (which are sometimes quite formidable) of their ancestors.

Service Dogs

While there is no currently recognized "service" breed, researchers have been trying to produce the perfect service dog for years, just as breeders tried to develop the perfect gun- or sheepherding dog in the past. Nowadays many guide dog organizations breed their own stock—a mix of, say, Labrador, Golden Retriever, and Standard Poodle. What the breeders look for in the breeding stock are such positive character traits as intelligence, confidence, and energy— qualities possessed by the aforementioned breeds (along with common sense and a calm demeanor). In like manner, dogs that show fear and suspicion are not considered good choices. It is well established, for instance, that nervousness is inherited, so breeding dogs with a tendency towards this trait is asking for failure.

Versatile Dogs

Many breeders, especially in Germany, attempted to breed all-purpose (or at least multipurpose) dogs that could hunt, guard, and herd sheep. They have been moderately successful in developing some multipurpose breeds; the trouble is that while these breeds can, in a sense, "do it all," they don't do any one thing as well as a more specialized breed. This is one of the problems that engage those who try to classify dogs into any reasonable, consistent system—some breeds were simply bred to do a whole bunch of things. There's nothing wrong with that, of course. The German Shepherd is probably the premier example of a versatile dog.

Chapter 4:
Walking the Walk, Talking the Talk: The Dog's Language Guide for Humans

"I've seen a look in dogs' eyes,
a quickly vanishing look of amazed contempt,
and I am convinced that dogs think humans are nuts."
—John Steinbeck

Because we dogs are social, we communicate; after all, there's no point in trying to communicate if you plan to live as a hermit. So in order to understand the argot, it's important to know a little bit about the social structure that sets the parameters of our discourse. Wolves and dogs use pretty much the same grammar, although there may be slight differences in vocabulary. For the most part, dogs do not use body language as fully or frequently as do wolves, even though we have most of the necessary equipment. Apparently our relative silence in this matter is due to different social structures and anatomical differences between us and wolves. Some researchers have also suggested that dramatic variations in modern dogs' appearance have led to incompatible visual signals among types and breeds.

> Among dogs only the Siberian Husky approaches the wolf in complexity of body language.

The first thing to know is that we dogs like an orderly society. On this subject, one exasperated and harassed editor said to me, "I really get tired of reading that dogs are pack animals in every dog book." "But dogs *are* pack animals," I pointed out (reasonably enough, I thought). "I know, I know," she said, "but I wish writers wouldn't keep saying it." Well, reader, I must say it: dogs are pack animals. But perhaps not as much as are we are given credit for—and a lot depends on what breed we are. Environment plays a big role in whether a group of dogs, wolves, or even (at times) coyotes will form a pack. (The conditions into which we modern dogs have been thrust often work against the pack mentality.) The long and short of it is that we can form a pack, but we are not compelled to do so. Sort of like you people. Hounds form packs easily; terriers don't. It also depends upon individual character and upbringing.

Dog groups are not much like wolf packs, either, no matter what you may hear to the contrary. Wolf packs are natural family or voluntarily formed groups. Conversely, a group of household dogs is usually unrelated; the "pack" is totally artificial, cobbled together by human beings. There is no reason for us to form a pack, particularly considering that we don't (as a rule) go off hunting together—which is the main reason wolves form a pack in the first place. (Packhounds, however, generally form packs because they do hunt together.) Like our wolf cousins, however, some domestic dog groups do have a definite "leader" or top dog, a role that is both acquired and learned. When we do form some sort of order, it's pretty fluid. Additionally, alpha status is not a permanent possession; it ebbs and flows with circumstance. Never assume that "once top dog, always top dog." It just isn't so. I have also noticed that if the leader is "deposed" by another, his personality may undergo a remarkable shift. He becomes sneaky, shy, and nervous, just as lower-ranked dogs and wolves are, while the previously shy, nervous, lower-status animal who deposed him becomes confident and self-assured. Wolves supposedly act the same way. It is shocking how much circumstances can alter one's personality, yet not really surprising; humans act the same way. When everything is going their way, they can afford to be nice; when their circumstances change, however, and they are forced to the back of the pack (so to speak), they get really dangerous.

One should remember, however, that there is no ultimate value to be placed on either dominance or submission—they are just strategies to get along in the world. For some dogs, dominance is best; for others, submissiveness is the better choice. We try to do what works and don't get hung up on labels. You folks should try this approach to life.

And you humans, by your very presence, vastly change the way we organize our lives—sort of like Heisenberg's uncertainly principle, if you get my drift. I have seen those books in which owners are advised to let household dogs sort out their own differences. That works sometimes—but only sometimes

It is true that some groups of dogs establish a chain-of-command that more or less (but usually less) resembles a wolf pack. In some cases there is a clear-cut order that is apparent to us, but not necessarily to you. One of the greatest mistakes an owner can make is to misinterpret the correct order—or, equally seriously, to attempt to reorder the group yourself. Honestly, you have no say in this; all you can do is respect the order we've established. You should try to figure it out, although it may not be an easy thing to do. Here are a few clues to help you.

For one thing, our hierarchy may not be uniform. We dogs have been known to develop one hierarchy for food, another for territory, and yet another for owner-attention privileges. To complicate things further, breed does make a difference. It has been shown that dominance tends to be linear in more aggressive breeds, while in less aggressive, more social breeds, several animals may hold the same rank. Some breeds tend to be aggressive regarding space (Shetland Sheepdogs), while other struggle more for food (Basenjis). It is also interesting that in non-aggressive Beagles and Cockers, there is no discernable tendency for males to be dominant over females; in quarrelsome breeds like Fox Terriers and Basenjis, however, males always assume the dominant role. Generally speaking, an animal of either sex can be dominant, although it more likely to be a male, especially in breeds with strong sexual dimorphism. There is some evidence that the tendency toward dominance is inherited, but since the studies were done with deer mice, I wouldn't put a great deal of stock in them. Deer mice are more trouble than they're worth.

Now this complex hierarchy may be partly based on what is important to each dog; say, for instance, that Fido, the normally dominant dog, just doesn't care all that much for petting, so he allows Buddy to have pride of place for that privilege. That's what cooperation is about; you pick your shots. Van Hooff and Wensing termed this sort of thing "situational dominance," a state of affairs in which the dominant animal chooses not to compete for a certain resource primarily because he is not interested in it—at least at the moment.[67] It has also been observed that, in many situations, the aggressor is the eventual loser. I should mention the sad case of Theo, a Shiba Inu–beagle mix, who had the personality of a Shiba Inu and the fighting ability of a Beagle. Theo challenged every dog he met and was always soundly beaten. He never figured out why.

In homes where a clear dominance hierarchy is established, fighting diminishes or ceases. However, in many contemporary pet homes, people who own several animals never allow a natural dominance order to be established because the fighting that takes place to establish it is unbearable. I am not making a value judgment here, but it is worth noting.

> If there is an abnormal amount of stress in a pack or household, the dominance order will be upset. Among wolves, stress seems to peak early in winter when females are beginning to come into heat and the food supply begins to dwindle; in human-run households, stress accompanies births, divorces, departures, additions to and deaths in the family, moving, shouting matches between humans, and similar events that provoke emotional upheavals. When the dominance order is upset, you can expect more infighting among the dogs.

Even if we don't form a pack, however, dogs are social creatures. And that's why communication is so important to us. By the way, we're much better at it than cats, who are solitary animals.

Like you, we use language to communicate our needs and our status—and sometimes just to play. As time goes on, people are learning a lot more about play behavior. They used to think that play was merely practice for hunting and such things. While it's true that hunting practice may be one function of play, adults (even experienced hunters) play, too—perhaps not as much as we did when we were young, but we still enjoy it. (Interestingly, older dogs will adjust their play styles to accommodate young puppies.) Researchers finally figured out that playing is an intrinsic pleasure, just as it is with humans. It also helps us maintain social cohesion, as it does with people. Of course, puppies need to learn to play nicely, just as human children do; learning the rules of play makes us better citizens. Wolves play too, but studies show that adult wolves play less frequently than adult dogs and that the amount of stimuli needed to get wolves to play is considerably higher than in dogs. Dogs also seem to play with a great deal more abandon than do wolves. Theories abound as to why this is so, with most observers returning to the neotenic theory—that dogs are just wolves in arrested states of development. Personally, I think that wolves just lead much more serious lives than mine.

Human beings can learn to initiate play behavior with dogs. The signal itself doesn't matter as long as you stick to it long enough to give us the general idea of what you want. We dogs are amazingly adept at distinguishing play behavior from other behavior. For example, consider the old adage "don't let your dog win at tug of war." Go ahead, have fun; let us win if you want. We know we're playing and it does not, contrary to the platitudes you hear all the time, affect our perception of dominance.[68] We are not so foolish as to assign leadership ability on the outcome of a frivolous game. I must say, however, that there are some attack or guarding breeds that take everything too seriously, so it's probably a good idea not to let *them* win. Researcher Patricia Simonet demonstrated that dogs regularly engage in dominant-submissive role-reversal during play.[69] (She also was the first to discover that dogs laugh.)

Speaking Dog

I'm going to give you a few tips on dog-reading in this section. We dogs spend a great deal of time figuring you out, watching your faces and memorizing your movements; you should return the favor. Watch us and listen to us. I am not going to ask you to smell us, but if you did, you might learn something there, too. Understanding dog language makes people better dog owners (guardians, baby sitters, parents, or whatever you want to call yourselves. Just don't call me late for dinner, ha ha).

We dogs (like our ancestors) have three systems of communication: visual, vocal/auditory, and olfactory. Our smelling ability provides us with a wealth of information, such as the age, sex, health, and territorial boundaries of a marker. You humans, however, haven't got what it takes, physiologically, to pick up the signals. (One of the great advantages of scent markings is that they are detectable for many days, unlike vocal and visual signals.)

Although dogs and humans have the same senses, we use them differently, which makes communication between us a little difficult at times. Things would be easier from my vantage point if humans had a better sense of smell, but that's life. Because you are lacking in the olfactory department, I'll confine most of this discussion to visual and auditory cues—even though in my world all three work together in dynamic harmony. Most dog signals were genetic heirlooms designed to work with wolves, but we've managed to carry some of them over to life with humans. For instance, most of have learned that your seemingly endless staring at us does not signal an imminent attack as it would in our society. (The vacant look in your eye gives away your harmless intent.) But it's something we have gotten accustomed to (more on that later).

Dogs and wolves both rely to a great extent on auditory and scent signals. The former can be read at a distance (howling) and the latter persist over time (scent markings), which give us a great advantage in communication. These abilities enable wolf packs to avoid direct confrontation and fighting, which sap energy. So even in inimical situations, wolves tend to work in harmony; they avoid physical confrontation when possible. Unlike people, wolves don't go looking for fights. We dogs wouldn't go looking for fights either if we had as much space as a wolf. We could just run away and…well, never mind.

When we're close up, we read facial expressions as well as ear and tail positions. Dogs whose faces are covered with hair (like Old English sheepdogs in show clip) and dogs with short tails, docked tails, or cropped or droopy ears have a lot more trouble in this department than those of us who prefer to go au naturel. Such altered animals must rely more strongly on olfactory and auditory communication.

Visual Cues: Walking the Walk

Visual cues do not work well over time or distance, but since they seem to be more readable to human beings, I suppose I should begin by talking about them. Some very important cues we give each other often go unnoticed or are misread by humans, so knowing them will make you a better owner. By the way, if you happen to meet a wolf, you can use the same cues—wolf and dog expressions are nearly identical.

Every dog and every situation is different, of course. Dog language is complex. For example, behavior that can be read as "dominant" in one context may be neutral or even "submissive" in another. For instance, growling, staring, raised hackles or tail, and other "dominant" or "aggressive" behavior is, in certain circumstances and with certain dogs, actually submissive behavior.

A Canine Visual Language Glossary

Here I have composed, with considerable effort (my alphabetic skills aren't quite what they should be), a little glossary of canine visual cues. Learn to read them, even though we don't always make it easy for you. For example, sometimes I get so confused that I give off mixed signals. I'd like to be friendly, but I'm not quite sure. My tail might do one thing and my ears or back another. If this happens, the smartest thing for you to do is to leave me alone; I'm confused and there's no telling what I might do. It's always best to err on the side of caution. On a deeper level, though, lots of apparently contradictory body language is perfectly consistent, although nuanced. Humans are just too thick-headed to read it.

If you are not sure what a dog (especially a strange dog) is trying to say, use caution. Always read a dog's body language considering its most dangerous possibilities.

Critical Body Parts

Back: Posture is so important in a social setting, isn't it? A straight back is a sign of self-assurance and dominance. Hunching the back suggests submission or insecurity.

Ears: When challenging another dog, I keep my ears erect, tense, and pushed forward; calm animals relax the muscular tension around the ears. An alert dog's ears are erect too, but they are not pushed forward unless the dog wishes to communicate a threat (very subtle, this dog language). Placing the ears back slightly is a sign of friendliness, but terrified dogs pin their ears back flat. One ear up and one ear down signals my confusion.

I am very sorry that, with the exception of a few freaks, you humans can't move your ears. I also feel sorry for Beagles, who are pretty much in the same predicament, and for those poor dogs whose owners have clipped off half their ears in the misguided impression that it makes them look better (no matter that the dog has been deprived of an essential means of communication). Originally, ear cropping it was done to make guard dogs look more ferocious—floppy-eared dogs always look sort of friendly, no matter how mad they are (remember Columella?), as well as to protect their ears in a fight (less to chew off, as it were). Give me a dog whose mood I can measure via his ears; it makes life easier.

Dogs with hanging ears, especially those breeds that also have hair growing down the canal, are prone to infection. On the other hand, dogs with big upright ears unprotected by fur (like Pharaoh Hounds) have problems with insect bites.

Eyes:

In the dog world, looking deep into another's eyes is not a declaration of love; it's a challenge. Having one's owner (not to mention a perfect stranger and therefore a potential enemy) stare at one takes quite a bit of getting used to. Even people understand this. "What are *you* staring at?" reflects the common wisdom that to stare is to challenge. Conversely, an averted gaze indicates submission or fear. Wide-open eyes suggest dominance, while dilated pupils usually indicate fear. Blinking suggests submission or friendliness. Casual, off-and-on glancing is a normal, contented pattern.

When a dominant and a submissive dog meet, the submissive animal will break eye contact first. If a dog (or sometimes a person) continues to stare after the more submissive dog has broken eye contact, it may initiate an attack. (See also "Staring," below.)

Eyebrows:

Dominant dogs have pronounced eyebrows, while the eyebrows of submissive dogs are barely discernable.

Forehead:

Aggressive dogs often develop unsightly forehead lines. (Botox, anyone?) Non-aggressive, mild-mannered types present a smooth, bland forehead to the world.

Hackles:

Hackles are the hairs on the dog's back. Most dogs can raise them, but how many they are able to raise is variable. Some dogs can raise their hackles from the neck to the root of the tail, which gives them an odd (but trendy) Mohawk look; other dogs can only raise the neck hackles, or at most those at the neck and base of the tail. At any rate, no many how many hackles are raised, take it as a sign of aggression. Be aware, however, that very long-haired dogs are usually unable to raise their hackles effectively.

Hair: A smooth coat means things are indeed going pretty smoothly. When I'm challenged, however, my hackles rise (and so does all the rest of the hair along my spine). I can't help it; it's involuntary. It makes me look bigger. I wish I could make the hair on my tail stand out like the family cat does when I chase him, but I can't.

Markings: Facial markings accentuate the expression. It is hypothesized that such markings are characteristic of social creatures because it makes expressions easier to read. It does seem true that highly social breeds (like hounds) are more likely to have facial markings than loners (like Chow Chows), but who really knows? Owners control the breeding. (Many all-white breeds do have a black "lining" to their lips that makes a snarl unmistakable.) At any rate, differently colored eyebrows, "eyelines," and other markings do make dogs' faces easier to read. Many social breeds also have a white-tipped tail that also facilitates communication.

Mouth: Mouths do more than bark and bite. Sometimes we yawn, for instance. Yawning usually signals nervous energy rather than exhaustion. It lowers the blood pressure and is relaxing. If I flick my tongue at you, I'm not flirting—I'm nervous about something (see also "Tongue-Flickering," below). If I mouth your hand, it means I trust you—unless, of course, I use my teeth. When a dog mouths your hand without crunching down, it's a greeting. You see this behavior most often in pointing and retrieving breeds. Harder mouthing can be a signal of attempted dominance.

A curled lip usually means a snarl, but some dogs do approximate a human smile. (See also "Smiling," below.) And most dogs do retract the corners of their lips (with the mouth open) when happy, which is a sort of a smile. It is extremely important for the owners of smiling dogs to learn to understand the difference between a smile and a snarl; confusing a smile with a growl may result in a mistaken attempt to punish a dog who is smiling, not snarling. This is disastrous. The dog then feels that its best offer of conciliatory, submissive behavior has been punished and he has no recourse other than attacking the owner the next time it feels fearful or threatened.

Neck: In dominant dogs, the neck is held straight; in more submissive dogs the neck is inclined like a bow.

Tail: Dogs with long, bushy tails have the easiest time communicating moods. Dominant dogs (and wolves) tend to carry their tails high (one problem with docked-tail and tailless dogs is that they have fewer means to communicate status and intent, which can potentially confuse other pack members). It is also true that we can use our tails to diffuse our own personal dog-odor to those in the vicinity. In fact, the higher the tail, the more dominant the message delivered (and the more smell, if you want brutal honesty). This is true of both wolves and dogs, but we dogs are flexible and understanding of breed differences. German Shepherds generally walk with their tails down, while Beagles always bounce around with their tails up. A German Shepherd would never make the mistake of confusing a cheerful Beagle with a dominant or threatening one (although that's hard to imagine, isn't it?). Many terriers have perpetually raised tails, it seems, while Greyhounds may habitually carry theirs between the legs even if they are not scared. We dogs have to learn to read all body language carefully.

If I'm scared, my tail swings down between my legs (of course, some sighthounds are always like that, but they're weird, in my opinion—bunch of scaredy-cats). If I hold my tail out straight and swing it slowly, I'm considering my options. If the tail is horizontal, it indicates supreme interest (an upright tail may signal the same). If I feel comfortable, I just let my tail hang down in a relaxed way. I feel sorry for those corkscrew-tailed dogs that are stuck with an unsightly pig-like appendage—it's not natural, I tell you. (Dogs with tightly curled tails have to use their entire bodies to wiggle with happiness and tend to wrinkle their foreheads a lot.) A dog who wags a lowered tail is probably feeling nervous.

A wagging tail does *not* always mean that I feel well disposed toward you. While a complete, fully realized tail wag indicates friendliness, a slow wag at the half-mast position may mean I'm going to attack you. If I wag my tail while it's in a lowered position, it probably means I'm not quite sure about something. (At least that's what I think it means—I'm not quite sure.) Tails with a different color at the tip (characteristic of many social breeds like hounds) are easier to read than self- (solid) colored tails.

Some dogs chase their tails. Sometimes they do it for fun, sometimes because their rear end itches, or sometimes because it's become an obsession (I am not joking).

Tongue-
Flickering:
This gesture usually signals uneasiness. Snakes do the same thing, but their tongues are better equipped for the job.

Behavior and Gestures

Ambush
Behavior:
This is a common behavior seen in both wolves and dogs in which the dominant wolf attacks (or pretends to attack) a subordinate or former rival. Cats are fonder of this sneaky ploy than dogs, but we'll use it if we have to.

Bowing:
Bowing is a play-eliciting behavior that is also seen in courtship. Even humans can figure this one out because of its unmistakably non-threatening nature.

Breathing:
Faster breathing indicates increased stress. The purpose is to get more oxygen into the lungs, which in turn helps prepare us to fight or flee—our usual responses to stress.

Champing:
Champing is a chewing motion (even though there is nothing being chewed) that usually signals friendliness and appreciation. The origin of champing has been traced to nursing behavior.

Chattering:
Chattering is a sign of happy excitement. You see teeth chattering in males around a female in heat; you also see it when dogs are about to start a field trial or some other thrilling event.

Circling and
Sniffing:
This is often a bossy, dominant behavior. It can hint at the beginning of an altercation.

Drooling:
While drooling is inherent in some breeds (Newfoundlands, Bloodhounds, Bassets and the like), any dog can drool. It's often a sign of nausea,

sickness, or fear. Not to mention hunger. You have heard of Pavlov, have you not?

Face Licking: In the wild, face-licking is a means of soliciting food; in dogs, it's a sign of affectionate subordination. When we dogs lick your face, we are acknowledging your alpha status. Feel honored. (Of course we may also be looking for remnants of food clinging to your skin.)

Greeting Behavior: I know, it's gross. We dogs prefer to make acquaintance by sticking our noses under each other's tails. Honestly, I don't know how we came up with it, because our wolf relatives prefer to face-to-face greetings that are accompanied by much licking. A submissive wolf usually approaches the dominant one and licks its mouth; the dominant wolf then averts his face as a signal of acceptance and non-aggression. Wolves also sniff each other's behinds, although such behavior is much more commonly exhibited by males than females (regardless of the other dog's sex). Females, however, may engage in it during the breeding season. In general, the dominant wolf freely allows subordinates to sniff its rear, while subordinates tuck in their tails so that their behinds are inaccessible (females are especially adept at this). In either case, it appears as if the animals are more interested in getting information than in giving it away.

With us dogs, however, somehow things got turned around (pardon the pun). You can learn a lot about someone by sniffing their butt. (That's why familiar dogs spend less time in greeting behavior than do strangers.) Some dogs simply grunt their greetings.

Dogs tend not to greet each other as joyfully as they greet their owners (after all, owners have the food and goodies). Wolves, however, do show such effusiveness towards members of their own species.

We also enjoy face-to-face greetings and can lick faces with the best of them (with the subordinate dog licking the mouth of the more dominant one) while perhaps lifting an appeasing paw. It seems to make humans oddly uncomfortable, however, when we try to lick their faces directly after sniffing another dog's butt. It's always something with you humans.

There is such a thing as equality among dogs, by the way. Dogs with equal status meet and greet by jumping around in each other in playful circles. If a dominance hierarchy has not been established the dogs may bump side to side, each one trying to place his chip on the shoulder of the other dog.

When you greet a strange dog, take a page from our own book. We regard frontal approaches as potentially confrontational, so it's always best to approach a strange dog from the side. Don't stare at us or move quickly toward us with your hand stuck out in the air as if you wanted a donation. Avert your gaze to show us your friendly intentions. You might even crouch down. (See also "Staring," below.)

Grooming: Dogs do engage in mutual grooming, although such behavior is not very common. When it does occur, it is restricted to animals that are well acquainted. In general, the only situation that stimulates this activity is an open wound (in which case it is often beneficial). Some dogs like to lick other dogs that have just had a bath.

Humping or Mounting:	I know you hate it and think it's gross. However, you'll be relieved to know that it doesn't mean I want to have sex with you; it's a sign of attempted dominance and is common behavior in both males and females. Most dogs outgrow it, and males are less apt to do it if they've been neutered. This behavior is also common in wolves, and the dominant wolf may even bite the neck of the subordinate one.
Leaning:	Sometimes a lean is a not-so-subtle attempt to get you to move out of the way—that is, an attempt to exert our dominance. Other times we are just trying to get close to you. Sometimes it's both. Of course, if we move back and forth, it means that we itch.
Limping:	If we limp, we might really be hurt. On the other hand, however, we might be faking to get your attention. Hey, it works. I knew a little dog that cut her foot and got a lot of attention; afterwards she'd continue to limp whenever she felt neglected or bored. It worked very well until she forgot which foot to limp on. She'd alternate them, trying to see which ones got her the most attention.
Nose Licking:	This is a gesture of appeasement, submission, or calming that is, supposedly, noted most frequently in black dogs—although this may just be because it is noticed more in black dogs. The pink tongue against the black fur is quite conspicuous.
Nudging:	Nudging with the muzzle is usually a demand to be petted; it has been linked to teat-seeking behavior in puppies. Hip-nudging is a friendly invitation to play—dogs hip-nudge both humans and other dogs. And—I almost hate to tell you this—it's a modified mating ritual.

Panting: Open-mouthed panting sometimes accompanies play behavior. However, stress and heat also produce panting. (See "Breathing," above.)

Pawing: Pawing with the front foot is both a pacifying gesture and an invitation to play. It is much a like person shaking hands.

Posture: We often use posture to clarify dominant and submissive status within our packs. When a dominant meets a subordinate, he tends to stand stiffly over him (making a T shape). As the more submissive animal approaches the more dominant, he will lick its face or roll over to present the groin. Wolves sometimes go overboard (in my opinion) with this sort of thing; the dominant animal may pin the other to the ground and put its jaws around the subordinate's throat. (It makes my blood run cold to think of it.) General skin tightness, especially around the shoulder and neck, signals fear or aggression. Bassets, Chinese Shar-Peis, and Bloodhounds are just incapable in the regard; they can't tighten their skins no matter how much they want to.

Rolling over: This is a very submissive behavior, especially when coupled with the lifting of a leg. Researchers trace it back to puppyhood when the mother dog rolls the puppy over and pushes up its leg in order to clean the genital area. Dogs often roll over for a belly rub, but generally do not break eye contact with the owner as they would in other submissive behavior. This demonstrates trust.

Scratching: Maybe I have fleas or a skin condition—or maybe I am just trying to relieve anxiety. Scratching the ground after defecation, which is most commonly (but not exclusively) seen in male dogs, is an attempt to spread the scent around as much as possible. This is a habit primarily of dominant animals.

Sideways look: This is my attempt to watch you while I am planning a dastardly act such as making a getaway or eating the pie on the counter. You're not supposed to notice I'm looking at you.

Sleeping Postures: Wolves generally sleep either curled up with their tails wrapped around their faces or stretched out flat on their sides. Dogs, while also adopting these positions, sometimes sleep on their stomachs with their legs stuck out behind like a frog, or flat on their backs. There's something about domesticity that makes us want to experiment, I guess.

Smiling: Some dogs do smile, an expression that superficially resembles a snarl although the meaning is precisely the opposite. Smiling appears to be an inherited characteristic and is invariably offered only to human beings, never to other dogs.

Sniffing the Ground: In addition to the obvious (the dog wants to smell who's been around), sniffing the ground around another dog is often a gesture of appeasement. We are saying. "Oh, hi, don't mean to offend, in fact I'm not all that concerned with you—just checking around here, you know how it is."

Staring: This is a common expression of dominance or attempted dominance in both wolves and dogs. In fact, beta dogs and wolves may engage in this behavior more often than dominant ones.

Stalking: Stalking (or creeping along with an intent gaze) is hunting (and play-hunting) behavior. You'll see it most in herding dogs or hunting breeds. A dog stalks with the front of the body lowered but with feet poised to take off at a second's notice.

Turning the Head Aside: This is an appeasing or pacifying behavior.

Urination:	Urination is a wonderfully versatile activity. To humans it's just emptying the bladder, but for us dogs it's a true art form and a subtle means of communication. You may not find it so subtle when I urinate on the corner of your chair, but I am only trying to stake my territory. That's one kind of urination—marking. It's usually (but not exclusively) engaged in by dogs who are out to stake a claim. Dogs have been recorded urinating as many as 80 times within 4 hours, until every bit of ammunition finally ran out. (Some didn't give up even then—they left "dry" markings instead.) On the other hand, depending upon the body posture involved, urination can mean submission. (Submissive dogs crouch to urinate.) We dogs can get a lot of information from smelling urine; in fact, every dog's urine is as unique as a fingerprint (or noseprint, for that matter). One sniff tells us if the previous dog was male or female, neutered or intact (urine contains important sex hormones), a friend or a stranger. Dog urine is a many-splendored thing!

Scott and Fuller discovered that dogs not exposed to the urine markings of previous dogs are not inclined to mark either.[70]

Yawn:	I do yawn when I am tired, but also when I am anxious or excited. It lowers the blood pressure, at least temporarily. And yes, it's contagious among us, too.

Vocalization: Talking the Talk

Vocalization isn't body language, strictly speaking, but it fits in this chapter anyway. The big problem with vocal signals is that they are so transitory. If only you could read my scent signals, I wouldn't need to tell you same thing over and over again by barking.

When people think about our ancestors the wolves, they think about howling—that ineffable, beautiful, yet frankly somewhat creepy sound that soars over the tundra. Some national parks in Canada as well as the International Wolf Center in Ely, Minnesota, offer "wolf-howling" trips to the general public.[71] Some people will do anything; to each his own, I say.

Howling may well be mesmerizing, but wolves whine, woof, whimper, yelp, and bark more often than they howl, as do most dogs (although wolf barks are lower pitched and less variable than dog barks). (For information on "nuisance barking," see Chapter 5.) Some guy who had nothing better to do than quantify wolf sounds estimated that howling makes up only 2.3 percent of all lupine vocalization. This sounds like a made-up number to me, but who am I to quibble?

At any rate, dogs and wolves have pretty much the same set of basic vocalizations: whining (an infantile wolf noise that is also used by adult dogs), barking (usually a warning, but it has other uses as well), growling (ordinarily a warning), howling (multi-purpose), yelping (pain or distress), and moaning (pleasure). To further complicate things, all of these sounds are nuanced and have subvarieties. It has been said that dogs have 10 separate vocalizations through which they can convey 39 different meanings.

The vocal range and talent of dogs varies by breed. Although the "barkless" Basenji can produce a fairly wide range of noises, it is more limited vocally than the average dog. Basenjis can bark, by the way, but generally prefer not to. It takes an extremely high level of stimulation to get them to do so, and the result is usually only one or two barks. However, the sounds they do produce have a particular advantage in their native habitat of Africa, where they are prey to leopards. Unlike a bark, Basenji vocalization conveys very little information as to exactly where the animal is located. Some researchers hypothesize that these vocalizations developed as a survival tool so the leopards would be unable to pinpoint the source of the sound.

Poodles and American Staffordshire Terriers, to take two dogs from opposite ends of the behavioral spectrum, are also rather limited vocally.

The Bark:

Compared to howling, I have to admit that the bark (defined as burst of sound lasting less than one-tenth of a second), is a pedestrian, lower-grade vocalization. I've also noticed that it's very annoying to non-dogs.

> The barkless Basenji has an oddly shaped larynx that accounts for their vocal deficiency—if you want to call it that. However, although the Basenji does not bark, it yodels, chortles, and makes a variety of other very odd noises. The New Guinea Singing Dog is another such animal; it looks like a fox but sounds like a rooster. This odd noise has great carrying power, which is useful in the mountainous regions where they

Different kinds of barks signal different things; of course, we dogs understand the meanings a lot better than you do. A few barks let our friends and enemies know not only that we are around, but also where we are, how far away we are, and the barker's level of excitement or investment in the barking.

The Howl:

Of all canid sounds, the howl, which is produced by vibrations of the vocal cords, is uniquely important in wolves because it is the noise that cements the pack together. It also helps maintain the proper distance between rival packs. A rival pack will tend to respond to howling if it has something to defend, such as a fresh kill.

> Wolf howling seems to elicit a response from other species as well, including coyotes, owls, and loons. Wolves may also howl back when people howl at them. It's only courteous to respond.

Some contemporary dog breeds also tend to howl. You know, there's an old proverb: "Live with the wolves, howl like a wolf." It is true that you can teach a dog to howl by howling yourself and that introducing a howling dog into a household can induce previously non-howling dogs to howl. I could go on in this vein for some time, although I have a feeling the author of the proverb was speaking metaphorically. Perhaps not, though; you never know with humans.

I wouldn't be caught dead howling myself, but the Basset Hounds that live here have convinced more than one would-be intruder that a pack of ravenous wolves waits just behind the door. Howls are modulated in such a way that it always sounds as if there are about five times as many wolves (or dogs) than there actually are. Here's the strategy wolves use to create the effect: instead of howling in a pure tone, the wolf-chorus uses wavering or modulated howls with rapid pitch changes.

The vocal cords also vibrate at more than one frequency, and that produces complex tones as well. Well-known wolf-researchers Mary and John Theberge, who have studied wolf howling intensively, have discovered that although human ears perceive the howl as one tone, the wolf actually produces one fundamental tone and several harmonic tones.[72] All this makes it difficult for an outsider to follow a howl and hence figure out how many wolves are participating. Throw in a few landscaping elements like ridges, trees, and cliffs that deflect and scatter the noise, and the listener is at a real loss. U.S. President and Civil War General Ulysses S. Grant related a story in his *Memoirs* about a time when a companion challenged him to determine how many wolves were howling. Wishing to be debonair by deliberately underestimating the number, he remarked that there were no more than 20; he was shocked and embarrassed to discover that there was a mere pair of them. This phenomenon is called the Beau Geste Effect. (I've never been sure who or what Beau Geste is or was, but I thought I'd throw that in.)

It is no coincidence that howling dog breeds like hounds and Siberian Huskies are also highly social pack dogs. The howl, with its signature qualities of low pitch and long duration, can be heard over a distance of 10 miles. (Even humans can hear a wolf howl from 4 miles off, if the conditions are right.) Each wolf (or dog) has an individual howl which can last up to 20 seconds, although it's more likely to go from about 1 to 11 seconds. (You try howling for 20 seconds. It's not easy.) Acoustically, howling has been described as a fundamental frequency which lies between 150 and 780 cycles per second with up to 12 harmonically related overtones. The pitch may remain constant or vary smoothly, and it may change direction 4 or 5 times. The intensity of the howl does not vary greatly throughout. An entire howling session averages about 35 seconds, although both domestic dogs and wolves can howl for much longer periods when we wish. We like to conclude a howling session with some short, snappy barks to give it a little punch. And there you have it.

Howls can mean a variety of things. A melodious howl is happy howl, but a mournful one signals loneliness. After living with a howler for a while, you'll be able to tell the difference. And yes, it appears that (at least according to some researchers) European and American wolves howl differently. The Theberges even postulate that there are semantic subtleties in the howl of a wolf.[73] They suggest that at one level, wolf howling is universal (decipherable by all wolves); however, individual wolves (and wolf packs) may have their own dialects, which are understood only by close acquaintances. Different howling styles have been noted in different packs.

What about baying at the moon? We don't. It's a myth you people cooked up for your own purposes. Wolves are just as likely to howl in the daytime as at night (early morning howling is just as popular as the late night variety) and they howl throughout the year, although midwinter is an especially choice time. However, they don't care for a lot of wind during howling time. Why? Well, the wind may carry the howl off in the wrong direction. Wolves also do not howl when hunting, for obvious reasons. They are "mute trailers." Some dogs, however, do bark or bay when following game; they are called "open trailers." Mute or open trailing appears to be an inherited behavior.

Low, dark barking ("wooing"):

This is a warning or protective sound. Some studies have shown that the deeper the bark, the more dominant the dog. This may be true, but it seems a shame that leadership would devolve upon one on such flimsy ground. Alas, such is the way of nature.

Several high-pitched barks:

Loneliness, worry, alarm. As the pitch rises and the bark becomes more rapid, it usually means something or someone strange has arrived; wolves sometimes bark this way if a threat is apparent. A study conducted by Dr. Karin Overall, Director of the Behavior Clinic at the University of Pennsylvania School of Veterinary Medicine; Dr. Arthur Dunham, an evolutionary biologist at the same institution; and Dr. Leslie Augulnick, a veterinarian in private practice, examined the barks of 30 dogs and found that the bark of a stressed dog is high-pitched, atonal, and repetitive.[74] Unstressed dogs have more harmonic, melodic barks.

Short, quick, chirpy barks:

Play-eliciting or prey notification.

Single bark:

Normal conversation—I wish to draw your attention to something. In wolves, a single bark may be an alarm.

Other vocalizations include:

Growling:

A deep-throated sound issued as a clear warning or threat; growling can be followed by biting. Conversely, many dogs also growl in play. There are various levels of growling, each of which is deeper and carries a more explicit threat: the grumble, the throat growl, and the belly growl.

Grunting:

A greeting or sign of contentment.

Whimpering or Whining:

A soft, high-pitched sound. In wolves, it is characteristically (but not commonly) used when begging or greeting a higher-ranked animal. Dogs, on the other hand, whine a lot and use whining primarily to communicate with their owners as opposed to other dogs. Whimpering and whining generally signal submission, pain, or defense. If a lot of stress is involved, the whining may be interspersed with even higher-pitched, eardrum-scraping yips.

Dog Moods

In the previous sections, I've gone into a fair amount of detail to explain just what certain body and vocal language may mean. Now I am going to approach things from the opposite direction. I'll list a mood, then tell you how we express it. (It's not written in blood or carved in stone, of course, and variations may exist between individual dogs.)

Aggression: If there's any single dog-mood you should learn, it's this one. Aggression is characterized by a fixed stare, wide-open eyes, upright ears, a curled or raised lip, a wrinkled nose, tail held high, and raised hackles (or any combination of these).

Anxiety: Anxiety is characterized by panting, dilated pupils, and often a gaze averted from the source of the anxiety. The ears will be down and back and the lips retracted. Although we are not able to sweat all over, our paws can sweat—and they will during anxiety attacks. We may yawn, scratch, or shake to relieve the anxiety.

Boredom: You'll recognize the signs immediately: glassy, blank stare; droopy ears (in breeds that can droop their ears); listless tail. Usually we lie on the floor with our chin resting glumly on our forelegs. Our tails lie limp like a dead snake. Sometimes we'll sigh pointedly and stare at the leash.

Defense Against a Dominant Animal: Our response is normally a submissive one, especially if we are a low-ranking dog. But we may respond to a perceived threat in a different way. Defense snapping, an unsure look, ears pinned back, tail down, and bared teeth all signal that we feel threatened by a dominant animal—which may be you. As a rule, the higher the rank of the threatened dog, the more aggressive the response to a threat.

Dominance: "On the muscle" (standing tall—up and forward, with the head held high), fixed stare, wide-open eyes, prominent eyebrows, straight neck and back, and possibly a curled lip. If one dominant dog meets another, a fight may ensue unless a hierarchy is quickly established. The posture is very similar to that of aggression, so take care.

Excitement: Lots of jumping around (on you, if you're dumb enough to permit it) and tail wagging. Our ears are pricked unless perhaps we hold them back when greeting a superior like yourself.

Fear: Fearful dogs do everything they can to appear smaller (even bending the legs), and they hide their tail between their legs. Some dogs will avert or narrow their gaze; others will stare intently at the fearful object (even to the extent that you can see the whites of the eyes). In extreme situations, we may close our eyes in hopes that the scary situation will dissolve.

I once knew a Bulldog named Milton. When stressed, Milton would shut his eyes and take off at a dead run. I saw him slam into the side of a barn doing that; it was very discouraging. Some dogs blink fearfully, apparently trying to combine staring with not looking. Usually the mouth will be closed and the ears flattened or flickering. If you see raised hackles in addition to all this, take care; the dog may be preparing to bite.

Friendliness: Narrowed eyes, blinking, flattened ears, and a full, relaxed, wagging tail will be seen in both wolves and dogs. Subordinate wolves (and dogs) are more likely to wag the entire rump (although tailless dogs don't have much choice about that).

Happiness:	Open or relaxed mouth with the corners slightly drawn back, loose tongue, forehead smooth, ears pitched forward. When standing, all four feet are placed evenly on the ground. The position of the tail is largely dependent on the breed. Very excited or happy dogs may alternate quickly between dominant and submissive postures. Heavy-flewed breeds like bloodhounds and bassets can't easily show some of the happy mouth positions, a disability that partially accounts for their somewhat gloomy expression (the drooping eyes don't help, either).
Interest:	An interested, alert dog will be on the muscle, sometimes with a paw raised. The tail is usually horizontal to the ground in long-tailed breeds; dogs with short or docked tails tend to hold them up slightly.
Pacifying:	Pacifying behavior, also called appeasement, is characterized by an outstretched paw, eyes narrowed to a slit (or even closed), flickering ears, the head turned aside, and ground sniffing.
Play-Eliciting Behavior:	Panting, hard and fast tail-wagging, play-bowing, fake "running away." We may utter a high-pitched bark.
Sorrow:	Very similar to submission. (See below.)
Submission:	Tail between the legs, lowered head, flickering or pricked ears, inclined neck, cringing, rolling over to the side or back, possible urination (often while crouching). The dog may blink excessively. Submissive dogs, like fearful ones, do their best to make themselves look smaller. Very submissive or intimidated dogs may roll over with their tails tucked between their legs and urinate. Wolves behave in exactly the same way. A Basset puppy we had in the house once did this when we visited a home in

which a large Chinese Shar-Pei of somewhat uncertain temperament resided. It worked. Submission does not always equal fear, however. We may roll over submissively for our owners to stroke our bellies, but as domestic beings we have learned to look confidently at them at the same time.

Threat: Wrinkled nose, raised lip, bared teeth (usually accompanied by a snarl), raised hackles, tail up, ears forward. The more wrinkled the nose and forward the ears, the more aggressive the mood. A snarling dog with a pitched (angled) back is both aggressive and fearful or submissive, which is a bad combination.

Uneasiness: This is characterized by tongue flickering It may also indicate a need to urinate.

Reading Your Language

Here is one trick I've learned—one which neither my lupine relatives (nor, so far as is known, any other animal) have not quite caught the knack of; I can read your face. Yes, even the the flicker in your eyes and the tightness of your lips. I alone have acquired this extremely useful skill. It wasn't easy. And, I've noticed, you are not so clever at reading my own body language, which is more straightforward and sensible. Researchers have concluded (tentatively, of course, but they've learned to be tentative about their conclusions when they deal with me) that perhaps this was the one factor that separated us dogs and wolves from the beginning. Those-who-remain-wolves just never learned the knack of reading the inscrutable (to them) human visage, while I did.[75] I, the Shapeshifter, can read my human partners' expressions and attune myself to their needs—the hunger or loneliness or sorrow in their eyes. "Ah, look," humans say in their gibberish. "Fido can read my mind." It's not your mind I am reading, just your give-it-all-away face. In fact, researchers such as Patricia McConnell, a zoology professor and dog-behavior expert who often works with aggressive dogs, suggest that as little a quarter of an inch of movement of a person's head can make the difference between a calm dog and one who attacks.[76] Think about that for a minute. However, be aware that a dog's vision doesn't mature until he is about 4 months old, so you'll have to expect mistakes before that time.

I grant you that some of us are much better at this sort of thing than others. Herding breeds tend to pay a lot more attention to gestures than the rest of us because they were bred for it.

Researchers have found that even if you raise a wolf cub from birth, let it live in your home, and treat it like your dearest child, the poor thing just cannot learn to read your face. I can. I can figure out where the treat is hidden by watching the movement of your eyes. I have made a habit of watching you very carefully since I never know what you might try to pull on me next.

Although we dogs can't understand most of the English language, with its annoying series of declensions, conjugations, and ablative absolutes (oh, wait, that's Latin), we are remarkably sensitive to tone.

> Perhaps we should make an exception for Poodles here, which have proved themselves amazingly adept at acquiring a very large human vocabulary.

We understand praise, commands, and reprimands. What confuses us is when your words contradict your tone. When that happens we read the tone every time—it's safer. For instance, are you really surprised that we don't come running when you call us (while you "hide" the toenail clippers behind your back)? It's not a mystery; we read the tension in your voice. Lie to your own kind—or to yourself, even—but not to me; I hear the truth in your tone. I can interpret even your mixed signals accurately, whether you think I can or not. I can even smell your moods. You probably have no idea how your body odor changes with your stress level.

> Some people have concluded that dogs respond to commands in German (a "tough" language) more readily than those in French, which is generally perceived as a more "gentle" language. No research has been done to support this strange theory, so far as I know. I suppose it stems from the observation

that many police dogs respond to German commands. But that's because they were trained in Germany.

Human Cues and How We Interpret Them

Every move you make carries a signal to us, whether or not you realize it. It will improve relations between us if you are just a little more conscious of what you are communicating.

Body Stance: People who stand tall with their shoulders back and head up present a self-assured, confident, dominant stance. When accompanied by a strong voice and purposeful walk, we dogs assume you folks are good leaders and know what you're about, so we'll follow you. People who exhibit neck rigidity may be perceived as threatening, so loosen up a little. And don't shove your hand in my face. A very slow, gentle extension of the hand is permissible so I can smell it, but don't do anything suddenly. Don't pat me on the top of the head, either, at least until I know you well and accept your leadership—it's considered provocative. A gentle stroking of the chest is much less intimidating.

Greeting: When greeting a strange but friendly dog, try kneeling down and opening your arms. Get down to our level and avert your gaze a bit. This establishes your friendliness. Of course, if you're not sure about the intentions of a strange dog, stand up straight and tall and don't stare—that's a challenge. Forget everything you've ever heard about "staring down a dog"; it's an invitation to conflict, take my word for it. We usually don't mind having our owners or other known friendly people stare at us, but if I don't know you, don't take any chances. When approaching, it's best to do it from the side rather than from the front—except with chow chows. They have practically no peripheral vision, and they're not the friendliest dogs to begin with. (Having been used as food for all those years, one can hardly blame them.)

Height: We dogs often equate height with authority, and in dog-play we try to establish ourselves on higher ground, even if it means dirtying up the furniture (which is even better, because it shows we own that, too). A tall person is more intimidating and authoritative than a child, so with a shy dog, sitting down next to it can be comforting. However, children should never do this around dominant, potentially aggressive dogs. In fact, it's best to keep them (the children) away completely.

Hugging and Kissing: Without practice, we dogs may not understand that a hug is a well-meant gesture of human affection. It doesn't seem a natural thing to us at all; in fact, it's a bit scary because it signals a threat or an attempt to dominate us. Therefore we may accept a hug from the adults in the home whom we know and trust, but may resent hugs, head pats, and kisses from kids, whose behavior is quixotic at all times and who seem to occupy a rather ambivalent place in the household. They pretend to be human, but they act like animals. Have you noticed this? Get your kids off the floor and teach them to stand tall and assert themselves. After we accept their leadership and we know we can trust them, they can kiss us. Of course this doesn't always apply to savior-types like Newfoundlands. They love kids and will protect them. There's always somebody like that around.

Movement: Because we can detect very low levels of motion, we often respond to a movement you made before you even knew you were making it. Unfortunately our responses may not always be appropriate, especially if the movements are unusual or quick. Fast gestures can be scary or overstimulating. Kids who run screaming through the house remind us of a tasty meal on the run or a large predator. Our response to either of those isn't particularly good.

Muzzle-Grabbing: A dog's muzzle and nape of the neck are very sensitive areas associated with admonishment from our superiors (starting with mom). You can get away with shaking our muzzles if we already consider you the boss, but do not try this with a strange dog. When we dogs fight with each other, that's the spot we go for. And, for that reason, when we fight, we'll go for your face. And a very effective strategy it is, too.

Petting: Dogs enjoy being stroked gently. We do not like being patted on the top of the head, although most of us get used to it after a while. This is a particularly annoying habit of children. A dog may perceive it as an aggressive rather than affectionate gesture. Wolves, by the way, do not like to be petted. They regard any such behavior as provocative and will try to kill you.

Staring: Since dogs regard staring as a threat, it's best not to stare back unless you want to provoke a fight. You don't want to cringe either, though, especially if the threatening dog looks dangerous. Compromise and stare at the tip of the dog's ear. That shows you are not threatening, but no coward either. It indicates that you are so far above him that you barely notice him. This is defusing behavior.

ESP in Dogs

I suppose I ought to say something about canine/lupine ESP. We have it; you know we do. We are eerily accurate in knowing when you'll be home or if there is something not quite right about a visitor—even if you don't. We know your intentions before you do; we can read your attitude. If you are ambivalent in your feelings about us, it shows.

Skeptics claim that I merely have super-acute senses and that I watch everything so carefully that I am aware of even the slightest dip in the breeze or angle of light. Call it what you will; I know things. I even know when it is my time to die—which is more than you do, for either yourselves or me, and more's the pity. You often keep me breathing with your latest technology and drugs when all I want to do is lie quietly under my favorite tree and breathe my last. You just won't allow that; you try to capture my spirit the way you've manipulated my body. But I elude you in the end—and I join the wind, time, and my ancestors. See you later, friend.

Chapter 5:
Challenges of Domesticity, or How We Live Now

"Every dog is a lion at home."
—H.G. Bohn

Believe it or not, life between us dogs and you people is not always a well-choreographed dance. We often have differing priorities. For example, my personal priorities are: (1) food (any); (2) running (anywhere); (3) getting attention (preferably from my owner, but anyone will do). My owner's priorities seem to be: (1) food (hers, of which I get none); (2) driving away in a car and leaving me alone with the other stupid dogs; (3) sitting like a lump in front of a book, TV, or computer. There's obviously some disconnect here. We seem to want opposite things, except for the occasions when we both want her food, in which case she gets it. Usually.

It should be obvious that differing priorities can result in difficulties, and in this chapter we'll deal with some of the more common ones that come our way. If you humans are as smart as you claim you are, it just stands to reason that *you* would be the ones to fix any little problems that might pop up in our relationship. After all, you're the owners, the feeders, the walkers, the trainers. No matter where the fault lies you have to fix it—I'm not going to. I'm just a dog. If I bark too much, bite too often, root in the garbage, chase the cat, steal food, run away, or act like a lunatic whenever it thunders—you fix it. You're probably the one who got me off-track to begin with. (Humans get off-track pretty easily themselves.) People can be physically or verbally abusive, rationalizing, subservient, manipulative, inconsistent, anthropomorphic, rigid, you name it—I've seen it all. (We're way beyond cause and effect and chickens and eggs here.) I can't help correct all such problems in one chapter, but I will give you a few hints.

There are no problem dogs, only problem dog owners. (That's not always the case, but it's a generalization I think we can both live with.) Every kind of problem dog-owner creates a different kind of problem in the dog. It's depressing to think of the number of dogs who have been choked, shocked, hit, hung, isolated, rolled over, shoved, and had their noses rubbed in you-know-what—all under the aegis of "training." Not surprisingly, this sort of treatment does not produce a happy, loving, well-balanced pet; it engenders a nervous, shy, depressed, confused, aggressive, phobic, neurotic heap of quivering muscle and nerve. Then you euthanize us.

In all fairness, however, I must make an admission. Studies have shown that most people who have a problem dog do not engage in bizarre, brutal, or outrageous behavior; most own or have owned other dogs who gave them no trouble at all. Sometimes certain dogs and certain owners just don't quite click, especially when one or the other of the pair is not very flexible in his approach to relationships. Or there can be a basic personality clash; weak owners and strong dogs (or vice versa) are usually a bad combination. For example, if a dominant dog is paired with a weak, uncertain, retiring person, the dog's dominant traits will quickly emerge. This doesn't mean the dog will bite his owner; it means he'll push him around. (But he might bite him, too—I've seen it happen.) Soft, gentle people do best with soft, gentle dogs. (I am not talking, in either case, about stressed dogs (such as the kind you often come across in canine rescue); they need special treatment that is neither overly attentive nor excessively tough. Such dogs need to be let alone long enough to chill out.

There are two main things to remember about our relationship: (1) Dogs generally group themselves into some kind of hierarchy. This is normal. (2) It's your job to be at the apex of the hierarchy. And there are two main things to remember when trying to get a dog to obey you: (1) Get us to pay attention to you. (2) Get us to trust you.

If There's A Problem

Most dog problems emerge when dogs are bored, insufficiently exercised, or lonely. I know that humans want it all, but too many people who own dogs are unwilling or unable to make time for them. They work all day, party all night (or stare fixedly at the TV with barely a grunt to the poor dog), then wonder why their dog isn't Rin Tin Tin. Ugh.

Many of the behaviors described in this section are termed "phobic" or "obsessive," but it's more accurate to call them adaptations to bad situations. We dogs are social animals, and it has been shown that dogs that develop obsessive or compulsive behaviors tend to be single dogs left alone for long periods every day. For example, certain stereotypical behaviors such as pacing, jumping, and other obsessive patterns can be ameliorated by providing a different feeding environment. Instead of slapping all the food in a bowl, putting it down, and letting us eat it in 20 seconds, make us work for it. Satisfy our urge to hunt and solve problems; use a feed hopper or Kong toy and hide the food in different places. In other words, provide some opportunity for us to think rather than behave mindlessly. Imitate the wolf environment (at least a little)—but do leave the heat on.

But let's say you spend a reasonable amount of time with your dog and give him plenty of attention and exercise, but there's still some kind of problem with, say, aggression, or housetraining (those are a couple of the big ones). Before you tear your hair out trying to decide what you did wrong or plunk down a fortune for behavioral therapy, have your dog checked out by a vet. Behavioral problems are not always rooted in psychological troubles, either mine or yours. They can be caused by parasites, hearing or vision problems, endocrine or hormonal imbalances (including thyroid dysfunction and Cushing's disease), hypersexuality, hyperactivity, spinal problems, medications, toxins, or a host of other reasons. In fact, over 50 percent of dogs dragged to the vet for "behavior problems" turn out to have either an underlying medical condition that requires treatment, a psychological problem that requires medication, or both.

Once a medical examination has ruled out such conditions, you can go to work on your attitude toward me. That's right. While it's tempting to start trying to figure out what *my* problem is, you will be off to a better start if you re-examine *your* set of expectations about me. If you humans continue to misunderstand our nature, we dogs will continue to have identity crises. Being a dog is tough enough under the best of circumstances. People say they want a dog, and then they want the dog to behave like something else—say, a cat or a robot. No wonder I'm frequently cast into a deep existential angst. Remember, we are not natural creatures—you made us. And in the process, you seem to have developed some misapprehensions about what you have wrought.

First of all, I am not your child. I'm not even human; our chromosomes don't match up. (I am, genetically speaking, a wolf, as I have tried to make clear to you. Several times.) You can't write me off as a dependent. Although I will never go to college, have a paper route, or get married, I am with you for life. If this disappoints you, I'm sorry; but if you think of me as a furry kid, I am bound to disappoint you when I (inevitably) show you my dog-wolf nature. Martha Scott's admonition "Don't make the mistake of treating your dogs like humans or they will treat you like dogs," is true, I'm afraid.

I'm not your best friend, either, despite all those silly sentimental sayings. I will never lend you money, take you out to dinner, or pick you up at the airport. I will listen your problems, at least for a while, but I don't really understand them and I can't give any useful advice. In fact, I depend on you to make good decisions for me.

I am not an object. You can't possess me the way you do a chair or a car. You cannot walk out of my life for hours and hours every day, come home, ignore me, and expect me to have been in suspended animation while you were gone. A tree may not make any noise if it falls in the forest with no one around to hear it, but you can bet your last dollar that I will carry on something awful if I am left alone too often for too long. I have feelings, needs, desires, and rights. If these are continually misunderstood, frustrated, or ignored, the outcome will be bad for both of us.

Most of the activities for which I am chastised are normal gene-embedded behaviors. If doggish activities such as barking, chewing, sniffing, and like are truly bothersome, get yourself a kid. See how well you cope with one of those.

Philosophically, I am a disciple of the American philosophers William James and John Dewey; that is, I am a pragmatist and a utilitarian. I do what works to make me happy. This simple, cheery doctrine has served me well. I do not need to complicate it by adding a convoluted and contradictory code of morality, a baffling metaphysic, or a perverted sense of aesthetics. It is you, not I, who decided that Jackson Pollack was a great artist. Let that speak for itself.

> I suppose I should say something about my limbic system here. (You have one too, by the way.) It's the area of the brain that includes the hippocampus (which is a weird little organ shaped something like a seahorse, which is what its name means in Greek—or so I'm told) The limbic system is a primitive part of the brain that controls not only new memory function (old memory gets stored in the cerebral cortex) but also much "instinctual behavior." If there's a clash between what you want me to do and what I want to do instinctively, you'll need an override switch—like food—if you want to have things your way. The hippocampus also plays a role in learning because it controls the degree of interest or arousal I feel in a subject. Studies have shown that when I'm interested in something, I learn faster. So do you. Thank your hippocampus.

Roger Abrantes astutely (for a human) noted that what makes social animals (like wolves, dogs, and people) successful is their ability to compromise.[77] Keep this in mind; living harmoniously requires give and take on both sides. We dogs have what Abrantes describes as "social awareness," which means that I know how to live in a civilized society and I expect that I need to be flexible to do so. Let's hope you do, too.

Dog behaviorists have noted again and again that the single most important aspect to controlling a dog problem is the owner's commitment to working things out. If you don't make an emotional and spiritual commitment to us, we won't commit to you, either. We dogs know when our humans are not fully committed to us, and this fearful knowledge adds stress to our lives. The more stressed we are, the more we act out. The more we act out, the more stressed and less committed our owners get. The next thing you know, we're in the pound. But if you're truly committed to us, you'll find it comparatively simple to solve the little misunderstandings that crop up from time to time.

In all fairness, I suppose I should acknowledge that the 55 million dogs in the country today are not always the pets of your dreams. We can bite you, pass on diseases, and cost you a lot of money in food, vet bills, insurance premiums, grooming supplies, and regular shipments of new furniture after we have chewed up the previous lot. I'm too polite to mention the 2 million tons of poop I drop in the street that you have to clean up. It all totes up to the tune of about a billion dollars a year, give or take. Look at the bright side, though; we keep the economy (as well as our bowels) moving.

I intend to discuss some common problems dogs and their owners face together. We'll do it alphabetically, just in case you need to look something up quickly. My first bit of advice, however, is so important that it can't wait: start training me when I'm young and involve all members of the family. Don't wait until bad habits have been established in either of us. You'll be surprised how much both of us can learn together in puppy kindergarten! And if the entire family helps in the training, I will bond more easily to each member rather than just to the person I consider the leader. Gather up a flat collar (no choke chain, please), a lead, some treats, a well-recommended trainer and class, and a couple of good dog-training books, and we're set to go. Remember, however, this is not a book about the mechanics of dog training. You can pick one of those up anywhere. I'm giving you just a bit of theoretical background.

> You may notice I avoid terms like "positive" or "negative" reinforcement, "classical conditioning," "operant conditioning" and other confusing terms that, frankly, don't make much sense to me.

Aggression

The worst problem a dog can demonstrate is aggression against people. *Aggression*, simply defined, *is violence or the threat of violence.* It can be directed toward prey animals, other dogs, or human beings—even those we like best. Different people, of course, define and measure aggression differently, and just as dogs have different "bite thresholds," humans have different levels of tolerance for antagonistic behavior. For some people, aggression is not a problem if directed against cats, dogs, or even strangers; for nearly everybody, however, it is a problem when directed at themselves or other family members. So for the purposes of this discussion, let's simply consider aggression *undesirable or inappropriate* hostility, since what is undesirable is what creates the problem. We'll concentrate on aggression against humans, since that's what everyone gets most worked up about.

When dogs get aggressive, people end up hurt or even dead—and we dogs get euthanized. (It's a fancy way of saying killed, but it means the same thing.) Unfortunately, such aggression is almost never dealt with immediately; it is often allowed to increase in severity until there is no other solution but the vet and the needle. For some reason, humans want to deny such things; they make excuses or blame others for the bad deeds of their pets, lose their temper, or become hopelessly depressed and do nothing. None of these tactics will work. *Aggression will not disappear. A dog with aggressive tendencies will probably always have aggressive tendencies.* With care and training (and sometimes even medication), aggression can be managed; however, it requires a savvy, committed, determined owner who will work faithfully with a canine behaviorist to get the problem under control. And if everyone in the household is not willing to go along, the effort is doomed before it begins.

> Standard obedience classes designed for non-aggressive dogs tend to increase rather than decrease stress, as do alpha rolls and other such interventions. Punishing an aggressive dog will not cure his aggression; it will only increase his stress, which generates further aggression.

Aggression is a mostly trait. It originates in the genes, although there is no single gene that dictates aggressiveness; it is largely the result of other genetically-controlled behavioral patterns. As is true of most behaviors, aggression is "polygenetic," meaning that a number of genes chip in to make a dog more likely to respond to a situation aggressively. The genes themselves just set codes for proteins which in turn set limits on behavior by making a dog more or less sensitive and reactive to certain stimuli. Such sensitivities can also be learned—but more on that later.

> Some tendency toward aggression is a normal part of everybody's makeup, including yours, although not all of us act it out. The first signs of normal aggression appear in puppies when they are between 3 and 5 weeks of age. This early aggression is directed toward their littermates and is partly a struggle for dominance. In fact, most aggression in the world of dogs (and wolves) is intraspecific—and why not? Our fellow dogs are our biggest rivals for food, toys, the best spot in the room, and our most valuable resource—you. Oh, we like you all right, but let's face it, your primary function in our lives is to provide us with food, attention, care, and the warm spot on the bed.

Aggression is part of the dog's natural inheritance, just as is running away. In fact, those are the two main ways we have of responding to adverse situations—fight or flee (or at least bluff the opponent into thinking we might fight). *In other words, aggression and flight are both stress-based.* Stress inhibits the cerebral cortex, the part of the brain where I reason and learn, but activates the primitive limbic system, which is what impels me to just react. Believe me, when a dog suddenly turns aggressive he is not thinking, he's reacting. Aggression toward humans may show up in a timid dog just as it does in a dominant one (this dominance/aggression stuff is mostly a myth). It is a common misperception that "dominant" or "alpha" dogs are those who show the most aggression, but that's just not so. Many "dominant" animals show very little (they don't have to), while certain subordinates ("middle manager" types, usually) display it frequently. Aggression appears when we are stressed and running away is impossible or seems not to be in our best interest. A calm, self-confident animal is must less likely to bite a person that a stressed-out, fearful one. But I should caution you that nothing is certain; anything with teeth can bite.

A better term than "dominance aggression" is "control complex aggression," which was coined by James O'Heare.[78] O'Heare states that dogs afflicted with this condition are "control freaks with low thresholds for frustration and anger…[who are] socially incompetent." These animals are not seeking status, nor are they confident dominant dogs; they are fearful more than anything else. This fear drives them to attempt to control their environment in order to make things "safe" (in their minds) for themselves. To call them dominant is exactly the wrong way to look at their behavior; it's almost the opposite. To understand how best to deal with such a dog, I highly recommend *The Canine Aggression Workbook*. It is, in my opinion, the best and most intuitive book on the topic. (That's straight from the horse's—er, dog's—mouth. My opinion should be worth something.)

The fight-flight strategy has worked well for us for millennia. That doesn't mean we go around biting everything we see; however, modern life has imposed considerable stresses on us that did not exist in the wild. Stressors can include uncertain, inconsistent, or overly emotional owners; a household crammed full of other dogs; or a gang of screaming kids. Normal stressors that existed in the wild (and still exist in our life with humans) include competition for sex or territory, defending our young or our possessions, or fear. The combination of modern environmental stressors plus those we've always been subject to can put a dog over the edge, shutting down the cerebral cortex and activating that primitive limbic system—hence the display of aggression. Most aggression can therefore be managed or eliminated by removing (or altering) stress in the environment.

The only kind of aggression that is not directly related to stress is the prey drive, also called predatory behavior or chasing. It's a whole different thing. We see little animals run and something tells us to go eat 'em. It's just dinner calling. I have to admit though that it sometimes stresses people to see us chasing the family bunny around the living room. Odd lot, you humans. Anyway, this isn't something you can train out of us—it's instinct. It runs, we chase, and if we catch it we might kill it. This depends on our breed and individual genetic makeup, but it's pretty much hard-wired.

> Most training methods rely on a system of rewards, but it's important to remember that certain behaviors are instinctively learned and intrinsically rewarding; that is to say that the behavior itself is pleasurable and gratifying. Just as a human child has an internal directive to walk (you don't need to reward a child with cookies to get him to do it), certain dog breeds have been selected for certain kinds of natural behavior. Scott and Fuller found again and again that different breeds, even when trained in precisely the same way, responded to that training in breed-specific ways.[79] In other words, different breeds like to do different things; for example, not all dogs are as crazy about running around in circles as I am. And although this should not come as a surprise to anyone, many trainers still lack the flexibility to alter their training methods to suit various breeds or individual dogs. Unfortunately, some of the behaviors most inherently rewarding to us are the very things that drive you mad; digging, chewing, and running away come to mind instantly.

In the wild, canids can (and sometimes do) resolve leadership arguments by duking it out, so to speak, even if one animal is injured, driven away, or killed in the process. Dogs living with humans are usually spared this possibly catastrophic ending (because people just don't allow it), but as a result dominance hierarchies (pack order) are sometimes never firmly established. In the canid world, unstable pack order results in increased fighting, displays of dominance, and other chronic, simmering problems among dogs. If your pack spends a lot of time fighting, there's a problem with them, you, or both.

The "bite threshold" in dogs is the point at which a stressed or provoked dog will bite. For some dogs, this threshold is very low— perhaps the mere sight of a hated person or object; for others, it is close to nonexistent (there are terrible stories of vivisected dogs licking the hands of their torturers). Many dogs prefer extremely submissive behavior to biting no matter what the provocation; most dogs, however, will bite when pushed to their limit (whatever that limit may be).

> Normal dogs have something called "bite inhibition," which means that we may close our mouths over a rival dog's body part but don't actually bite—at least we don't if we were left with our littermates long enough to learn this important skill. We found that biting a littermate too hard made him squeal and then he wouldn't play any more. Good bite inhibition allows us to play and even squabble (with lots of noise), but usually no real damage is done. It's kind of fun.

However you measure it, aggression is now one of the most commonly reported problems in dogs. That's too bad. My ancestors, the wolves, are generally a friendly, peaceable lot; they had to be, or they would never have managed to rouse the cooperative effort needed to take on a herd of caribou. In group work, nonviolence is a very useful tool. Among modern-day dogs, hounds and sporting dogs have best retained this aspect of wolf-character; they are social animals capable of tremendous cooperation with one another. Herding dogs are great cooperators as well, but they prefer to do so with humans.

> Aggression seems to be getting more common in today's breeds. According to the *Journal of the American Medical Association*, about 334,000 people in the United States are admitted to hospital emergency rooms annually because of dog bites, another 466,000 report to other medical facilities, and thousands more go unreported.[80] A dog bites 1 of every 100 Americans every year (but it's probably not the same person—or

the same dog, for that matter). There seems to be a plague of biting dogs, a problem caused partially by irresponsible breeding and, to a degree, by some humans getting a little cozier with dogs than is wise.

Much aggression among dogs is ritualized—we go through the motions, but nothing serious happens. Its main purpose is to maintain order. In general, species with strong aggressive tendencies need rituals; it really is the only way to keep things under control. I have noticed that people have rituals of aggression too (like, say, football).

We don't always act on our aggressive instincts. Like you, most of us are capable of self-control. We may wish to eat the family cat or even bite your hand when you take something away from us, but prudence prevails. We know, or should know, where our self-interest lies. However, problems do sometimes arise when we perceive our masters as competitors for important resources.

Regarding the great nature vs. nurture debate—it is probably impossible to disentangle inherited aggressive behavior from that which is learned. For example, it has been noted that a dominant bitch may growl at her own humans if they come too near her puppies, while a more submissive bitch may not. The puppies of the dominant bitch may then copy their mother. Is their behavior inherited or learned? Probably some of each. One indication that at least some of it is learned has been observed by many breeders: the temperament of puppies tends to be more like that of the mother than of the father (whom most puppies never see. I certainly never saw mine—and I dare you to say something about my mother).

Inappropriate aggression could probably be largely eliminated or at least ameliorated by strict breeding guidelines (in Germany, for instance, the Parson Russell Terrier Club Deutsche requires stud dogs to pass a temperament test before breeding), but of course that's not done in this county (it's not democratic or something). On the other hand, my German-Shepherd-dog friends outside America have fairly serious aggression problems. That's because the majority of them descend from Canto vd Wienerau (1968–1972), whose temperament was, well, not quite perfect, no matter how admirable his other qualities.

Although we dogs are now almost exclusively pets (with too much spare time on our paws), it wasn't always so. We used to spend a lot more time working outdoors and less time indoors being jumped on by kids. Outdoor working dogs were not hugged, coddled, or kissed repeatedly on the nose; they got enormous amounts of exercise. Guard dogs stayed outdoors and no one came near them. This lack of closeness resulted in fewer bites. Today, however, you ask us to be much more social without ever really socializing us. You want to us submit to behavior that frightens us, like hugging and kissing, without clarifying that you are not committing an aggressive act. You stare at us, "alpha-roll" us, and run around us screaming, then expect us to act as though you are not some dangerous creature to be purged from the face of the earth. We dogs become very puzzled.

It's not always easy for humans to clearly identify a dog that has aggressive tendencies. If a human owner is a strong, consistent, trustworthy leader, a dog may never exhibit aggression; however, certain "control-freak" dogs will test their owners over and over again. By the way, a strong human leader is not a violent one. No muzzle-shaking or alpha rolls are needed to establish your dominance. (Those alpha rolls—who came up with that idea? We roll over on our backs in extreme submission on our own. Pushing us into it is scary unless we already accept you as a strong, dominant person and know you're just going to rub our bellies. We do like having our bellies rubbed.)

Sex matters. Male dogs, especially intact males, are more likely to demonstrate aggression toward other dogs and their owners than are unspayed females; spayed females, however, tend to be more aggressive to other dogs than those who are not spayed. Neutering a male dog may help reduce aggression, and it's a fact that cryptorchid dogs (who have one testicle undescended—that is, still hidden in the groin) often show unusually high levels of aggression. Between 70 and 90 percent of canine aggression incidents are perpetuated by intact male dogs. (I was neutered myself at an early age, and don't think I've missed anything important. I wonder if you humans have ever considered how much trouble you get yourselves into with your uncontrolled sex drive? Perhaps you to ought think about—oh, never mind, you'd never agree. Hypocrites.)

One of the most ambiguous accomplishments of human beings is their having bred some modern dogs to be *more* aggressive than our wolf ancestors. The thanks goes to people's interest in protecting themselves from other (aggressive) humans, seeing dogs tear each other to pieces in dogfights, and similar high-minded activities. All this is the result of artificial—not natural—breeding.

A perfect example is the rather extreme aggression of certain fighting breeds,which are programmed to attack dogs and humans. In fact, they will continue to attack no matter how tired or injured they become. This quality is (stupidly) termed "gameness" by their breeders. Additionally, such dogs have been bred to have a higher pain threshold and a lower attack threshold. Wolves and dogs that have inherited wolflike behavior respond to natural "cutoff" signals (facial, vocal, or postural) from their opponents. Dogs from fighting lines, however, neither convey nor respond to such signals. They are social misfits. They may fight for hours, which is unheard of in normal animals. Some researchers think that this kind of aggression is misdirected prey-drive—in other words, the drive normally directed towards dinner. In the case of fighting (and guard) dogs, the natural prey drive has been redirected toward other animals, dogs, or humans.

Historically, when dogfighting was a legal sport, dogs were specifically selected to be aggressive only toward other dogs, *not* people; those that were human-aggressive were killed or removed from the breeding program. This is not the case today, however. Since dogfighting has been made illegal (as it should be), illicit breeders no longer take the time or effort to separate dog-aggressive dogs from those that are also human-aggressive. This problem is compounded by a criminal market for human-aggressive dogs. Conversely, careful breeders of some historical fighting breeds have drastically reduced their intraspecific (dog-dog) aggression since there is no longer any point in keeping it. The problem, however, is that non-aggressive, dog-aggressive, and people-and-dog aggressive animals look alike. There is no morphological difference between a Pit Bull and an American Staffordshire Terrier, and certainly no way to tell by looking which animal comes from a fighting line and which does not.

One recipe for aggression is to tie up a dog; it leaves him feeling vulnerable. By tethering a dog, you eliminate one of his two major coping options—flee or fight. When fleeing is impossible, fight is all that's left. Karen Delise, in *Fatal Dog Attacks*, discovered a direct correlation between fatal attacks and a dog's being tied up.[81] Although killing humans is certainly not acceptable, immobilizing a fearful dog while a perfect stranger enters his territory is an invitation to tragedy. Remember, the dog does not know your motives; attacks occur even when the "intruder" is trying to untangle the dog from the chain. Delise writes, "Chaining a dog is arguably the single most dangerous condition in which to maintain a dog. Statistically, chained dogs are more dangerous than free-running packs of dogs." Note carefully that more than half of fatal dog attacks are perpetrated by chained dogs. Additionally, dogs that are kept chained have probably never had the opportunity to bond and form normal relationships with other dogs and humans. It's a cruel, foolish, and potentially dangerous way to keep a dog.

Competition and fear are both accompanied by high levels of stress, so both can result in aggression. It's scary to have to fight for food or bite out of fear. Fear biting should never occur; it happens because people don't read and respond to our submissive signs. For example, dogs fearful of children often just leave a room when kids come into it. Unfortunately, this unmistakable sign is often overlooked or ignored by the feared object (the child), who will continue to approach despite our giving every signal in the book that we are scared half to death. A normal creature would back away to show us they mean no harm; instead, the human comes closer and closer until we have no recourse but to bite, growl, or snarl. And if it continues to happen, we won't wait until the child starts to follow us because the more reasonable strategy is to attack first.

Sometimes, especially in more excitable dogs, a series of apparently minor things can build stress incrementally. For example, an owner may do weird things like shake a finger in our faces, whack us with a newspaper, scream at us, and so on until one day, "for no apparent reason," it all explodes. This is sometimes termed "rage syndrome," and the attack is usually characterized as "unprovoked." It *was* provoked, but the owners were just too dumb to see it coming. Rage syndrome is the ultimate acting out of a desperate dog. It has been noted particularly in Cocker and English Springer Spaniels (who do tend to be an excitable lot), but it can occur in any dog or breed. In most cases, the solution lies in reducing the stress that lead to the explosion.

Fighting for Food

Food aggression stems from our days in the wild. Food is one of the great prizes, and the deliciousness of the food directly increases the competition and stress to claim it and, hence, the likelihood of aggression. For example, meaty bones rank pretty high on the delectability scale, as Scott and Fuller discovered in their experiments.[82] They found that a bone was "one of the few cases in dogs of a specific primary stimulus producing a behavior pattern." That's fancy language for saying that dogs readily fight over bones.

> Scott and Fuller have shown that just feeding a dog, without any other interaction, will not forge a bond between owner and animal.[83] In other words, if someone feeds the family dog but does not play with him, exercise him, or cuddle him, the dog is no more likely to bond with that person than it would with an automatic feeding machine. Dogs do not live by food alone; we have feelings, too. Scott and Fuller also noted that littermates can form very close attachments despite the fact that one puppy never fed another—in fact, they competed for food, which supports their thesis quite well.

Even in the case of highly desirable meaty bones, however, the results are not all that clear-cut. For example, in order to test the establishment of dominance, experimenters placed a bone in a pen with two wolf cubs (littermates). The idea was that the pup who got and kept the bone the longest was the dominant one. The cubs mostly shared the bone, however, which sort of ruined the whole test. When the same sort of experiment was tried with dogs, the results were largely breed-dependent. Beagles and Cocker Spaniels never bothered fighting over the bone at all, although some dominance patterns were established. (In fact, Beagles turned to be non-aggressive under any circumstances.) Basenjis squabbled until they were a year old, but other tested breeds settled into dominance hierarchies by 11 weeks of age.

While wolves do bring leftovers home to the pups, dogs usually don't; we leave that to you. Other than parental provisioning, however, wolves are not great sharers. Each wolf just attempts to grab a hunk of food and sneak off to eat it in relative peace. Dogs can be even less community-minded than wolves; it depends on the breed. In general, a dog with a bone is best left alone. (This is the first line of a poem I have been working on; unfortunately, I have not been able to get any further with it.) At any rate, it should not surprise you that I choose to go off alone with my rawhide bone. Leave me alone with it or risk awakening my completely natural desire to keep my food for myself. And keep that kid away from me as well.

If there is by chance an overabundance of food, I will bury it and perhaps return to it later. Wolves do the same thing; that's where I learned that behavior. Technically, it's called "caching." Of course, the hiding place may be under the couch cushions or behind the smelly sneakers in the closet—but, hey, that's your lookout. Dogs seldom if ever display aggression regarding liquids, however, This is probably because water, when found at all in our native lands, was plentiful. No sense squabbling over a river.

In wolf packs, as mentioned earlier, alphas eat first and get the best of everything. At home, however, everyone gets more or less the same food; the only difference is who eats first. To make things simple, just feed your dogs in the same order every day, starting with the most demanding animal. Providing each animal with a secure place in the eating order increases our comfort zone and decreases stress and aggression. Also, by making yourself the assured and firm dispenser of food, it is more likely that the dogs in the house will see you as the source of all good things. In the old days (when I was a true wolf), the alpha male provided food for nursing females, so I instinctively understand that the provision of food equals power. I respect that.

If you happen to have food-aggressive dogs, feed them in separate areas with their heads facing away from each other, or even in separate rooms if the situation demands. If, however, a dog's food-guarding behavior extends to belligerence toward you, the best thing is to do is begin a desensitization program. There are many excellent books on the topic, but all suggest the same basic technique: start by hand-feeding the dog so he associates you with the source of all good things. This won't make him like you better, but it will certainly get his attention. At the very beginning, do not even allow a food-aggressive dog to have his own bowl. Hand-feeding entire meals takes time, but it's worth it. In the next stage, place a little kibble in a bowl, but hand-feed him something he likes much better (a "high value" treat like liver). If you are consistent, you will eventually be able to approach the bowl and make "trades." (Don't try to overpower the dog and get him to accept taking food away without getting anything in return. It's not fair.) Soon the dog will regard your standing around the bowl as a positive thing. It is, as Aristotle so often proclaimed, "the product of habit." This same technique can be used if a dog is in the habit of guarding an object, or if he fears your insane habit of clipping his nails every time he turns around.

Unfortunately, as James O'Heare notes, aggression "generalizes."[84] What may begin as a specific response to a particular stress- or fear-inducing incident may, if the stimulus is repeated over and over, broaden. For instance, let's say a dog fears the vet (something bad happened there once). If he continues to be taken to the vet despite his fear-induced aggressive responses, his threshold of aggression may become progressively lower. To avoid repeating a bad experience, the aggression may generalize to include men in coats, people with something in their hand, and so on. This doesn't mean you shouldn't take me to the vet; it means you need to start making it more pleasant for me. Maybe just drop by and give me some treats while we're there, then leave. The next time, maybe I'll let the vet tech pet me. Keep cool (no fussing or panicking) and let me cool off, too.

Babies and Dogs:

There seems to be a human rule that all human beings are in charge of all dogs. This, however, is difficult for some of us to accept—especially regarding juvenile humans, who do not look, sound, smell, or act like normal humans (or humans at all, sometimes). Until it is made very clear to me by Alpha Bitch Mama Human that little kids have a place in the hierarchy over me, I will test them. If they are very tiny, I might eat them. Listen, humans who are too stupid to keep their young safe and supervised in a nice, safe, cozy den get what they deserve. Sometimes it's really difficult to tell an infant human from a really good roast, if you know what I mean. Not all dogs feel this way, of course; some unaccountably take to guarding the kid as if it were a prized possession. Others ignore it (or pretend to), and a few even try to play with the thing. But until it becomes entirely clear to us that a kid is part of the family, don't expect us to figure it out. The same is true for other pets, including cats and tiny dogs. (See "Chase and Predatory Behavior.")

Internecine Squabbles:

Many breeds have kept some wolf traits and lost others. For example, terriers, Bulldogs, and Bull Terriers, among others, really can't stand the sight of other dogs. They have inherited and retained the wolf's exclusivity (its intense suspicion of strangers and its predilection for keeping themselves to themselves), yet because of their antipathy toward other dogs they have lost the wolf's aptitude for cooperative effort. Such breeds are obviously much less social with other dogs than are hounds, the great cooperators. But although hounds have retained the wolf's knack for cooperation, they have lost a different wolf trait—protection of the pack. Still other breeds, notably guard dogs, have retained the rare ability (among dogs) to comprehensively understand the world more the way wolves do—

they are friendly to all in their "pack" (which centers around the humans in the family) and exhibit eternal enmity to those outside it. Most of us dogs, however, either like or dislike all other dogs without discrimination. We probably won't change our attitudes, either, after we've passed three months of age.

Most dogs get along pretty well with each other, but in some breeds, it's a stretch. Scott and Fuller studied aggressive behavior in some 7-week-old littermates when a bunch of the puppies attacked another.[85] They note: "In most breeds this 'ganging up' is temporary and playful. In the Fox Terrier breed, however, such group attachments are persistent and become so serious that the victim has to be removed in order to prevent serious injury. In one litter of 6 animals there were 3 males and 3 females. The group began 'ganging up' on the smallest female. When she was removed they began to attack another, and when she was taken out they attacked the third."

Once a stable "pack mentality" is formed, however, everything usually works out; most problems usually occur in the beginning stages. People who bring large numbers of new dogs into their homes, such as rescue group "foster parents," are apt to experience more difficulties.

Dog-dog aggression not linked to hierarchical instability is generally the result of undersocialization. If a dog is undersocialized, the fault belongs to a human. Dogs that grow up with other dogs as well as meet and (more importantly) play regularly with other dogs develop sophisticated social skills. They're less apt to start or enter fights and they arouse less aggression from other dogs. There's another payoff when you let your dog develop healthy relations with other dogs; it makes it easier for us to apply the same social skills to relationships with humans. It's true that we have to learn that different rules guide dog-human play than dog-dog play, but it's not hard if the owner teaches them to us consistently.

Agoraphobia

Dogs that have never been properly socialized or brought into contact with the outside world can develop a fear of open places and strange people. An agoraphobic dog will move slowly and fearfully, in mincing steps, with his legs pulled under and neck extended (the better to look out for the enemy he imagine lurks everywhere). This behavior is frequently seen in young wolves when they enter large pen spaces for the first time. Dogs can be desensitized to open spaces and strange experiences, but it takes a long period of committed effort. Small dogs, by the way, should not be picked up and carried everywhere, especially in strange situations; it reinforces their fears. Let them stand on their own four feet, so to speak.

Barking

I like to bark. Nearly all dogs do (with the exception of those primitive Basenjis). Barking, howling, whining, et cetera (we can make 38 different vocalizations) is a way of life for us dogs. We are much more vocal than wolves, for instance. After all, we don't *have* to be quiet, do we? We don't have to sneak around hoping to ambush some hapless rabbit.

Although adult wolves bark very infrequently, juveniles bark often. And since much of dog behavior is simply juvenile wolf behavior, you shouldn't be surprised—it comes with the package. Speaking of which, adult dogs whine more than adult wolves. This, of course, makes sense. If I were an adult wolf, to whom would I whine? However, since I'm an adult dog, guess who's sitting around waiting to fulfill my every need? Huh? Even so, most of the barking that gets barked is barked by young dogs—those who really don't know the ins and outs of things yet. As they mature, they'll learn your subtle body language and probably quiet down.

> Dogs encouraged to be vocal when chasing game (like Fox-hounds) will tend to be vocal even when there are no foxes around. Conversely, dogs like sheep guardians tend to bark only when something is really wrong (so as not to alarm the sheep).

Dogs usually bark for a very simple reason: we wish to draw your attention to something—either to ourselves or to some suspicious or interesting activity like an old lady with a walker or a kid on a bike. I have to admit, however, that I once knew a Beagle named Topper who spent a lot of his time barking at the ground. Apparently he was on the trail of something, all day, every day. Topper always seemed to be talking to himself. "Hmm…a chipmunk passed this way an hour ago—whoops, what have we here? Mouse tracks…and that's where the kid next door short-cut across the yard." Although this behavior seemed to get on people's nerves, I found it endearing, though primitive. Barking is a tension reliever for us dogs, even though it may drive you nuts; frankly, we just don't care.

> I suppose I should mention allelomimetic (which means copying others) barking. That means we bark because other dogs are barking. This behavior is pretty typical of us social animals in general. Don't tell me you never did something just because everybody else did—say, staring up at the sky just to see how many other people you could get to copy you or experimenting with tobacco or drugs. (At least we dogs don't have those problems.) Howling is particularly allelomimetic, especially when started by the alpha wolf. (In the dog world, the initiator is called the "bell hound," and he may or may not be the "alpha dog." He certainly isn't in my house.)

While scientists don't know for sure why we dogs carry on vocally more than wolves, they guess that it's because there are more of us packed into smaller spaces than are typical of wolves. Common politeness encourages speaking. Conversely, one researcher reported a livestock-guarding dog that carried on continuously for 7 hours when there was no other dog around. Well, maybe he was just hoping; sheep make lousy company.

Between 13 and 35 percent of behavior complaints by dog owners concern what is termed "nuisance barking." Some breeds are particularly barky—Beagles, Shetland Sheepdogs, Dachshunds, and Yorkshire Terriers, for example. This is an inbred characteristic; when you get the dog you get the bark.

In any case, the first step in solving the problem is identifying the cause. While some experts suggest that nuisance barkers bark for "no particular reason," it's not true. Just because you don't know the reason doesn't mean there isn't one. Take my word for it.

Excessive barking can become an obsessive behavior that is difficult to correct; however, it is easier to fix if you can figure out why the dog barks. If he's barking because he's lonely, bring him in and work on your stamp collection together, or go out there and play with him. What he's asking is probably not unreasonable, after all. It won't do any good to ignore him; chances are he'll outlast you. Barking doesn't bother us any more than talking bothers you. Besides, if you want any kind of a relationship with your neighbor, you'd better pay attention. One the other hand, if he's barking just for fun, bring him in. He may figure out that the only way to enjoy the yard is to do so quietly.

Now, if he barks indoors while you're gone or if you absolutely must leave him outside for some reason and he still barks, you must resort to the citronella collar. There are electronic shock collars too, but they are not as effective. (They are also inhumane.) The electric collar delivers an adjustable jolt of juice when a vibration sensor in the collar detects barking; the citronella collar releases a spray of citronella fragrance (a nasty smell to us, although people don't seem to mind it) when a microphone in the collar registers barking. It has one downside, though—you have to be careful in adjusting it. A poorly adjusted citronella collar can pick up the sound of other dogs' barking and unjustly release a puff of citronella into your dog's face.

Remember, barking is a natural behavior, so it can't be "cured," but it can be managed. Also, like begets like: if you start yelling at a barking dog, he'll bark louder; he assumes that you're joining in, not telling him to stop. And even if a dog figures out that "Shut up!" means "Stop barking," the fact is that you have rewarded him by paying attention to him—and you'll get more barking. Some authorities will tell you to remove "barking stimuli," meaning shut the curtains, keep the dog indoors all the time, et cetera. Such an approach, however, is not the best. When you remove normal, healthy stimuli, you could redirect my energy elsewhere—like the couch or the cat. The best plan (after figuring out why I'm barking) is to find healthy outlets for my energies. Tire me out; a tired dog is a good dog, humans say.

While we're on the subject of "good dogs," let me say that people's values are warped in this regard. Why is it that everything we like to do, such as barking, digging, chewing, chasing, and biting are labeled "bad," and we are only labeled "good" when we do *nothing*? Does that make any sense?

Chase and Predatory Behavior

As I mentioned earlier, predatory behavior is really a variety of aggression, but it's so specialized that it deserves its own section. Chasing is a deeply ingrained canid behavior. It is part of the prey drive and can be activated by sight, smell or sound. Although wolves try to sneak up on their quarry in the wild, it generally ends with an all-out chase. Researchers have observed that when the prey animal hesitates, the wolf pauses as well; it usually does not dash in for the kill unless it has the stimulus of a fleeing animal. It's the same with us dogs. There's something about a fleeing child, bicycle, or car that is almost irresistible; we just can't help it. You humans can use this impulse to their advantage, if only you would. It's really the easiest way to teach us to come when called; just walk in the other direction and we'll chase—um, I mean, follow you. (If we do grab you, we tend to get the back end first—after all, it's the closest—then we go for your head. We wouldn't want you to suffer any more than is necessary.) On the other hand, if you don't want your kid chased by every goofy dog in the neighborhood, teach him to stand still. That will quiet the wolf-instinct in the local Labrador.

There is also the "fluffy dog" problem—you know, those little puffballs who are so covered with hair that we normal dogs can't read their body language. We find it best to treat them like game.

Virgil wrote, "A sad thing is a wolf in the fold." Actually, the sheep in the fold are usually a lot sadder than the wolf when the wolf gets in. Predatory behavior is a natural drive in nearly all dogs (although it is quite attenuated in some breeds, like sheep-guarding dogs) although it has been strongly selected for in certain breeds (or accidentally came along for the ride). Sometimes it is profoundly related to chase behavior, but sometimes it is not—plenty of dogs will chase a cat but never hurt it, while others chase to kill. Still others apparently don't intend to kill until the chase is actually on, then something kicks in that triggers the behavior.

If you own a breed that has a strong prey drive or an innate dislike of other animals (including dogs), it's best to have an only pet. Don't push things unless you like the idea of shredded cat on your rug; that's just how it is with some breeds. Even we dogs who actually like cats can be goaded into chasing them around the house. If you introduce us properly (don't force it), we'll usually accept Fluffy as part of the family as long as she doesn't run—I can't guarantee what will happen then. In fact, it's easy to set off the chase instinct in young, inexperienced dogs by wearing loose, flowing clothes, trailing scarves, or even loose shoelaces.

Chewing and Destructive Behavior

Dogs are chewers by nature, and you must expect that all young dogs will chew things. I'm not talking about the neurotic destruction perpetrated by bored, lonely animals (a dog chewing due to anxiety is like you biting your fingernails)—just the everyday stuff. Chewing is also essential to the teething process, and all dogs up to the age of six months at least are going chew things. (The major chewing stage is from 4 to 6 months.) We do have specific preferences in this regard; they include new things, expensive things, irreplaceable things, and dangerous things—not necessarily in that order. We also like things that smell like you, which is reason the TV remote is such a hot item. It not only smells like the popcorn and potato chips you've been munching on, but it carries your scent, too. We love the smell of your greasy hands.

While some dogs will chew nicely on a chew toy for hours and make it squeak in a civilized way, most of us take the next pro- grammed step after bite, which is dissect. If you have a dog who likes to chew things, don't waste money buying an endless array of chew toys—he'll destroy all of them. Get one of those indestructible Kong-things, fill it with something delectable (they even make a commercial dog treat filler, if you have the bucks), and let him go to work on it. Or devise something safe yourself. And if I eat the toys I've shredded, go for *only* the hard rubber things unless you want an unscheduled trip to the vet.

As a pup, I got a big thrill out of ripping all the bark off the back yard fruit trees. According to L. David Mech, this behavior is practice for tearing the hide off a moose.[86] I hope so. I haven't had the opportunity to try moose, but I would like to.

At any rate, the best way to restrict puppy chewing to appropriate items is to make sure that he has plenty of acceptable chew toys—none of which should be your clothes or shoes. In fact, it's a bad idea to do anything that rewards chewing, so try to avoid putting your hands all over your puppy's face. Once your start allowing a puppy to nuzzle your hand, the next step will be a tentative lick, then a full-force slobber, and pretty soon he will be nipping away. I guarantee it. Just stroke his back gently instead.

If you haven't listened to me and the pup has already started nipping, you need to redirect his attention immediately—not five seconds later. One easy way to do this is by startling him with a squirt of water or by shaking something noisy (like a can containing some pennies). Naturally, you have to have this stuff ready beforehand. Once you have his attention, give him something acceptable to chew and praise him lavishly. Avoid rawhide unless you are sure your dog won't swallow the thing whole and choke (I did that once). Hard rubber Kong toys and Nylabones are excellent and safe chew toys.

> I shouldn't have to tell you (but I will anyway) that you should never strike your dog for any reason. And striking a dog anywhere near his head produces a snapping or biting reflex. Just don't do it.

Coprophagia

Coprophagia is the eating of feces. It can occur in several forms: auto-coprophagia (eating one's own feces), intraspecific coprophagia (in which one eats the feces of other dogs), and interspecific coprophagia (in which the dog eats the feces of other animals, such as deer). Some us of develop all three kinds at once, and it's most common in puppies, who are far too curious about everything. And, lest you begin lamenting the degeneracy of modern dogs, let me hasten to assure you that wolves engage in the same behavior; we learned it from them, thank you very much.

While not all dogs engage in coprophagia, enough of us do for it to be a problem for humans. No one knows the cause, although it's not for the lack of guessing. Some people suggest that it is compensatory behavior for a nutritional deficiency or a disease (like exocrine pancreatic insufficiency—apparently the deoxycholic acid in the waste will fix us right up). However, this view is not widely held. Other physical causes might include transient pancreatitis; intestinal infections; food allergies that contribute to malabsorption; overfeeding, which leads to undigested food in stools (which makes them palatable); and allelomimetic behavior, in which we observe you collecting the stools and decide it's a good idea for us to do the same (most experts say that cleaning up secretly is the best choice around dogs that have this problem). Then again, we might just be bored—that plague of modern dogs. This behavior is seen in both extremely submissive and extremely dominant dogs. Perhaps the submissive dog is trying to avoid detection, while the dominant dog is too selfish to allow anyone to have anything of his—including his feces.

The most likely cause is behavioral (boredom). Then again, some dogs just like the taste. Cat poop is irresistible to most of us and I must confess that, at times, even I—never mind.

Cures include:

▼ Cleaning up feces the moment they appear rather than letting them lie around the yard all day.

▼ Feeding me a better diet with higher quality protein (yes!).

▼ Commercial products like For-bid and Deter.

If you have a cat, keep the litter box in a place inaccessible to the dog. Some of the newer designs make it practically impossible for dogs to get at it, and you can always raise the litter box or put it in a room that dogs are not able or allowed to go into. Or you could just make the little feline demons go outside.

Digging

"But keep the wolf far thence that's foe to men/ For with his nails he'll dig them up again," wrote playwright John Webster. Although you (hopefully) don't have to worry about the family dog digging up dead bodies in the back yard, I have to admit that this behavior can be annoying.

Digging is common in terriers and northern breeds. The former are driven to find vermin; the latter to dig themselves a warm (or cool) spot in the yard. L. David Mech reports that two wolves he raised from cubs spent most of their summer days in Minnesota trying to cool off.[87] They rested in the shade and dug beds in the soil for sleep. Every time a cub would reuse a bed, it would dig away the warm top layer to expose the cool soil beneath. This is also a natural behavior in canine or lupine mamas of all breeds. And despite the proclamations of many dog experts, dogs watch people dig, then they dig too; or they watch another dog dig and follow suit. And finally, dogs often dig when they are bored and have nothing else to occupy their minds. Digging is most characteristic of high-energy dogs that spend a great deal of time alone in the backyard, especially when it's hot and sunny. In rare cases, the dog may be suffering from a nutritional deficiency and is trying to balance his diet with roots.

Since this too is a natural behavior, you can't eradicate it. Try to manage it instead—don't punish the dog. Give him a special place of his very own where he can dig, such as a sandbox. And give him company and exercise; digging can also be a sign of plain old loneliness. It will help if you install a doggy door that lets the dog go in and out of the house (and your company) at will.

Disobedience (General)

"Why, that dog is practically a Phi Beta Kappa. She can sit up and beg, and can give her paw—I won't say she will, but she can" (Dorothy Parker). My guardian (who calls herself my owner) is constantly saying stupid things like "Dogs are just smart enough to learn a task and just dumb enough to do it." I think that's over-simplifying, don't you? For one, thing, I often do not carry out required or suggested tasks. I don't mind easy ones, like "sit"; it gets me off my feet and then I get a dog biscuit (hopefully a liver one). Other commands, like "Come," are a lot dicier.

I have to disagree with some of the newer lights in the world of dog obedience on this matter. In their desperation to deprive dogs of any "human" motivations, they resort to the machine model. Raise the motivation, they say, and you'll get the result you want. Of course you will. It'll work with people, too. I admit that it takes a lot of motivation for my owner to get me to jump into the bathtub; in fact, she hasn't found it yet. She ends up just lifting me into the tub. And there is probably not enough motivation in the world to keep me at her side when a rabbit runs by. For me, a rabbit is the ultimate motivation because it appeals to my intrinsic prey-drive. This behavior does not make me an automaton—unless you want to confess that you're an automaton too. You do everything you do for a reward, just like me. That's another way in which we're alike—except in the way opposite from what you might think. Neither one of us does anything unless there's something in it for us.

There is another new way of thinking among dog trainers. They have apparently made the amazing discovery that dogs do not bear moral responsibility. Barbara Woodhouse wrote a book entitled *No Bad Dogs*, and there aren't any. Dogs are not morally capable of being evil—or of being good, either, if you wish to push the point. (Whether people are any different from us in this respect is touched upon in the last chapter.) However, I do agree with Walt Whitman, one of my favorite poets. He wrote that animals "do not lie awake in the dark and weep for their sins." That's true. We don't.

At any rate, these new trainers mean well. They wish to save us from the emotional stupidity of owners who punish us for things that are their own fault. These trainers have a laudable agenda; however, one should not sacrifice truth for the sake of an agenda, no matter how noble.

The truth is that "human" emotions and other qualities do exist in dogs. We have feelings. We can think, we are conscious and aware, and we can make reasonable decisions. It's not that I don't know what you want, at least sometimes; at other times it's a total mystery. And at yet other times I think you don't know what you want, either. Take, for example, the come command. Yes, I understand that you want me to stand next to you. But it's often not clear why you want me to, and even if it is, maybe I just don't feel like it. Does that make me evil? Does it make me "good" when you I perform the desired behavior because you bribed me with food? If you do it enough, perhaps I'll get into the habit of coming when called, although that happens mainly because I have nothing better to do, or because I know that sometimes you'll give me a treat. That doesn't make me a machine, friend; it makes me like you. Do you never do something just because you've gotten into the habit of it? As Aristotle proclaimed, virtue is "the product of habit." Your job as our teacher is to get us in the habit of doing what you want.

I will admit, if pushed, that we dogs have developed something of a Stockholm syndrome towards our captors; we ascribe benevolent motives to them that aren't always present. I suppose I can say that we charitably give you the benefit of the doubt, although I have creepy feeling we are stuck with you no matter what. I don't even know how to find and run down dinner on my own any more.

It is frequently said that dogs have no spite. Ha! Spite may be a purely human emotion, but we can mimic it. We collect toys that we don't want just to keep them from other dogs that do (that's one of my own favorite activities). However, we do not urinate or defecate on your bed to get back at you (at least not precisely). We do it because the products of our renal and digestive systems have a somewhat different symbolism to you than they do to us. (We tend to poop and pee when we get stressed. Sometimes, when owners act strangely or disappear for hours at a time, we search out the place where their odor is strongest. It's comforting, but sometimes not comforting enough to quiet our stress. Hence the leavings.)

Remember, the secret to getting a dog to obey is to get his attention and to get him to trust you. (Or the other way around.) Trainers call this "focusing." The best way to get most dogs (including me) to focus is to reward us with treats when we look at you. That's right. Looking at you focuses our attention on you rather than on the ground or some other interesting place. (On its own, your face really isn't that fascinating—don't kid yourself.) However, a nice little treat held up close to your face works wonders. (Don't try this if you haven't taught me to stop jumping all over you, though. I might leap up, grab it, and scratch you on the way up or down. And don't try this with a wolf. A wolf will bite your face off.) Once I learn to focus, you can start working on training. Remember that we dogs normally tend to look down or straight ahead at the level of our faces; that, historically, has been where the food is. We have to learn to look up to you in more ways than one, and that's where trust comes in. If you want us to trust you, do not punish us. Punishment breeds fear (not to mention stress and violence), and where there is fear there can be no trust. They are antithetical states of being.

I suppose the most difficult exercise is the old "recall" command. We often do not come when called. Sometimes it's because we suspect you're going to do something like give us a bath, medicate us, or clip our nails: that's the fear factor at work. (Remember fight or flee?) Other times we are distracted, especially if there are other dogs or perceived prey animals around. To get us in the habit of obedience, try using food and gesture at our level as mentioned above. You can also try kneeling with open arms; I'm sucker for that. Nothing is certain, however. It is true that most dogs don't look into the future as most humans do, so it's difficult to us forgo a present pleasure because of the possibly of a greater reward in the future. You know how it is. Sometimes you'll have to use force (not pain) to convince me to take a bath, meaning you will just have to carry me there. And I will just have to trust that it won't hurt.

As a rule, female dogs are more trainable than are males and some breeds are more inclined to obey than others. Researchers have found that dogs are more likely to obey low, dark tones of voice than happy, excited ones. The low tones remind me of my mother in a stern mood. That doesn't mean you should yell at your dog; it may get his attention, but it will probably make him too nervous to listen to you. In fact, sometimes it helps to whisper. You may be surprised at the results.

Forging Ahead

Wolves generally don't walk on leads, although they can be taught to do so. (Heeling, however, is out of the question.) Dogs have inherited just the slightest tendency regarding this, too. For some reason, though, humans never walk fast enough to suit me—or, conversely, they walk too fast when I want to investigate something. In the long run, although it takes some effort, the best approach is to getting me to walk next to you is to make me want to walk at your side. Oddly enough, one of the best ways to do this is to encourage me to walk *off* the leash next to you first (deploy those treats again). However, don't start this exercise until you've taught me to come reliably. If you get me to associate walking with you with a pleasant treat, it will be no time at all before I'm anxious to do so at all times. Then those devices that force us to walk alongside you, such as the choke chain, prong collar, head halter, no-pull harness, et cetera are unnecessary.

In a few cases, my pulling at the lead may be the result of an attempt to take leadership from you; most of the time, however, I'm just in a hurry to see what's up ahead. In a large pack of dogs (like, say, foxhounds), the same dogs always charge out first, but this behavior is not automatically carried over into relationships with humans. Hounds are bred to run ahead of you so they can lead you to the game; this does not mean they are trying to take over your lives. To find out if a dog is truly displaying control-freak behavior, you have to look at all the signs, not just pulling on the lead.

Garbage Eating, Counter-Crusing, and the Like

We are opportunistic feeders like our ancestors, the wolves. If it's edible, we're all over it. To us, stealing food is not stealing; it is taking advantage of the ineptitude of the food-guardian. We dogs are honoring our long and noble heritage when we empty the trash compactor, rifle the garbage pail, and devour decaying roadkill. Wolves could sustain themselves on salvage, although they preferred large ungulates when they could get them (and who wouldn't?).

It is up to you to make food unavailable to us. Some people have had some luck applying sticky tape to the edges and fronts of counters (we hate the feel of it on our paws), but it's easier and neater to just keep food off the counter. Trash bins should be dog-proofed or put in places we can't get to. You can try to make the trash unattractive by spraying it with some nasty-smelling stuff like citronella; it may work, but it's better to circumvent the whole problem. We dogs like to keep you people in the habit of doing the right thing. You'll thank us later.

Housetraining Problems

We dogs generate about 4 billion gallons of urine and millions of tons of poop every year. (Only some of it is destined for your house.) As a rule, female dogs are easier to housetrain than are males. And when a dog seems to forget housetraining or begins doing "spiteful" things such as soiling your bed, remember—you can bet that if it's not a physical problem (and get that possibility checked out first), it's a response to stress.

Marking has nothing to do with housetraining, really; it's a sign of territoriality and dominance. It is usually characteristic of males, although females (both dogs and wolves) may indulge when no dominant male is present. In wolf communities, usually only the alpha pair mark, and even then it's done close to the den. In places where two packs have adjacent territories, marking behavior increases along the boundaries. Marking doesn't scare one wolf from another's territory; it's more a notification system than anything else. L. David Mech observed an adult female member of a high arctic wolf pack dominating a nursing female; she lifted her leg to urinate in the absence of an alpha male.[88] In dogs, leg lifting doesn't begin until we start to mature and find our place in the pack. Neutering male dogs reduces the incidence of marking about 50 percent of the time. Back in the 1900s, someone named Bekoff actually studied canine urination patterns; he found that males lifted their legs 97.5 percent of the time and females squatted 67.6 percent of the time. Both sexes, however, reversed postures on occasion.

Nothing will sell a book a faster than the claim that you can housetrain a dog in an hour, a day, or a week. Such propaganda just appeals to human fantasies. Okay, there are maybe one or two dogs in a hundred who will accommodate you immediately, but it's rare. First, dogs' sphincter muscles aren't sufficiently developed to control their bowels and bladder until they are 12 to15 weeks old. Second, little puppies have little bladders, so they just can't "hold it" for very long. (Incidentally, forcing a dog to hold it longer than is really comfortable puts him on the fast track to bladder stones and urinary problems.) Yet people insist on taking home an eight-week-old puppy, then wonder why…well, it's beyond me.

> It has been reported that domestic dogs defecate more when they are not on a leash and also when the owner is not present.

While a crate is a necessary component of easy housetraining, you do need to take the puppy out of it frequently enough to make it possible for him to become housetrained. Go outdoors with the little tyke. Don't just toss him out the door alone; he will perceive that as exile and punishment. If the puppy seems too interested in pottering about while you're standing there freezing in your nightie, be patient. It's his nature to investigate his surroundings. After all, you're dealing with a highly intelligent mammal. A big mistake lots of folks make is running the dog out and then running him back in the second he accomplishes his mission. Just when the poor puppy feels that the fun can begin, it's back in the house. No wonder he tries to prolong his outdoor time as much as possible!

The most basic rule of housetraining is this—reward your dog every single time he eliminates in an appropriate place. Jump for joy, pass the dog biscuits, praise and pet and do whatever it takes to make the dog understand that he has accomplished a veritable miracle. Repeat this performance the next time the dog achieves your goal (for it is your goal and not his), and again and again and again until he acquires the habit of this virtue. Belong long it will be second nature.

Incidentally, we dogs can and do develop definite preferences regarding where and when we eliminate. Certain surfaces, for example, are more appealing than others. Your job as owner is to try to steer us toward liking the idea of urinating in the yard better than using the wall. Take us to where you want us to go and, again, praise us mightily when we succeed; you can't overdo things in this department.

It is essential to differentiate between physical and behavioral causes of housetraining missteps. Physically, I just mentioned the physical limitations of a puppy. And a dog of any age, especially a submissive or timid one, can urinate due to overexcitement or fear. Older dogs may experience incontinence; older spayed females may "leak" at night. Surely they cannot be blamed for this; be understanding. (You may have such problems someday yourself.) Certain disease conditions may also contribute to incontinence. If a previously housetrained animal starts making mistakes, a trip to the vet is in order.

The behavioral causes of housetraining errors are nearly always a response to household stress. It's just the way we dogs react to tension. Sometimes the stress is a result of family spats; sometimes it's a direct result of the stress you incur while trying to housetrain us. How's that for a cycle?

The biggest and most common error dog owners make in this department (and in administering any discipline, in fact) is to punish a mistake long after (and 2 minutes is "long after" by my canine clock) the error is made. Typically, the owner comes home, finds a mess on the floor, and starts yelling or even hitting us. As a result, we immediately associate the owner's return with yelling and hitting. Bingo! We develop a weird kind of separation anxiety sparked not by longing for the owner's return but fearing it instead. What do we do when we are afraid? Eliminate. Rather indiscriminately. Hey, it's your fault—you increased our stress load.

The Crate Debate:

Most people know by now that having a refuge is extremely important to us. Robert Hubrecht of the University of Cambridge for the Universities Federation for Animal Welfare did a study of kenneled dogs and found (surprise!) that providing a shelter satisfied our needs for a resting place, playpen, and a refuge from other dogs when the going got rough.[89] You too should provide your dog with a crate—not to be used as a prison or baby-sitter, but a place he can go to when she wishes to retire from the world for a while. We can be quite possessive of our "place." As Rudyard Kipling wrote on one of his finer days:

> *The Lair of the Wolf is his refuge,*
> *and he has made him his home*

> *Not even the head wolf may enter,*
> *not even the council may come.*

On the other hand, though, the desire to have a haven is not lupine, as some people would have you believe. One reads a great deal about shelter-seeking behavior among wolves and all that kind of thing. Shelter-seeking, however, is not particularly well-developed in adult wolves; turning around three times is about it. Because they are nomadic animals, a "home" is not important to them—home is where the pack is. (They may seek cover during bitterly cold, blowy weather, though.) Wolves generally den up only to produce a litter; the den itself is usually a hole scraped out of sandy soil, preferably on an elevated place near water. (In the tundra, such places are called "eskers.") Although wolves can make their own dens, they will readily take over those built by other animals. In the wolf world, the purpose of the den is to provide a safe place for the young. Litterless adult wolves usually do not occupy a den.

Wolf dens are usually just enlargements of natural caves— our ancestors didn't go about digging big holes in the ground the way groundhogs and true burrowing animals do. They usually have no problem sleeping outside even in bitter weather. Sometimes they tuck their noses into their tails (the way Siberian huskies do), but they often stretch out as comfortably as you please. I couldn't do it, but few dogs have the mechanisms for maintaining heat that wolves have.

For us dogs, home is where you are. This stands in contradistinction to true denning animals, like cats, who hate new places. Dogs do seek shelter slightly more than wolves because we are, behaviorally, stuck at that more juvenile wolf stage. Also, many dogs don't have the very thick double coat of the wolf.

Although we are more den-oriented, we still need to be trained to the crate as puppies. Our little ones prefer small, crammed places to open spots and will sometimes demonstrate a little agoraphobia if they venture too far from the den. Dogs that have never become acquainted with crates, however, aren't crazy about them: they don't jump for joy and shout, "Aha! Just what I've been missing all these years!" Instead, they're liable to develop barrier anxiety and other phobias. Take advantage of our childish needs and train us to crates while we're still quite young. It will come in handy later when you need to take us to the vet or on a trip.

Once we get used to a crate, it can become a sort of home to us—but don't lock me up in it for hours on end unless you want to stunt my mental and physical growth. The *Journal of the American Veterinary Medical Association* reported: "Dogs that spent most of their time during the day in crates (odds ratio 3.12) were at increased risk of relinquishment [to shelters] compared to dogs that spent most of their time unrestrained in some portion of the living area of the family home."[90] Maybe this is because the crated dogs went bonkers when they were finally released. Or maybe it just shows that people who stick their dogs in crates all day don't really want a pet in the first place.

Hyperactivity

Genuine, medically-diagnosed hyperactivity (hyperkinesis) is rare in dogs. Owner-diagnosed "hyperactivity" is usually the result of a dog not getting enough exercise. Sporting breeds and other dogs selected for physical activity need more exercise (and more stimulation) than, say, a bulldog.

Some medications, such as thyroid hormone supplements and bronchodilators, can produce hyperactivity in some dogs. Check with your vet.

Additionally, many of us have learned that running around, barking like maniacs, and jumping up-and-down get us the Big Prize—your attention. Ever notice how often we start to bark or charge around the house when you're on the telephone? If you stop talking to scream at me, I got what I wanted—your undivided attention, even if only for a moment.

I would probably exhibit better self control if you exercised me adequately and trained me in basic obedience (both of which are nice bonding activities, by the way). While you're working on that, try keeping a head collar and a leash on me even when I'm just hanging around the house. If simple obedience training doesn't work, I'm afraid you'll have to dish out some cash to a professional behaviorist-trainer. I might even need medication, but I hope not.

Jealousy

Yes, jealousy occurs in dogs. Every pet owner knows this all too well. However, my human recently read an article claiming that dogs don't really feel jealousy—they're just guarding their resources. To my mind, it's the same thing; I want what I want and I don't want certain others to have it. In our species, such possessiveness is inextricably mixed with the desire to assert rank-order. For instance, when a new baby is brought home, I have no idea what it is. It doesn't look, sound, smell, or behave like any human I know. And the owners of the thing ("parents," they call themselves) are obsessed with it. Nearly all cases of trouble between dogs and babies are caused by suddenly ignoring a previously beloved dog in favor of an infant. If people would just take the time to reassure the dog that all is well and maybe give us some special, high-value treats whenever the kid is in the same room with us, we might decide we like the little beast after all.

Nevertheless, a wise parent/owner *never* leaves a dog and a small child together unsupervised. I am of the wolf—never forget that. We dogs kill children every year, often newborns, because the parents stupidly leave the kid alone with us long before we're even aware of what it is. Until a child is at least 3 months old, I have no idea that it's human. Do not kid yourself (no pun intended) about this. (In some cases, we don't even mean to harm the child; we just carry it around like a big stuffed toy.) Karen Delise reports that in the 37-year period she studies (1965–2001), there were only 8 cases in which an established family dog killed an infant aged 3 to 11 months.[91] (After that, it's the toddler stage, and things get dicey again.) In most cases, the fatal attacks occurred when the child was staying with a relative or the dog was new to the household.

Jumping Up

Jumping up is a greeting; it's a holdover from our wolf days. In the kingdom of wolves, face-to-face greetings are more common than the nose-to-tail sort that occur among dogs. Additionally, puppies (of both the wolf and dog variety) learn to beg for food by licking the face of a parent or a senior dog. So that's it in a nutshell—we're just trying to say hi and perhaps get a little treat. You may have (inadvertently, of course) rewarding us for jumping up by reacting to it. Remember, almost any kind of reaction, even a negative one, is a reward. You can stop the jumping by kneeling to greet us, or reorient us by ignoring all jumping behavior and giving us a treat only when we are calm and quiet. Either works for me; I just need to know.

Of course, we jump all over other dogs as well. In that case, we're often trying to assert dominance. Once in a while we try the same trick on people.

Rolling In It

Dogs are terribly fond of rolling in anything nasty, including garbage, carcasses, feces, and other smelly material. No one knows why, although some suggest that this behavior serves to mask our odor from a predator. On the other hand, you don't see cats behaving in this fashion. They'd die first.

Running Away and Roaming

Wolves are nomadic animals, especially in the fall and winter when there are no young cubs. For a wolf, living means hunting and hunting means running, and that's all there is to it. Wolves have been clocked running up to 40 miles an hour, and they can lope along just about forever. Their trotting pace is 5 to 9 miles per hour.

Wolves have an extensive territory (up to 30 square miles, compared with only a square mile or so for a deer) and will only return to a den when they have cubs—in the spring and early summer. Many dogs have inherited this ancestral urge to roam. Those who have not, like guarding dogs, are neotenous in this respect. Young wolves remain at rendezvous points to wait for their parents; when the cubs do venture out, it is with them.

Some kinds of domestic dogs, especially hounds, will often not return home after they've taken off. They are wanderers by nature—bred to follow a scent. They expect you to follow them; after all, they know where the rabbit is and you don't. The Lassie-come-home instinct just doesn't exist in hounds. They must be fenced or kept on a leash. I hate to admit it, but it's true.

> Although it is undeniably dangerous to allow pet dogs to chase around all over the neighborhood, the sad fact is that tie-down, line-runs, and even the sacred fenced yard have some harmful effects. First, they are frustrating because they hinder my desire to chase stuff. Even though it's for my own good, my reflexes don't know it and bingo, you can end up with a very frustrated animal on your hands. Second, as discussed earlier, my ability to flee danger is severely restricted which can result in dog bites (remember, being unable to flee forces me to my only other choice—fighting). Third, a fenced-in yard, while necessary to modern civilization, increases our territoriality (and our urge to protect it).

Additionally, the critical period between 4 and 8 months is called the "flight instinct period." If your dog gets loose during this time and has a positive experience (finding something dead to roll around in, a bunch of kids to play with, some tasty food, or something equally pleasurable), it's practically impossible to make him forget it; the memory of the joyful time is permanently imprinted. Those four months are not necessarily inclusive—in fact, the critical period itself may be only a few days within that time frame—but the question is, which few days? It varies from dog to dog, so to be safe, keep your dog under wraps pretty much the entire time.

> L. David Mech reports one Alaskan wolfpack covering 5,000 square miles of territory in 6 weeks.[92] That's pretty amazing. I stick a lot closer to home than that.

When we dogs get out as group and take off, we can become dangerous to small prey. Confidence lies in numbers.

> While many breeds (like hounds) are preprogrammed to roam, neutering can reduce the frequency in 90 percent of cases.

Separation Anxiety:

While separation is a real problem for us dogs, humans tend to think of it in relation to themselves. (That shows how selfish you are. While we dogs are pining for our loved ones, said loved ones are worried about their furniture, carpets, and what the neighbors think.) For humans, our separation anxiety has three negative aspects:

1. Separation anxiety-related barking, howling, whining, crying, baying, yipping, yapping, and moaning.

2. Separation anxiety-related ripping, tearing, eating and chewing of the owner's furniture, valuables, and shoes.

3. Separation anxiety-related urinating and defecating in the house.

See? It's all about you! But wait. Let's look at the real culprits—you humans. After all, you bred to us to be family members and to depend on you for everything—food, comfort, companionship—and what do you do? Leave! Go to WORK! Almost every day! You walk out that door and I have no idea if you'll ever come back. I watch a lot of TV when I'm home alone—I know what goes on. "Hey, Molly, just going out for a box of dog biscuits—be right back!" And pow! You're gone and never come back. It happens all the time—some poor emaciated little dog is found in an abandoned apartment, and where's the owner? In Las Vegas!

It's no wonder we get nervous when you walk out the door. This is particularly problematic if we've been abandoned before. While some researchers have concluded that separation anxiety is higher than average in Labrador Retrievers, German Shepherd dogs, and English Cocker Spaniels, more careful analysis reveals that mongrels and dogs who were once turned over to shelters suffer from it most often—understandably, too. The incidence is also very high in pet-store dogs (who have pretty much the same lousy experience as shelter dogs). Dog raised by breeders, even casual backyard breeders, have much more temperamental stability—but that shouldn't surprise anyone.

Even in the healthiest, most well-adjusted dogs (like myself), understimulation and sheer boredom can eventually lead to separation anxiety. There's nothing more detrimental to an intelligent, active mammal than boredom. And humans suggest that the perfect solution is to put us in a crate. Argh!

Well, it may not be the perfect solution, but the simplest solution—for humans—*is* the crate. You betcha. Your dog has separation anxiety? Just shove him in the crate. That way he won't eat the furniture or crap on the floor. Maybe not, but I'll scream until the neighbors call the cops if I don't tear my teeth out first trying to get out of that cage. A crate is no comfort to most of us separation-anxiety-ridden dogs. Crates do not always remind us of a comfy den; they can remind us of the pound and a time when we were trapped and couldn't get out. It just makes us worse. After all, our wolf ancestors weren't locked into crates; they weren't even left alone. Their relatives looked after them until we were old enough to follow along. In like manner, some of us can handle separation better if we have a pal to keep us company, but it's not a sure-fire solution.

Many books will give you specific instructions for dealing with separation anxiety. Most of them include toning down the guilt-ridden affection you lavish upon us in the brief time you're home. Stop petting, kissing, and fooling with us every second you're around; that strategy makes it less traumatic for us when you leave again. And it is true that we are flexible and can get used to such a situation. However, we'll tend to grow less dependent on you and instead of feeling acutely lonely when you're gone, we'll feel vaguely alienated all the time. But we're not ripping up the furniture. After a while you can resume your attentions if the "switch" for separation anxiety has been turned off.

But you know what? If you're going to be gone long hours every day, maybe you should rethink having a dog in the first place. Even though we can indeed grow used to being alone, most of us don't like it. We want you to be there, if not every second (after all, wolves often spent time alone) then at least more often. Dogs were not domesticated under such conditions, and it will take some time to get used to them. Breeders may have to work to develop more independent dogs, but they're no fun. If you're gone all day and still want a pet, get a cat or some nice goldfish. Or both.

It is difficult to say whether or not separation anxiety is increasing because all the studies on the subject are relatively new. If it is, there are a few intriguing explanations for the upsurge. One is that humans are selecting for overly-dependent, super-affectionate types of dogs—the very sort who would be most distressed by their leaving. These traits are assuredly heritable and so breeders may be loading the gene pool with cry-babies. On the other hand, maybe we've always been like this, but in earlier times, it was (a) much more likely someone was at home all day baking dog biscuits, and/or (b) the people at home treated us much more casually. It has been shown that what leads to a crisis in separation anxiety is a period of intense bonding and affection that is followed by leave-taking. You humans feel so guilty (as you should) leaving us alone all day that you shower us with addictive affection when you are home. It's heavenly, but then you leave. We can't stand that sort of thing. Please be more consistent!

There is a medication (Clomicalm) that works well for reducing the symptoms of separation anxiety. Another (and the latest) approach is the use of dog-appeasing pheromones, which are available from your local pet supply store in a plug-in delivery system (like a room freshener). It turns out that nursing mammals release these appeasing pheromones that comfort their babies, and the stuff from the pet store reproduces that effect. It is also works to calm a dog during a stressful situation. One brand, Comfort Zone (Farnum), covers 500–650 square feet and lasts about 4 weeks. The stuff is odorless and does not affect people.

Sexual Displays

While we dogs are definitely not attracted to humans, you people sometimes give us unintended sexual stimulation. I'm not talking about mounting behavior here; that's not always sexually provoked and may be a sign of dominance. A dog that's always mounting you may be trying to establish a position of superiority. (Neutering a male dog will result in reduced mounting behavior 60 percent of the time.)[93]

However, you may—without knowing it—stimulate a sexual response form us through rough play. It reminds us of courtship and the good old days on the tundra, and we'll grab you with our forelegs. And that's just the start of it.

Prolonged stroking on the chest between the forelegs, on the neck, or scratching the base of the tail may elicit the same response. And so will bathing, if you're washing down our private parts. Just watch what you're doing.

Shyness

Shyness is largely inherited. Certain breeds (and lines within breeds) tend to be skittish. While shyness had its uses back in the days when we were wolves, it doesn't help most modern dogs at all. However, socialization with humans at the right developmental period is also crucial. In their classic study on canine behavior, Scott and Fuller raised some puppies in a large field where they had no human contact.[94] If one of the pups was brought in to a passive human observer at 3 weeks of age, he toddled over to the person almost at once; but by the age of 7 weeks it took an average of 2 days for the puppy to approach. Fourteen-week-old puppies were so fearful they never approached the human, even after a week. They had to be confined and "tamed" by forced, continual close contact. If properly socialized, adult dogs tend to be less shy, more adaptable, and able to meet new objects and people with aplomb. The more you socialize your dog, the happier we will both be. My own opinion is that the best way to socialize a dog is to get everyone you know to hand-feed us. Just little treats. That will assure us that the world is a friendly place.

I'd like to complain again about fenced yards for a moment. I understand that they are necessary in today's world of whizzing cars and dog-hating maniacs, but too many people use a fenced-in yard as an alternative to a walk. There is no real replacement for getting out the leash and walking us so we can meet everyone of every race, sex (there seem to be a lot of them these days), uniform, size, and speed. This is world of wheelchairs and folks in pairs, talkers and walkers, crazy hats and old bats, teenagers and pagers, boys and noise, llamas and lamas, huggers and muggers, runners and gunners, nappers and rappers, clappers and tappers, balloons and Walloons, skates and straights, gays and strays, cops and lollipops, preachers and creatures, cell phones and ice cream cones, bikes and mikes, canes and Janes. We need to know about them all. Take us out and expand our horizons.

But if a dog is very shy, too much activity can be overwhelming. Then you need to go slowly, desensitizing the pup and rewarding every bit of courageous behavior he shows. It may not seem like much to you, but failing to run from a scary object is a big victory when you're shy.

Territoriality

Wolves are strongly territorial for a reason—they need to protect their food supply. We dogs have inherited this tendency, and it is reinforced when our territory is marked off by a fence. Stray dogs, who have no specific territory, are usually rather friendly; it's the snippy little terrier who goes charging along the fence line barking like a mad thing that you wonder about. Yet, if the fence is gone, many times the dog will just trot up to meet the stranger.

Unfortunately, today's average yard is approximately equal in size to a wolf's denning area, and that gives us an additional reason to protect it. The larger the territory a dog has to call its own, the less defensive of it he is. One can only do so much, after all.

This does not mean that you should let your dog run wild—and I do mean wild. First, it's not safe for the dog. Dogs running loose can be hit by cars, taken home by strangers, shot by farmers, poisoned by garbage, attacked by other dogs, skunked, or suffer any number of other horrors. To make things worse, stray dogs often tend to group up in memory of the old wolf pack and run around—if not terrorizing the humans in the area, then doing a good job running deer and killing sheep or cattle. Then someone will surely kill us.

Thunderphobia

Let's get one thing straight; where there is thunder, there is lightning. And lightning, in case you haven't heard, is dangerous. Very dangerous. Dangerous enough to kill. This is why many of us fear thunder—because we know there's lightning around somewhere. And while a lightning flash may be visible only in a smallish area (and who's looking up every minute, anyway) you can hear thunder a long way off, especially if you're a dog. (Remember what I said earlier about our super-hearing?) Research shows that sheepdogs are the ones most likely to fear thunder. This should not be surprising; sheepdogs are out in all weather, so they know how scary it can be. Hunting dogs are terrified of thunder for the same reason. On the other hand, indoor-type dogs tend to be less fearful. (Of course they are; they're inside.) Terriers aren't afraid of thunder either; they were bred to be unafraid of anything.

Is there a cure? Well, you can buy one of those "desensitizing" tapes that have real thunderstorms recorded on them, but they won't work for a couple of reasons. First, I bet the speakers in your house can't reproduce volume four-and-a-half-times softer than you can hear, and that's what it would take to really simulate the experience. And, even more importantly, we don't gauge a coming storm just by a few rumbles of thunder. Approaching storms are heralded by changes in barometric pressure and variations in atmospheric ionization. So don't waste your money on the tapes. It's also not a good idea to cuddle us. That only reinforces the idea that something is very wrong.

So what can you do? Well, just act normal, even happy. That'll help. It may also help to try some Valium; we won't get addicted because you control the supply. Some people have had good luck with melatonin, a substance our bodies produce anyway. You might also want to try the plug-in dog-appeasing pheromones described in "Separation Anxiety," above. There are even body wraps that are supposed to help make us feel comfortable.

Summary

There is lot of complexity to living in today's world. Sometimes I would like to go back to the good old days, but I confess I've grown rather dependent on central heating, modern medicine—and, well, you, even though you have managed to botch up so many things. Let's be honest. Choke chains, anti-bark collars, and ear-cropping were not the products of your finest thought processes. But you'll get better; you have to.

Chapter 6:

The Lethal Alloy—Wolf Hybrids

"The dog has seldom been successful
in pulling man up its level of sagacity, but man has
frequently dragged the dog down to his."
—James Thurber

Should people breed or own wolf-dogs? In a word, no. We're beyond that stage. Remember that wolves selected themselves out for us. When we breed a wolf-dog (*Canis lupus* x *Canis lupus familiaris*), we are selecting a random wolf, one who has not the least interest in himself or his progeny becoming our pet. The dog-half of the equation could be anything too, although Malamutes and German Shepherds are more frequently chosen than say, Poodles (although that would be an interesting cross). A wolf-dog is an unnatural animal with the worst traits of wolves and dogs rolled up into one nasty package. You're probably better off with a real wolf for a pet; he'll try to avoid you—at least until he gets used to you. Then he may kill you. Shakespeare wrote, "He's mad that trusts in the tameness of a wolf…" (King Lear 3. 6. 20), and he wasn't kidding. Even more worrisome is my suspicion that people don't really want to domesticate their hybrids; they like the idea of having a wild animal (or a half-wild animal, as the case may be) in their house. Such people fantasize that they have a special skill or knack with wild creatures that is outside the ken of ordinary

185

people. This hubris often results in severe attacks upon humans and a mongrelization of the wolf population.

I should say, however, that people have been breeding dogs back to wolves for thousands of years. It is not a new phenomenon, despite it's being a fad. It was widely practiced in colonial America, for instance. But it is still a dangerous thing to do.

A wolf-dog is ideally half wolf and half dog. (Of course, other combinations are possible as well—three quarters wolf, one quarter dog, or vice versa. The whole thing is limited only by your knowledge of fractions.) However you slice it up, though, this is an unstable, dangerous cross. While, theoretically, any similarly-sized dog can be bred to a wolf, the most common wolf hybrids are crossed or otherwise mixed with Alaskan Malamutes, Alaskan or Siberian Huskies, or German Shepherd dogs. Such animals are almost entirely the result of deliberate breeding, as wolves and dogs do not frequently encounter each other in the wild. When they do, the result is more often bloody than romantic.

Owners hope the dog will look like a majestic wolf and act like a tractable dog. And sometimes, especially when a wolf is crossed with a beautiful animal like a Malamute, the result is physically even more impressive than a wolf. That is the ideal, but it's an elusive one. All too often the creature acts like an intractable wolf and looks like a mongrel of particularly infelicitous ancestry—which is just what it is. There is no wolf hybrid "standard" because there is no purpose for breeding wolf hybrids; there is nothing that one could even theoretically construct a standard around.

Wolves and wolf hybrids are unsuitable as companions because they are just not trainable. Think about this: you've seen wild animal shows with tigers and lions—maybe even with leopards. But how about wolves? Seen any trained wolves lately? (A somewhat analogous case is that of the zebra. You don't train them to pull carriages or trot around the equestrian ring with you because they look like horses.) When I say "trainable" regarding wolves, I am not talking about fancy tricks; I am talking about the simple commands that enable dogs to get along in our world. That's all beyond wolves. They don't sit on command, fetch, heel, lie down, or roll over—and chances are better than good that your wolf-dog won't either. It might, but you're taking a big risk.

Additionally, wolf hybrids rarely signal their intentions the way a wolf or even a dog might. They have a habit of attacking without the customary preliminaries, almost as if some important set of genes got lost in the transfer—which may be the case. Because wolf-dog mixes can be so eclectic, it's often difficult to distinguish among them (there are no reliable, consistent physical attributes) except perhaps by genetic testing now being developed.

> Researcher Erik Zimen tried hard to train some wolves to pull a sled.[95] He used captive-bred, hand-reared animals. They were totally uninterested and eventually got into such a fight that Zimen and his wife ended up pulling the sled themselves—which shows just how smart wolves are. If you're interested in participating in this sport, try a Siberian Husky, an Alaskan Malamute, or a Samoyed. If you want to race, get an Alaskan Husky (which is more a type than a breed). It'll work out better for you. Those dogs are not only faster and stronger than wolves, but they also like people.

Because wolf hybrids carry both wolf and dog characteristics, it is uncertain at what age the animal will develop sexually. As mentioned earlier, female dogs become adult between the ages of 6 and 8 months, while the female wolf does not achieve maturity until at least 2 years of age. The hybrid may go into heat once a year like the wolf or twice a year like the dog—there is no telling. The same is true for males. Male dogs reach sexual maturity at 8 months (when it will lift its leg during urination), while male wolves don't fully mature until 5 years of age. A wolf-dog may not exhibit leg-lifting until it reaches 2 to 4 years of age. (Incidentally, not all male wolves lift a leg to urinate. In the tundra, there's often nothing to lift one's leg against, after all.) Although anything can happen with a wolf hybrid, the general tendency is for it to behave more like a dog in this regard. Wolves, as noted earlier, achieve sexual maturity early if raised in captivity without parents to repress its sexual development. Also, the mental development of the wolf-dog is often slower than that of the domestic dog, so he requires special handling.

> While we are (once again) on the fascinating topic of urination, I should remind you that wolf hybrids are usually (but not always) much more difficult to housetrain than a dog. This is because they use their eliminative functions as much to mark territory as to empty their bladders and bowels. Wolves generally can't be housetrained at all.

Additionally, the social needs of these animals are highly developed—much more so than those of the average dog. It is particularly dangerous to try to raise a wolf or wolf hybrid without the company of its peers. Unless it learns the consequences of aggression from others like himself, he will never learn them—and you will be on the receiving end. In other words, if you plan to have one wolf-dog, have several instead. Then, of course, you have an entirely different set of problems; but if you don't, you are dooming your "pet" to life of terrible loneliness and psychic turmoil.

If you're looking for a guard dog, get a well-trained German Shepherd. Wolf hybrids tend to be either extremely shy or unpredictably aggressive; this is not something you want in either a pet or a guardian. And even if they do alert you to the presence of strangers, they are not particularly likely to protect you if you are attacked. My friend, Dr. Rob Russon, a veterinarian who practiced for many years in Alaska, says of wolf-hybrids: "These animals are a liability to their owners—and to other people as well." He adds, with a faint twinkle in his eye, "You can take the wolf out of the wild, but you can't take wild out of the wolf."

Then there's the legal problem. Every state has different rules about owning such animals; it may be illegal to own one in yours. Check with your local authorities if you are determined to risk this mad course of action. If you decide to get such an animal illegally, then you risk its being destroyed when you're found out.

Wolf-dogs also have special dietary needs. Most of them, for instance, cannot digest soy, a common ingredient in many commercial foods.

Yet despite all this, the Humane Society of the United States estimates that there are about 300,000 of these animals in the United States, and their popularity seems to be increasing—despite the fact that they kill people every year.

Perhaps due to widespread public apprehension about wolf-dogs, the United States Department of Agriculture (USDA) withdrew a proposed rule that would have included wolves and wolf hybrids on the labels of vaccines manufactured for dogs. Originally the rule redefined the word "dog" to include all members of the *lupus* and *familiaris* species. Officially, the USDA decided that it had insufficient safety and efficacy data on giving vaccines to wolves and wolf hybrids; unofficially, opponents feared it "would have set a serious legal precedent by allowing wolves and wolf hybrids to be called dogs," according to Bonnie V. Beaver, DVM, a member of the American Veterinary Medical Association's Executive Board.[96] A veterinarian may refuse to vaccinate the animal at all, which leaves the owner (and the animal) in a real predicament.

Wolf hybrids can bond to their owners, but they retain a much higher prey drive than do normal dogs. This sets the scene for dangerous aggression toward humans—and the most common victims are children and strangers. One former breeder of these animals, Terry Jenkins, who is now curator of the Folsom City Zoo in California, estimates that only about 5 percent of hybrids make good pets.[97] Even the tamest of wolf hybrids resent sudden moves. While some wolf-dog owners maintain that these animals can form a bond of sorts with their owners, they do admit that they require very special handling in order for that to happen.

To make matters worse, these animals have inherited the wolf's miraculous powers of escape; they have a passion to run as far and fast as they can. If there is anything worse than a wolf hybrid, it's a runaway wolf hybrid. They require at the very least a 30-by-30-foot outdoor area with a non-climbable fence at least 8 to 10 feet high.

> The state of Alaska has tried a new tack. Instead of trying to ban wolf hybrids (which are, in fact, already illegal), the Alaska Board of Game passed a regulation that makes the sale of wolves (or wolf hybrids) illegal if they are advertised as such. The state has had to resort to banning advertising because it's often impossible to distinguish a wolf hybrid from a dog except by time-consuming and expensive genetic testing. Also, all such animals must be neutered and microchipped. There are thousands of such animals in Alaska, most of which are husky types.

In areas where wolves abound, the breeding of wolf hybrids is a threat to both the natural population and the people. True wolves fear people; wolf hybrids don't. As attacks upon people increase, the wolves will get the blame.

And what happens to these animals when their owners decide that a wolf hybrid is dangerous, untrainable, or requires more attention than the owner can give? Well, most shelters will euthanize such animals immediately, even if they have shown no aggression. A few rescue groups have the facilities to house them, but there are more unwanted wolf hybrids than refuges that can keep them. Many are dumped in the woods where they either (a) die, (b) take to ravaging dumps and other local hotspots, perhaps killing pets or even children, or (c) manage to hook up with a wolf pack, in which case they infect the highly evolved wolf with dog genes, which weakens the pack's chances of survival.

The hybrid problem is not limited to dogs; hybridization of wild wolves and coyotes remains a perennial problem. First of all, it is unclear right now how "pure" coyotes, red wolves, and other canids are, even in the wild. The famous Isle Royale gray wolves, the best-studied wolf pack in history, all have coyote mtDNA. Every one of them. Yet these wolves look and act like other wolves, not coyotes. Proponents of delisting wolf subspecies on the grounds they are really wolves anyway frequently play the DNA card, but the United States Department of the Interior (USDI) is not buying it—yet. Controversy even exists about how long subspecies must be isolated from each other before they can be considered truly separate. (A lot of this dispute has to do with different populations of sandhill cranes, a subject thankfully outside the scope of this book.) Since even the purest of pure species are dynamic and undergo constant change, the whole problem is difficult to get a handle on or even, in some circles, discuss without rancor.

As far as hybrid wolves go, however, one thing is clear; we have taken something away from them. Just as the dog occupies that strange land between the animal world and ours, the hybrid wolf is caught between wolfdom and dogdom. He is neither. We have condemned him to a life in which he can never be free and never be trusted. This is our crime, not his.

Chapter 7

The Personhood of Dogs: The Mirroring Spirit

"A dog has the soul of a philosopher."
—Plato

When we look at dogs, we stare into a funhouse mirror—a dim, distorted reflection of mist and shadows. For a moment we think we glimpse a fellow human being; we recognize familiar motivations, desires, and needs. An instant later, we encounter a wolf.

Both images tell the ambiguous truth, for the funhouse mirror *is* a mirror. It shows us a creature capable of measureless devotion and sudden fury, a being who comforts us and who needs comforting, one who rages, fears, hungers, and loves. The mirror reveals in its flickering images the rich psychological and spiritual complexity that characterizes a person—which is what dogs are.

In this context, the word "person" does not, of course, mean "human." As should be apparent by looking at them, dogs are different from human beings in many ways—starting with genetics. Humans have 23 pairs of chromosomes, while dogs have 39. Humans have only about 40,000 genes; dogs have about 100,000. Their large number of genes may be responsible for the enormous adaptability of their species.

Physically and genetically humans, have much more in common with apes than we do with dogs; we look more like gorillas than Irish Setters. Dogs do, however, share about 18,000 of the 24,000 clearly identified "human" genes with us; in time as the Canine Genome Project is completed, more similarities will probably be discovered.

But gorillas and chimps and gibbons and orangutans are wild creatures. They are not ours in the way dogs are "ours." Apes would be much better off without humans in the world. So would wolves. Without humans, however, dogs as we know them would cease to exist. They are, for want of a better term, social parasites—not unlike children. Because of their amorphous position between the wild and human world, we are always mistaking them for one or the other—human or wolf—when they are neither.

Of course, not everyone considers dogs human beings or even housebound wolves. Some people make the opposite mistake—the mechanistic one. Because dogs do indeed somehow belong with us and to us but are so obviously "other" in their appearance, we sometimes consider them our possessions—in other words, warm, furry objects. There is not too much to say about this, because I have little comprehension of or sympathy for anyone who can mistake a Chihuahua for a chair or a terrier for a tablecloth. Objects cannot feel and have no desires, needs, or preferences; dogs do.

To depersonalize animals by categorizing them as "things" is a more grievous logical error than anthropomorphizing them, since animals are not inanimate objects like stones and weathervanes; they are sentient creatures like ourselves. Nor are they mere neural-possessing automatons; dogs react individually to the same stimulus. Some dogs will run up to greet a strange child with joy, some will back away, some will attack, and some will ignore it. Some dogs cower and shake at the approach of a storm, while others seem oblivious. It is readily apparent to anyone who has ever owned a dog that each has a distinct personality, an individual quality that separates him radically from others of the same species. This is also true of people; it cannot be said of a machine.

To find our way out of the morass of mechanism and the abyss of anthropomorphism, we must be brave and make a bold assumption. It is this: dogs (and other animals, each in its own way) are persons, in the philosophical, if not legal, sense of that term. Some folks will accuse me of anthropomorphizing here, but that isn't exactly true. Anthropomorphizing is assigning traits that belong only to humans to animals. I suggest instead that humans and dogs share enough significant traits to place us both into the larger philosophic class of persons just as, biologically, we both belong to the class of mammals.

My assertion that dogs are persons is not based on whim, fancy, or sentiment, but on what I see as truth. The consequences of such a declaration may be a bit unsettling, but surely they are less destructive than the opposite view (animals are not persons), which has ruined most of the earth and crippled our own development as a species.

Persons? Are animals human? Of course not. Animals are skunks or voles or muskrats or dogs or tigers—or human beings. There is no more honor attached to one classification than the other. Animals are as glorious (or inglorious) in their way as we are in ours; that doesn't make animals and people identical. Besides the genetic differences, we are different culturally and behaviorally—although dogs share our culture and behavior to an extent that is extraordinary. That does make it easier to refer to a dog (rather than a chipmunk) as a person, I must admit.

Why does one have to belong to the species *Homo sapiens* to be accorded the label of person? Are only those with a particular genetic code allowed in the club? What other criteria might reasonably be applied? What is a person, anyway? What, if anything, precludes dogs, giraffes, trout, or salamanders from this august grouping?

We do. It is difficult (as I hope to show) to argue that anything special in the way of talent, spirit, or intelligence separates us completely from our fellows; we do, however, have the power to decide whom to admit to our club. And considering that we have regularly and historically excluded members of our own species from that sacred grouping (fetuses, slaves, prisoners, women, the mentally ill, the physically handicapped, and those who differ from the elite in any way the group designates have all been barred from the club at various times), it only makes sense that the opposite would be true—we can admit anyone we choose. We have accorded membership to serial killers and other such egregious individuals, so why exclude the family dog?

Historically, humans have attempted to define personhood (and the privileges associated with it) in a way that automatically reserves the term for ourselves. The method has been one of exclusion rather than inclusion. We begin with our conclusion already drawn: "person" equals "human." But do we have an adequate reason for assuming this—other than to salve our own vanity? Isn't this just an example of petitio principii—begging the question? That's what my high school Latin teacher, Mrs. Badger, would say. (It is nice to have had a Latin teacher named Mrs. Badger for the purposes of this piece.)

Another tactic humans apply in our never-ending attempt to raise ourselves above the beasts is to craft the definition of "person" in such a way that it establishes not only an unbreachable wall between humans and animals, but also reifies the measureless superiority of the former over the latter.

Before genetic studies, it was hard enough to define "human being," let alone "person," which is a considerably more abstract concept. Aristotle, one of the first people on record to give it a try, opined that a human being might be defined as a featherless biped—until another Greek offered the snide counterexample of a plucked chicken. (Most subsequent definitions of human beings have been equally silly, inadequate, or just plain wrong.)

Once it was agreed upon that genetics, rather than culture, brains, or even appearance clearly demarcated the human being, it became incumbent upon some thinkers to attempt to show how the term person entailed a deeper difference—one outside the realm of hard science. After all, it is not the business of geneticists to decide which genetic package is better than another; they leave that to the arbiters of culture. Thus many humans claim to be not just humans, but also persons. But if nothing separates us from animals but a bunch of genes, how can we be superior to any of them? The scramble was on—the race to find a philosophically satisfying barrier to erect between Us and Them. (Oddly, most people have no trouble acknowledging that persons, meaning human beings, are animals. The concept that animals are persons, however, seems a bit harder to swallow.) The problem got knottier and more urgent as every new piece of scientific research suggested that we are much closer to the beasts than most of us wanted to be.

We were getting desperate to show that we are special enough to be persons, but animals are not. There's more to this than idle curiosity, of course; there's an agenda. We don't want to admit that the only thing that really separates us from animals is our power over them—our ability to kill them almost at will (with the exception of ticks, mosquitoes, and disease-dispensing cockroaches, who seem to be better at killing us than the other way around, and which by that standard must be considered superior to us). But for us to be comfortable in doing whatever we like with animals, we have felt it necessary to come up with a reason, no matter how specious, to show that we somehow deserve this power. We need that barrier, and we'll take it where we can get it. Here are some examples.

The Tool Barrier

For a long, rather dull while, scientists speculated that it was the use of tools that elevated us above the beasts—until we discovered just how creative apes, birds, and other creatures can be with tools. I knew a blind dog that carried a stuffed toy in his mouth as a bumper; it guided him away from walls. And chimpanzees not only use tools, they make them as well. If we want to employ tool-use as the supreme principle, then I suppose one would have to concede that the guy who built my patio is more of a person than Albert Einstein.

Of course, humans as a group are much better toolmakers and users than are other animals, but that is a difference of degree rather than kind. Most of our cleverness is due to the chance arrangement of our digits, including our indispensable opposable thumb—something we certainly cannot take any credit for. Additionally, some of us are really terrible tool users. As far as making tools for ourselves, crafting a pointed stick to toast marshmallows is the beginning and end of that ability for many of us. I am frankly more amazed at the ability of birds to make nests without tools than ours to build houses with them.

The Language Barrier

Not all scientists are impressed with tool use as a major divider between Us and Them. They have instead proposed language as the sine qua non that makes humans the only persons in the universe. Language is verbal communication. In that sense, birds have language; so do wolves, dolphins, and dogs. Dogs can understand large chunks of human language. My own dogs understand English better than I understand Spanish. Most of them know the difference between "Let's go for a ride!" and "Want a bath?" even when each phrase is spoken in the same happy tone. Apes can be taught American Sign Language, and dolphins appear to have a complex language of their own. And if we require that one speak a human language in order to qualify (and what a piece of hubris that is), I can only offer the examples of African grey and Amazon parrots who can not only copy human speech and song with a disquieting exactitude, but who can also use human words to make meaning. The famous African grey parrot, Alex, has been quoted in scientific journals. Of course, humans use human speech better than parrots; what is surprising about that I have no idea. I will even grant that we humans can make more complex meaning than animals, but again, the difference is one of degree. A parrot can say, "I want a cracker" when he's hungry, but most humans cannot discuss Immanuel Kant's categorical imperative competently, which puts us closer to parrot level than to Kant. I will even venture to say that most people would get more pleasure out of discourse with a parrot—at least it would make sense.

The Intelligence Barrier

Language and tool use both seem to be rooted in intelligence, so maybe intelligence is the magic barrier that separates Us from Them. Intelligence, however, is not an impermeable barrier, since some dogs can be more knowledgeable or intelligent than certain humans or classes of humans, such as newborn babies or mentally defective people. (I'd bet that a working Border collie is smarter than about 27 percent of the human population, although I must admit that I can't say this about my step-Border collie, Boo, who allows the sheep to herd her.) As a general rule, of course, people are smarter than dogs, but there's enough overlap to make one wonder. Like people, dogs have a highly developed cerebral cortex, the organ responsible for intellectual behavior. If damage is done to this part of the brain, the dog becomes "slow," just as we do. It is true that most humans are capable of more complex thinking than are dogs, but, again, it's a matter of degree. Although no non-human animal has yet been able to do calculus or write a symphony, the same can be said for most people. Can we assert that a child born with a mental deficiency is less a person than an honor student? Or that geniuses have more personhood than the average person?

Some people offer that old standby, abstract thought, as the barrier criterion. One problem with this approach is that it is simply impossible to know what goes on in another's head. We are, however, pretty sure that babies are incapable of abstract thought—yet they are undeniably persons. Dogs may or may not be capable of abstract thought, but they can generalize, which is surely the first step. A dog that has been terrified by one letter carrier will soon learn to fear all letter carriers—and probably anyone in a uniform. Dogs are also probably able to count, as least to a limited degree.

My Basset Hound, Mugwump, was highly intelligent and displayed a breadth of foresight and scheming that was truly Machiavellian. For example, if I gave her a rawhide treat, she would begin to chew it immediately. If, however, I gave a rawhide treat to each of my 5 dogs, she would immediately bury hers in an out-of-the-way spot. She would then race toward the far reaches of the yard, barking furiously, as if the most exciting activity in the world were occurring next door. The other dogs would immediately drop their rawhides and tear after her. Mugwump would then stop about halfway and, as the other dogs charged past her toward the nonexistent distraction, pick up speed in the opposite direction, collect the other rawhides, and gather them between her paws. She didn't chew them—yet. She just waited for the other dogs to return. Then she would growl at them, pointedly chew each one of their rawhides, and bury them when the others were not looking. This happened over and over again, and the other dogs never caught on. No one taught her this trick; she figured it out herself. She pulled much the same ploy when she wanted a particular bed that one of the other dogs was lying on. Now that I have recounted this story it gives me pause. Perhaps I am not making that case that Mugwump was smart so much as I am that the other dogs were stupid. But I'll let it stand; I'm fair-minded.

We also know that if we compare the mean IQs of any 2 groups of people (left-handers vs. right-handers, baseball players vs. football players, Kansans vs. Iowans), one group will average higher than the other (even if only by a teeny bit) due to statistical variance. It's practically inevitable. Can we say that the group that scores higher is superior (and proportionately superior to the degree to which it scores higher)?

Once we start using differences of degree as a demarcation between persons and non-persons, there is nothing to stop us from placing superior people (judged by whatever standard) in a class above inferior ones. Many of the social inequalities between men and women arose because men (who had the physical power, the only thing that apparently counts) decided they were the superior sex— better at using tools for instance, which, as we noted earlier, is no standard at all even if it were true, which it isn't. In other words, males developed the criteria for superiority—criteria which did not include nurturing ability, empathy, or common sense.

Okay, agrees the skeptic; any meaningful differences between animals and person must reside in the realm of philosophy, art, religion, or ethics. Yet the same arguments apply. Men claimed superiority over women because of their supposedly better developed talents in the arts, their higher ethical capacities, or their God-given place in the universe (the top). You should read what Aristotle and some early church fathers had to say about women. For a long time they weren't quite sure whether or not they even had souls (while simultaneously expressing no doubt that males are ensouled).

The Spiritual Barrier

Speaking of which, we could claim that personhood depends on the existence of an immortal soul and that only humans have that important commodity. That, however, is a chauvinistic opinion and one that is not universally held. Some people and some faiths assert that all creatures have an immortal spirit or soul (like the Jains), while others (such as Buddhists) maintain that no life form does—including *Homo sapiens*. As for Christians, there is no uniform agreement about the matter. Martin Luther, in fact, assured his little dog that when resurrected, he would have a golden tail. The truth is that we don't have a clue as to whether any being has an immortal soul or not. (The idea of a golden tail is seductive, though, isn't it?)

The concept that only humans are ensouled has no philosophical foundation. In fact, those who assert that only humans have immortal souls are generally ensnared by a circuitous reasoning which goes something like this: "Only human beings have immortal souls because human beings belong to a special order of creation. The special order of creation to which only humans belong is that of ensouled creatures." This is yet another example of begging the question or rationalizing the conclusion we so desperately wish to prove.

The Self and Self-Consciousness Barrier

We might reduce the religious grandiosity of the "only human beings have souls" concept to a more modest, philosophical, "only human beings have self," but that doesn't help either. First, "self" can be used as a synonym for "soul." It also seems obvious that whatever one can posit about the selfhood of humans must apply equally to the selfhood of animals. (The Buddha declared that all beings are empty of self, and our final delusion is the belief in a permanent self.) I see no credible philosophical reason for reserving selfhood to human beings. Even if we were able to prove (which we are not) that only human beings are conscious of our selfhood, that would not disqualify animals from having a self—whether they are conscious of it or not. Consciousness can't be a criterion. Is a newborn baby of conscious of self? Are we conscious of self when we fall into a dreamless sleep, or when we are under anesthesia? Are we unselfed non-persons in those states? If so, animals are just like us in that regard. They are, at various times, wakeful, dreaming, or in deep sleep. Perhaps not all animals dream, but dogs certainly do—at least their rapid eye movement, running motions, moans, yips, and whines give every indication that they are dreaming.

Is the self present in animals only when they are awake—or never? If never, what differentiates the wakeful human from the wakeful animal? (Whether a human being born with such severe brain damage as to be unaware of his surroundings has personhood is an interesting question, but one which has an answer—which is "maybe.") Animals certainly behave as if they know who they are and what they want, at least to the extent humans do. And the fact that only humans may ask the question "Who am I?" suggests only that we have no idea ourselves. Animals seem a bit more confident in this regard.

Besides, I don't think that self-consciousness is so rare a commodity as human-centrists imagine. Research indicates that self-awareness and the ability to respond creatively are hallmarks of many life forms. It may not exist in amoebae, but is certainly present in octopi, crocodiles, camels, and dogs. There is also evidence that it exists in honeybees.

George Berkeley and his trees falling in the forest notwithstanding, we all know that an object continues to exist whether or not it is perceived or we are conscious of it. A chair in a room stays in the room when you leave it; it doesn't pop in and out of existence like a magic yoyo. In the same way, the soul, if it exists, continues to exist whether or not we are paying attention to it. For those who claim that the self is a different sort of entity than a tree because it is not material—well, that supports the claim that the soul is a fabricated notion, which doesn't help the "only-humans-are-persons" case. Invented, intangible terms like "soul," "love," and "person" can mean pretty much what we want them to mean, as opposed to a word like *chair*, about which there is nearly unanimous agreement. *Chair* may still mean what we want it to mean, but at least we have an objective correlative to base our argument upon. So if each of us wishes to privately define *person, love, soul,* or *God*, we can, but we should be aware that's what we are doing. There is no objective correlative to the term "person"; a person is what we say it is. And when we say only human beings are persons, we are making a decision—not discovering a truth. There's a difference.

The Moral Barrier

Let's forget religion and metaphysics and talk about morals and ethics instead. We could posit that our fine-tuned moral sense gives us the edge over, say, dogs. Dogs certainly seem to have no highly developed moral scruples, although British novelist and philosopher

Iris Murdoch wrote that "Dogs are very different from cats in that they can be images of human virtue. They are like us."

It is true that humans have used morality as a stick to beat dogs over the head with. "The damn dog did it on purpose; he knows it's wrong." This statement is only partially true, as I will show. Dog trainers get the best results by assuming dogs have no moral sense; it's also the best way to keep people in line. The truth may be somewhat more complex when we delve into what exactly morality is.

Animals are sinless. Even the most religious of persons must grant that whether humans are or are not born with original sin, animals have to be let off the hook. One cannot be a "bad" or "good" owl, dog, or caterpillar. One is what one is. Animals have not erected for themselves the elaborate and confusing moral edifice we humans have made for ourselves. Is war moral? Capital punishment? Abortion? Lying to protect another? Serving in the military? Avoiding the military? One might reasonably ask what good a moral code serves that has no agreed-upon answers for these and other critical questions. Yet it is this murky and contradictory set of rules (which we have made up) that we claim is one of the markers that separates us from the animals, who act in their own best interest—just as we do, although we are usually too hypocritical (and self-serving) to admit it. We need that barrier for practical reasons; if we don't keep telling ourselves how great we are, we might cease to believe it.

Even we enlightened human beings are not born with a moral sense, and our concept of morality changes from culture to culture and century to century. Dogs at least appear to have developed (thanks to us humans) a rudimental sense of—well, if not right and wrong, then of what is acceptable and what isn't, even if what is acceptable conflicts with their perceived best interest. And let's face it, most humans aren't much further along than that themselves. We refrain from stealing, lying, and mayhem mostly because we're afraid we'll be caught and punished—by the law, by God, or by a culturally-contrived guilty conscience. And, of course, there exists a fairly large number of people who commit crimes and behave unethically despite any societal restraining factors. So even if you believe that dogs have no true moral sense, which is certainly possible and perhaps even likely, it's hard to develop a firm theory that accounts for human morality and its supposed origin. After all, humans have not infrequently used their intellectual superiority to create new and interesting crimes and obscure methods of torture that would never occur to a dog. I suppose that make us superior.

Here's a case in point. Humans have been known to act with (apparently) complete selflessness (and get a lot of credit for doing so) from time to time. We call this altruism. But dogs have been known to exhibit exactly the same kind of behavior—rescuing their owners, for example, at great danger to themselves. But we should be fair; dogs are more likely to behave selfishly, just as we are.

It is true that animals can develop what seems to be a guilty conscience after, say, having eaten a good portion of the living room couch (or the baby) during a dull afternoon, but that guilt is probably closer to a realistic apprehension regarding the owner's response to the dining adventure than a moral crisis. How different is that, really, from most of us? While we may feel guilt, it was originally imposed upon us from without. Guilt is also highly individual—an act that makes one person feel guilty may fill another with pride; it has nothing to do with a universal human condition. Can dogs feel pride? We may never know, but it certainly seems as if they do, at least sometimes. I have seen show dogs behave as if they knew they'd done something well, and this afternoon I worked with a Border Collie who had herded her first sheep. She seemed extremely pleased with herself.

While no dog has attained the saintliness of Mother Theresa, none has sunk to the depravity of Adolf Hitler. Most dogs, like most people, live somewhere between those two extremes. I readily grant that dogs cannot be found morally culpable for such acts as stealing the bacon; like Adam and Eve, the temptation may just be too much. It's up to you to keep bacon away from your dog. (And you probably shouldn't eat it yourself.) Moral culpability is, however, a slippery term. Certainly dogs can be taught to behave themselves, which is all we ask from people. We don't really care how people really feel about murder and stealing; we just don't want them to do it.

Just as it is unrealistic to expect animals to understand calculus or even long division, it is not sensible to hold them to a higher ethical standard than that we set for people: behave yourself or you'll get into trouble. It is not necessary for them to internalize these values, especially since humans are in the habit of changing them at will. Dogs have learned that it's better to adapt than memorize.

The Emotional Barrier

I almost skipped this one as being too feeble to withstand even mild scrutiny until I realized how many people refused to acknowledge that animals have feelings and emotions until very recently. While it is impossible to feel any emotions but one's own, we can say that most higher mammals seem to exhibit jealousy, love, anger, grief, fear, and joy. Dogs do so to an almost extravagant degree. Although the latest training psychobabble claims that dogs do not feel jealousy but are rather guarding resources, the difference between the two is unclear to me. People who are jealous are also guarding their resources—real or imagined.

Dogs mourn their owners and their fellow dogs. When our English Springer Spaniel died, our Irish Setter fell into a deep depression for well over 6 months, never leaving her couch except to eat and eliminate. She eventually got better, but she never regained the joie de vivre that that been so characteristic of her up until that time. Those who maintain that animals have no emotions have never owned a pet.

The Aesthetic Barrier

Let's turn to another branch of philosophy—aesthetics. We could assert that human superiority lies in the fact that we create art. But as mentioned earlier, this is far from a universal talent. Most of us can't paint, sing, or play the oboe. And what about those chimps and elephants who show an uncanny knack for the visual arts (at least on the level of Jackson Pollack), and the bower-birds who are masters at home decoration? My own Mugwump was always thrilled when I got her costume box out of the closet—wagging her tail like mad and barking excitedly. One may posit that the dog enjoyed the attention she got while wearing the costume (in this case a homemade mummy outfit) rather than the wearing of it, but I daresay that the same is true for humans. We wouldn't wear costumes either unless we thought someone were going to pay attention to us when we did so. Few people sit alone around the house, then suddenly jump up and say, "Hey, I'm going to put my ghost outfit on!" (But then again, you never know.) In fact, I doubt people would bother wearing anything but sweatsuits if no one were around to judge appearance. I have to say that dogs have the moral advantage there; they don't care what they (or we) look like. Their minds are one higher things.

Let's grant that true art (as opposed to the frightening smears of monkeys and abstract painters) is indeed a uniquely human quality (and even then restricted to only some humans). So what? Does a unique ability make us the only "persons" in the universe? What is so unique about uniqueness? Why should that be a criterion? Other animals have unique abilities too. So, although you might claim that art makes us superior to, say, mako sharks, let's offer a counter-proposal. Since mako sharks can swim 40 miles an hour, they are superior to us. Both painting a picture and being a fast swimmer are skills. Is one inherently superior to the other? It depends on the situation. Sometimes being able to swim fast is a definite advantage (as when a mako shark happens along); and most of the time one must agree with Oscar Wilde that "All art is quite useless." Differences between species do not spell superiority, or, by any objective standard, mark personhood.

Survivability and Superiority

In the school of evolution, superiority is measured by one factor only—the ability to survive. And if survival is the key to superiority, both dogs and humans are in trouble; most scientists think cockroaches will be here long after we've gone to oblivion. They are superior to us by the only objective standard I can come up with: survival. The one real evolutionary advantage we seem to have acquired over the millennia is our capacity to destroy the planet before the rest of creation out-evolves us. Does our ability to destroy everything around us make us superior? If yes, then let's forget about spirit and art and intelligence and talk about the one thing that really counts: power—the power to choose and the power to enforce our choices.

We have power; animals don't. At the present moment, humans rule the earth despite occasional sniper attacks by snakes, hippopotami, and sharks, as well as the persistent terrorism of mosquitoes. How we use our power is up to us. Power includes the power of nomenclature—we decide who persons are. We decide, in other words, who gets the care, consideration, and love reserved for that class of beings.

If we are as noble as we often claim, then we should stop dreaming up self-serving criteria designed to assert our separateness from animals. The old distinctions are based upon human values, not scientific fact or even common sense. We are already separate from animals genetically, which is where it counts. Any artificial construct designed to prove our overall superiority is based on a prepackaged bias. It is much more interesting, creative—and ultimately human— to discover commonalities rather than differences.

The Superiority Barrier

Even if we *could* somehow prove that human beings are by any standard (including that of power) superior to animals, we would fail logically to make the case that animals are not persons. One human may be superior to another in every sense. Alice may be very dull; she may have no developed moral sense; she may have no musical or artistic ability. Jean may have all these things in abundance, and be better looking besides. She may also have complete power over Alice. Does that mean Alice is not so fully a person as Jean? Of course not. Superiority is not the benchmark of personhood. I will tell you what is.

What Makes A Person?

I don't pretend to be particularly original here (Jeremy Bentham, John Stuart Mill, and the Buddha are all way ahead of me), but I think we can reduce personhood to one simple criterion—the capacity to suffer. It is not incidental, by the way, that human beings are the direct cause of much of the suffering experienced by animals. In the United States alone we kill 10 billion animals every year just for food—not to mention the numbers we use for research, the fur trade, and such entertainments as rodeos, dog and horse racing, dog and cock fighting (illegal but widely practiced), and so on.

Maybe the real reason we are so anxious to deny the personhood of animals is that we benefit materially from their captivity, suffering, and death. It is more practical to regard them as non-persons in the same way we once regarded slaves as non-persons. We had to. Once we acknowledge another being with attendant rights, we make ourselves monsters (even in our own eyes) by not honoring that personhood. And who wants to admit that humans are greedy, selfish, and basically amoral? That wouldn't seem right. No, it is much better to say that the Other is "sub-human," "vicious," "stupid," or even, as René Descartes claimed, a mere automaton unable to feel pain and capable only of reacting. (This idea is so absurd that it makes one wonder about the rest of his philosophy. He may have ushered in the Enlightenment, but there is something odd about someone who got all his best ideas while he was in bed, as he claimed.) However, it cannot be denied that every oppressed group in history, whether relegated to that status by virtue of race, gender, religion, or ethnic identity—or, in this case, different DNA packaging—has been marked as Other.

At any rate (Descartes notwithstanding), anyone who has ever owned a pet knows that it feels pain when its tail is trod upon—or it gives every possible indication that it feels pain, which is all we can ever know. After all, a human may claim to feel pain when he does not. This is called lying and has also been observed in animals on occasion; many a dog will "limp" to obtain sympathy from his owner, once he has learned that it works. However, occasional dissimulation about pain does not mean that one is not capable of feeling genuine pain, either person or animal.

To feel pain is the benchmark of personhood—not because it makes the sufferer superior, but because it makes him a victim. It is a place we all know well. Suffering is a mark of sensitivity to and awareness of the environment. Saint Thomas Aquinas believed that suffering is the inescapable price we pay for living. It is also the silent companion of caring, and the suffering of others calls upon us to respond with caring and love.

People suffer; animals suffer. Therefore they are persons. Rocks don't suffer. They are not persons. People undergoing surgery may or may not be suffering—we don't know, so we should probably give them the benefit of the doubt.

I choose suffering as a criterion not because of what it does to animals, but because of what it calls upon us to do as humans. To be fully human is to be able to respond to suffering; those who are not fully human cannot. In fact, they do the opposite—they cause suffering. I could use other criteria—love, for instance. But not all animals, or even all dogs, love us. Those who have been most abused may no longer be capable of love. (The same may well be true of human beings.) If anything, that increases their claim upon us.

So What and Now What?

Okay, animals suffer. They're persons. Big deal. What does that mean to Us? It means they have a claim upon us, upon the deep compassion we pride ourselves upon. The word "kindness," which we often use when we are speaking about the proper treatment of animals, carries within it a hint about the true nature of that relationship. "Kind" comes from "kin"; kindness means recognizing a deep kinship.

We may not agree, after all this, that animals are persons. Perhaps I have not made a convincing case for personhood, which can be defined in various ways. But we can't dispute the fact that animals suffer. Those who suffer offer us the opportunity to exercise those human virtues of caring and compassion. The challenge to those who doubt the personhood of animals is to prove their own humanity by caring for the "least of these." Our own human-ness is challenged by how we confront their agony.

But compassion is not a guarantee. If we do not make a claim for the personhood of dogs, then they are forced to rely on human mercy, and our performance in that department has not been good. Animals deserve compassion, as most well-meaning persons recognize—hence the proliferation of animal welfare organizations. But we have to go further and declare for their legal rights as well (both the animal-welfare and the animal-rights movements rest upon the philosophical basis of animal suffering).

Steven M. Wise, in his exciting book *Drawing the Line: Science and the Case for Animal Rights* (and elsewhere), suggests that many animals deserve fundamental legal rights, a theory based largely on the mind-power of the animal in question.[98] As is obvious, my own case is a bit broader. In the largest view, I am far from convinced that humans are more important than cockroaches. This does not mean that I think animals should have the same rights as humans. Well, perhaps I do, but pragmatically and as a matter of self-interest I would not allow it. I am parochial enough to retain a certain sneaking fondness for my own species. So I don't think animals should vote. We don't allow many humans to vote (and in some countries nobody votes). Besides, animals don't know how to vote, which is a good thing. I would not care to be outvoted by cockroaches.

I think that it is probably necessary for human survival to use animals in medical research—provided we take extensive measures to limit their suffering as much as possible, not experiment with animals unless it is absolutely imperative, and only use animals when no other model will serve. The killing and eating of animals by human beings is a long-established part of our culture; this does not make the eating of flesh moral, healthy, or economically wise. Until the time comes when our culture prefers beets to beef, however, we have an obligation to prevent suffering among such animals by raising and slaughtering them as humanely as possible.

I think wild animals should be left alone and have as much of their territory as possible returned to them (and humans should practice some pretty strict birth control to make it possible). I include birds (with the exception of certain fowl) among wild animals. They were not meant for life in a cage.

I think all domestic animals deserve good food, fresh water, love (when asked for), and an interesting life. They should not be abused, neglected, or abandoned. Dogs should be treated with dignity and love, not contorted into fantastic shapes to satisfy some warped aesthetic which result in movement and breathing problems. They should not be made to fight other dogs. They should not have their ears and tails cut off to suit our whims, or be debarked because we find this natural behavior annoying. They should not be left chained in yards or crammed into crates for hours and hours every day.

> Just to show you how selfish I really am, I will tell you right now that I have no sympathy for ticks. There is nothing remotely charming about them.

And why dogs, among all other animals? Because we have so thoroughly made them our own. As discussed earlier, we have so thoroughly altered the structure and temperament of our familiar wolves that they are no longer capable of living without us. And we are in their debt for that.

Let's go back to the mirror. It is not a mistake to see ourselves partially reflected in the dog, our mirroring spirit. Doing so shows us how far and deep our fellow-feeling can run, the sweep of our empathy. And I have shown how similar we truly are. But it is a mistake to see only ourselves. Although the dog is of our making, he is not us. We have seen that, coiled deep in every gene, is the wolf. But as we have also seen, the dog is no longer purely wolf either. He walks a different path. Like ourselves, and like every being on earth, he is a unique creation. Failing to respect that unique creation diminishes us.

Today's dogs encircle our human consciousness as their ancestors sought the edges of human campfires. They are watching and waiting—not for scraps of food this time (although, being dogs, they will graciously accept these too), but for scraps of our true humanity. The salvation of animals can come only when we become fully persons and completely human. They are in our hands, God help them.

Endnotes

1. At one time, people thought that perhaps several canids…Jennifer Leonard, et al., "Ancient DNA Evidence for Old World Origin of New World Dogs," *Science* 298 (22 November 2002).

2. One of the first recognizable canid forebears…"Evolution of the Dog," *The Dog*, www.lookd.com/dogs/evelution.html.

3. For example, using the taxonomy…Juliet Clutton-Brock, G. B. Corbet, and M. Hills, "A Review of the Family *Canidae*, with a Classification by Numerical Methods," *Bulletin of the British Museum (Natural History) Zoology* 29 (1976); J.R. Ginsberg and D.W. Macdonald, *Foxes, Wolves, Jackals, and Dogs: An Action Plan for the Conservation of Canids,* (Gland, Switzerland: IUCN, 1990).

4. Besides the gray wolf…Robert Wayne and S. M. Jenks, "Mitochondrial DNA Analysis Implying Extensive Hybridization of the Endangered Red Wolf *Canis rufus*," *Nature* 351 (1991): 565–568; Leonard, "Ancient DNA."

5. Formerly, many common classifications…C. Vilà, P. Savolainen, J.E. Maldonado, et al., "Multiple and Ancient Origin of the Domestic Dog," *Science* 276 (1997): 1687–1689.

6. Here is that list, which includes…Liz Harper, "Subspecies of the Wolf," *Scientific Classification of Wolves,* International Wolf Center, www.wolf.org/wolves/learn/intermed/inter_sci/wolf_subspecies.asp.

7. To show how perplexing the classification of wolves…Peter Steinhart, *The Company of Wolves* (New York: Random House, 1995).

8. And all this fuss is about just one variety!…"Timeline: The Red Wolf in the Southeastern United States," *Wolf Basics*, International Wolf Center www.wolf.org/wolves/learn/basic/history/red_timeline.asp.

9. L. David Mech observed several such events…L. David Mech, *The Wolf: The Ecology and Behavior of an Endangered Species* (Minneapolis: University of Minnesota Press. 1970).

10. In fact, L. David Mech, a premier expert on wolves…L. David Mech, *The Way of the Wolf*.

11. Interestingly, Woolpy and Ginsberg have shown…cited by James Serpell and J. A. Jagoe in "Early Experience and the Development of Behaviour," in *The Domestic Dog: Its Evolution, Behaviour, and Interactions with People*, ed. James Serpell (Cambridge: Cambridge University Press, 1995).

12. L. David Mech observed that wolf leaders…Mech, *The Way of the Wolf* (Stillwater, MD: Voyageur Press. 1991).

13. Jared Diamond, among others, has theorized…Jared Diamond, *Guns, Germs, and Steel: The Fate of Human Societies* (New York: Random House, 1997).

14. Raymond Coppinger, noted canine researcher…Coppinger Raymond and Lorna Coppinger, *Dogs* (New York: Scribner, 2001).

15. L. David Mech recounts how…Mech, *The Way of the Wolf*.

16. Experiments that compared reproductive parameters…E. Haase, "Comparison of Reproductive Parameters in Male Wolves and Domestic Dogs," *Z. Säugetierkunde* 65 (2000): 257–270.

17. L. David Mech observed several…Mech, *The Way of the Wolf*.

18. Prolactin, a hormone that stimulates nurturing behavior…National Park Service, "Wolves in Denali Park and Preserve," *U.S. Department of the Interior*, www.nps.gov/akso/ParkWise/Students/ReferenceLibrary/DENA/WolvesInDenali.htm.

19. While no one is really sure what this is supposed to accomplish…Mech, *The Way of the Wolf*.

20. All animals go through critical learning…John Paul Scott and John L. Fuller, *Genetics and the Social Behavior of the Dog: The Classic Study* (Chicago: University of Chicago Press. 1965).

21. The Swedish Dog Training Center experimented…Serpell, *The Domestic Dog*.

22. J. A. Altman at the Pavlov Institute of Physiology…J. A. Altman and I. V. Kalmykova, "Role of the Dog's Auditory Cortex in Discrimination of

Sound Signals Simulating Sound Source Movement," *Hearing Research* 24, no. 3 (1986): 245–253.

23. Katherine Houpt of Cornell University…Katherine Houpt, P. Shepherd, and H. F. Hintz, "Two Methods for Producing Peripheral Anosmia in Dogs," *Laboratory Animal Science* 28, no. 2 (1978): 173–177.

24. During the Hundred Years' War…Desmond Seward, *The Hundred Years War: The English in France, 1337–1453* (London: Constable, 1978).

25. Russian biologist Dmitry K. Belyaev…Lyudmilia Trut, "Early Canid Domestication: The Farm-Fox Experiment," *American Scientist* 87, no. 2 (1999): 160–169.

26. Here are some characteristics…Edward Price, *Animal Domestication and Behavior* (New York: CABI Publishing, 2002).

27. In 1963, F. E. Zeuner noted…. Frederick Zeuner, *A History of Domesticated Animals* (New York, Harper & Row, 1963).

28. Dog Genome Project is completed…Jasper Rine, "Dog Genome Project," University of California, Berkeley, http://mendel.berkeley.edu/dog.html.

29. Furthermore, as Stephen Budiansky reports…Stephen.Budianksy, *The Truth About Dogs,* (New York: Viking, 2000).

30. One factor that may have played a part…Helmut Hemmer, *Domestication: the Decline of Environmental Appreciation* (Cambridge: Cambridge University Press, 1990).

31. A related theory is offered by Raymond Coppinger…Raymond and Lorna Coppinger, *Dogs.*

32. Evolutionary geneticist Robert Wayne…Vilà, C., et al., "Multiple and Ancient Origin of the Domestic Dog," *Science* 276 (1997): 1687–1689.

33. Biologist Jennifer Leonard, from the Smithsonian Museum …Leonard, "Ancient DNA Evidence."

34. Leonard's work reinforced that of Peter Savolainen…Vilà, C., et al., "Multiple and Ancient Origin."

35. Konrad Lorenz, the Nobel-prize winning ethologist…Konrad Lorenz, *Man Meets Dog* (Houghton Mifflin Company, Boston, 1954).

36. Scott and Fuller discovered…Scott and Fuller, *Genetics and the Social Behavior.*

37. Wayne and company push the wolf domestication date…Vilà, C., et al., "Multiple and Ancient Origin."

38. As Ray and Lorna Coppinger observed…Raymond and Lorna Coppinger, *Dogs.*

39. Those like Coppinger and Schneider…Raymond Coppinger and Richard Schneider, "Evolution of Working Dogs," *The Domestic Dog: Its Evolution, Behavior and Interactions with People* (Cambridge: Cambridge University Press, 1995).

40. Stephen Budiansky, in his wonderful book…Budianksy, *The Truth About Dogs.*

41. As Steven Pinker shows…Steven Pinker, *The Blank Slate: The Modern Denial of Human Nature* (New York: Viking, 2002).

42. Elaine Ostrander, a molecular geneticist…"Dog Genome Project."

43. If the observation that breeding matters…Scott and Fuller, *Genetics and the Social Behavior.*

44. Stephen Budiansky suggests that…Budianksy, *The Truth About Dogs.*

45. Juliet Clutton-Block presents…Juliet Clutton-Brock, "Origins of the Dog."

46. For example, Bruce Fogle notes…Bruce Fogle, *The Dog's Mind: Understanding Your Dog's Behavior* (New York: Howell Book House, 1990).

47. As Dr. Vicki Adams…Dr. Vicki Adams, quoted in Jonathan Amos, "Pedigree Dog Health to be Probed," *BBC News/Science/Nature*, http://news.bbc.co.uk/1/low/sci/tech/3413581.stm.

48. The "Current Eye Disease Overview"…Kirk Gelatt, "Current Eye Disease Overview," *AKC Canine Health Conference, 1999*, www.spinone.com/AKC_CHF99/26EyeDisease.htm.

49. Jane Brackman writes…Jane Brackman, "Working Hard to Hardly Working," *AKC Gazette* (December 2003).

50. Dr. Irene Stur, of the University of Vienna Animals Genetic Institute…Irene Stur, "Genetic Aspects of Temperament and Behaviour in Dogs," *Journal of Small Animal Practice* (1987).

51. As long ago as 1944…F. C. Thorne, "The Inheritance of Shyness in Dogs," *Journal of Genetical Psychology* 65 (1944): 275–279.

52. DNA studies of the famous Isle Royale wolf pack…Christopher Eckert, "Inbreeding Depression and the Evolutionary Advantage of Outbreeding," in *Proceedings of the 15th Annual Workshop/Conference of the Association for Biology Laboratory Education* (ABLE), ed. Corey Goldman (Association for Biology Laboratory Education, Incorporated, 1993), 215–238.

53. Peter Steinhart has declared…Steinhart, *The Company of Wolves.*

54. Scott and Fuller write…Scott and Fuller *Genetics and the Social Behavior.*

55. Plant and animal breeders…Eckert, "Inbreeding Depression."

56. Interestingly, Coppinger found that…Coppinger and Schneider, "Evolution of Working Dogs."

57. Biologist Christopher Eckert explains it this way…Eckert, "Inbreeding Depression."

58. Dr. John Armstrong, a geneticist…John Armstrong, e-mail to *The Canine Genetics List*, available at www.filadog.com/inbreedingdepression.htm.

59. And Dr. Hellmuth Wachtel…Hellmuth Wachtel, "Breeding Dogs for the Next Millennium (1997)," *Lhasa-Apso Organization*, www.lhasa-apso.org/health/hellmuth.htm.

60. Dr. Armstrong observed in "Longevity in the Standard Poodle"…John Armstrong, "Longevity in the Standard Poodle (2000)," *The Canine Diversity Project*, www.canine-genetics.com/lifespan.html.

61. Over a quarter of a century ago…Scott and Fuller, *Genetics and the Social Behavior*.

62. And as Raymond Coppinger and Richard Schneider point out…Coppinger and Schneider, "Evolution of Working Dogs."

63. In the early 1960s, Scott and Fuller…Scott and Fuller, *Genetics and the Social Behavior*.

64. In fact, a study by J. Green and R. Woodruff…J. Green and R. Woodruff, "Is Predator Control Going to the Dogs?" *Rangelands* 2 (1980): 187–189.

65. Raymond Coppinger and Richard Schneider tried very hard…Raymond Coppinger and Richard Schneider, "Evolution of Working Dogs."

66. Scott and Fuller found that…Scott and Fuller, *Genetics and the Social Behavior*.

67. Van Hooff and Wensing termed…J. van Hooff and J. Wensing, "Dominance and its Behavioral Measures in a Captive Wolf Pack," in *Man and Wolf: Advances, Issues, and Problems in Captive Wolf Research*, ed. Harry Frank (Boston: Kluwer Academic Publishers, 1987), 219–252.

68. We know we're playing…Nicola J. Rooney and John W.S. Bradshaw, "Effects of Playing Tug of War with Golden Retrievers," *Applied Animal Behaviour Science* 75 (2002): 161–177.

69. Researcher Patricia Simonet demonstrated…Patricia Simonet, Molly Murphy, and Amy Lance, "Laughing Dog: Vocalizations of Domestic Dogs during Play Encounters" (paper presented at the Animal Behavior Society Conference, Corvallis, Oregon, July 2001).

70. Scott and Fuller discovered that…Scott and Fuller, *Genetics and the Social Behavior*.

71. Some national parks in Canada...The International Wolf Center, www.wolf.org/wolves/index.asp.

72. Well-known wolf-researchers...Mary and John Theberge, "Wolf Music," *Natural History* 80 (4): 36–54; John Theberge and J.B. Falls, "Howling as a Means of Communication in Timber Wolves," *American Zoologist* 7 (1967): 331–338.

73. The Theberges even postulate...ibid.

74. A study conducted by Dr. Karen Overall...Mark Derr, "Dogs' Vocalizations Aren't All Bark," *New York Times News Service* (21 April 2001).

75. Those-who-remain-wolves just never learned...Brian Hare, M. Brown, C. Williamson, M. Tomasello, "The Domestication of Social Cognition in Dogs," *Science* 298 (22 November 2002): 1540–1542.

76. In fact, researchers such as Patricia McConnell...quoted in Marsha Walton, "15,000 Years with Man's Best Friend," *CNN.com Science and Space* (22 November 2002), www.cnn.com/2002/TECH/sci-ence/11/21/coolsc.dogorigin/.

77. Roger Abrantes astutely...Roger Abrantes, *Dog Language: An Encyclopedia of Canine Behavior* (Naperville, Illinois: Wakan Tanka Publishers, 1996).

78. A better term than "dominance aggression"...James O'Heare, *The Canine Aggression Workbook* (Ontario: Gentle Solutions. 2001).

79. Scott and Fuller found again and again...Scott and Fuller, *Genetics and the Social Behavior.*

80. According to the *Journal of the American Medical Association*...Harold B. Weiss, Deborah I. Friedman, and Jeffrey H. Coben, "Incidence of Dog Bite Injuries Treated in Emergency Departments," *Journal of the American Medical Association* 279 (Jan. 1998): 51–53.

81. Karen Delise, in *Fatal Dog Attacks*...Karen Delise, *Fatal Dog Attacks: The Stories Behind the Statistics* (Manorville, New York: Anubis Press, 2002).

82. For example, meaty bones rank pretty high...Scott and Fuller, *Genetics and the Social Behavior.*

83. Scott and Fuller have shown that...ibid.

84. Unfortunately, as James O'Heare notes...O'Heare, *The Canine Aggression Workbook.*

85. Scott and Fuller studied aggressive behavior...Scott and Fuller, *Genetics and the Social Behavior.*

86. According to L. David Mech, this behavior...Mech, *The Way of the Wolf.*

87. David Mech reports that 2 wolves he raised...Mech, *The Wolf.*

88. L. David Mech observed an adult female…Mech, *The Way of the Wolf.*

89. Robert Hubrecht of the University of Cambridge for the Universities Federation for Animal Welfare…Robert Hubrecht, "Comfortable Quarters for Dogs in Research Institutions," in *Comfortable Quarters for Laboratory Animals,* ed. Viktor and Annie Reinhardt (Washington, D.C.: Animal Welfare Institute, 2002), 56–64.

90. Patronek, G. J., L. T. Glickman, A. M. Beck, G. P. McCabe, and C. Ecker, "Risk Factors for Relinquishment of Dogs to an Animal Shelter," *Journal of the American Veterinary Medical Association* 209, no. 3 (August 1996): 572–581.

91. Karen Delise reports that in the 37-year period…Delise, *Fatal Dog Attacks.*

92. L. David Mech reports one Alaskan…Mech, *The Wolf.*

93. Neutering a male dog…Helene Rugbjerg, Helle Friis Proschowsky, Annette Kjær Ersbøll, and Jørgen Damkjær Lund, "Risk Factors Associated with Interdog Aggression and Shooting Phobias among Purebred Dogs in Denmark," *Preventive Veterinary Medicine* 58 (April 2003): 85–100.

94. In their classic study on canine behavior…Scott and Fuller, *Genetics and the Social Behavior.*

95. Researcher Erik Zimen tried hard to train…Erik Zimen, *The Wolf, a Species in Danger* (New York: Delacorte Press, 1981).

96. Officially, the USDA decided…"Wolf and Wolf-Dog Crosses Not Eligible to be Added to Dog Vaccine Labels," *Journal of the American Veterinary Medical Association News* (1 June 2001), www.avma.org/onlnews/javma/jun01/s060101pp.asp.

97. One former breeder of these animals…Terry Jenkins, "How High the Price?" *Humane Society of the United States News* (Winter 1991): 18, 21.

98. Steven M. Wise, in his exciting book…Steven Wise, *Drawing the Line: Science and the Case for Animal Rights* (Cambridge, MA: Perseus Books, 2002).

Bibliography

Abrantes, Roger. *Dog Language: An Encyclopedia of Canine Behavior.* Naperville, Illinois: Wakan Tanka Publishers, 1996.

Adams, Vicky. Quoted in Jonathan Amos, "Pedigree Dog Health to be Probed." *BBC News/Science/Nature.* http://news.bbc.co.uk/1/low/sci/tech/3413581.stm.

Altman, J. A., and I. V. Kalmykova. "Role of the Dog's Auditory Cortex in Discrimination of Sound Signals Simulating Sound Source Movement." *Hearing Research* 24, no. 3 (1986): 245–253.

Armstrong, John. E-mail to *The Canine Genetics List.* www.filadog.com/inbreedingdepression.htm.

———. "Longevity in the Standard Poodle (2000)." *The Canine Diversity Project.* www.canine-genetics.com/lifespan.html.

Brackman, Jane. "Working Hard to Hardly Working." *AKC Gazette* (December 2003).

Budiansky, Stephen. *The Truth About Dogs.* New York: Viking, 2000.

Clutton-Brock, Juliet. "Origins of the Dog: Domestication and Early History." In *The Domestic Dog: Its Evolution, Behavior and Interactions with People.* Edited by James Serpell. Cambridge: Cambridge University Press. 1995.

Clutton-Brock, Juliet, G. B. Corbet, and M. Hills. "A Review of the Family *Canidae*, with a Classification by Numerical Methods." *Bulletin of the British Museum (Natural History) Zoology* 29 (1976): 117–199.

Coppinger, Raymond, and Lorna Coppinger. *Dogs.* New York: Scribner, 2001.

Coppinger, Raymond, and Richard Schneider. "Evolution of Working Dogs." In *The Domestic Dog: Its Evolution, Behavior and Interactions with People.* Edited by James Serpell. Cambridge: Cambridge University Press, 1995.

Delise, Karen. *Fatal Dog Attacks: The Stories Behind the Statistics.* Manorville, New York: Anubis Press. 2002.

Derr, Mark. "Dogs' Vocalizations Aren't All Bark." *New York Times News Service,* 21 April 2001.

Diamond, Jared. *Guns, Germs, and Steel: The Fate of Human Societies.* New York: Random House, 1997.

Eckert, Christopher G. "Inbreeding Depression and the Evolutionary Advantage of Outbreeding." In *Proceedings of the 15th Annual Workshop/Conference of the Association for Biology Laboratory Education* (ABLE). Edited by C. A. Goldman. Association for Biology Laboratory Education, Incorporated, 1993.

"Evolution of the Dog." *The Dog.* www.lookd.com/dogs/evelution.html.

Fogle, Bruce. The Dog's Mind: Understanding Your Dog's Behavior. New York: Howell Book House, 1990.

Gelatt, Kirk. "Current Eye Disease Overview." *AKC Canine Health Conference, 1999,* www.spinone.com/AKC_CHF99/26EyeDisease.htm...

Ginsberg , J. R., and D. W. Macdonald. Foxes, Wolves, Jackals, and Dogs: An Action Plan for the Conservation of Canids. Gland, Switzerland: IUCN, 1990.

Green, J., and R. Woodruff. "Is Predator Control Going to the Dogs?" *Rangelands* 2 (1980): 187–189.

Haase, E. "Comparison of Reproductive Parameters in Male Wolves and Domestic Dogs." *Z. Säugetierkunde* 65 (2000): 257–270.

Hare, Brian, M. Brown, C. Williamson, and M. Tomasello. "The Domestication of Social Cognition in Dogs." *Science* 298 (22 November 2002): 1540–1542

Harper, Liz. "Subspecies of the Wolf." *Scientific Classification of Wolves.* International Wolf Center. www.wolf.org/wolves/learn/intermed/inter_sci/wolf_subspecies.asp.

Hemmer, Helmut. *Domestication: the Decline of Environmental Appreciation.* Cambridge: Cambridge University Press, 1990.

Houpt, Katherine, P. Shepherd, and H. F. Hintz. "Two Methods for Producing Peripheral Anosmia in Dogs." *Laboratory Animal Science* 28, no. 2 (1978): 173–177.

Hubrecht, Robert. "Comfortable Quarters for Dogs in Research Institutions." In *Comfortable Quarters for Laboratory Animals.* Edited by Viktor and Annie Reinhardt. Washington, D.C.: Animal Welfare Institute, 2002.

International Wolf Center. "Timeline: The Red Wolf in the Southeastern United States." *Wolf Basics,* www.wolf.org/wolves/learn/basic/history/red_timeline.asp.

Jenkins, Terry. "How High the Price?" *Humane Society of the United States News* (Winter 1991): 18, 21.

Journal of the American Veterinary Medical Association News. "Wolf and Wolf-Dog Crosses Not Eligible to be Added to Dog Vaccine Labels." 1 June 2001. www.avma.org/onlnews/javma/jun01/s060101pp.asp.

Leonard, Jennifer, et al. "Ancient DNA Evidence for Old World Origin of New World Dogs." *Science* 298 (22 November 2002).

Lorenz, Konrad. *Man Meets Dog.* Houghton Mifflin Company: Boston, 1954.

Mech, L. David. *The Way of the Wolf.* Stillwater, MD: Voyageur Press. 1991.

———. *The Wolf: The Ecology and Behavior of an Endangered Species.* Minneapolis: University of Minnesota Press, 1970.

National Park Service. "Wolves in Denali Park and Preserve." *U.S. Department of the Interior.* www.nps.gov/akso/ParkWise/Students/ReferenceLibrary/DENA/WolvesInDenali.htm.

O'Heare, James. *The Canine Aggression Workbook.* Ontario: Gentle Solutions. 2001.

Patronek, G. J., L. T. Glickman, A. M. Beck, G. P. McCabe, and C. Ecker. "Risk Factors for Relinquishment of Dogs to an Animal Shelter." *Journal of the American Veterinary Medical Association* 209, no. 3 (August 1996): 572–581.

Pinker, Steven. *The Blank Slate: The Modern Denial of Human Nature.* New York: Viking, 2002.

Rine, Jasper. "Dog Genome Project." University of California, Berkeley. http://mendel.berkeley.edu/dog.html.

Rooney, Nicola J., and John W. S. Bradshaw. "Effects of Playing Tug of War with Golden Retrievers." *Applied Animal Behaviour Science* 75 (2002): 161–177.

Rugbjerg, Helene, Helle Friis Proschowsky, Annette Kjær Ersbøll, and Jørgen Damkjær Lund. "Risk Factors Associated with Interdog Aggression and Shooting Phobias among Purebred Dogs in Denmark." *Preventive Veterinary Medicine* 58 (April 2003): 85–100.

Scott, John Paul, and John L. Fuller. *Genetics and the Social Behavior of the Dog: The Classic Study.* Chicago: University of Chicago Press, 1965.

Serpell, James, ed. *The Domestic Dog: Its Evolution, Behaviour, and Interactions with People.* Cambridge: Cambridge University Press. 1995.

Seward, Desmond. *The Hundred Years War: The English in France, 1337–1453.* London: Constable, 1978.

Simonet, Patricia, Molly Murphy, and Amy Lance, "Laughing Dog: Vocalizations of Domestic Dogs during Play Encounters." Paper presented at the Animal Behavior Society Conference, Corvallis, Oregon, July 2001.

Steinhart, Peter. *The Company of Wolves.* New York: Random House, 1995.

Stur, Irene. "Genetic Aspects of Temperament and Behaviour in Dogs." *Journal of Small Animal Practice* (1987).

Theberge, John and Mary. "Wolf Music." *Natural History* 80 (4): 36–54.

Theberge, John, and J.B. Falls. "Howling as a Means of Communication in Timber Wolves." *American Zoologist* 7 (1967): 331–338.

Thorne, F. C. "The Inheritance of Shyness in Dogs." *Journal of Genetical Psychology* 65 (1944): 275–279.

Trut, Lyudmilia. "Early Canid Domestication: The Farm-Fox Experiment." *American Scientist* 87, no. 2 (1999): 160–169.

van Hooff, J., and J. Wensing. "Dominance and its Behavioral Measures in a Captive Wolf Pack." In *Man and Wolf: Advances, Issues, and Problems in Captive Wolf Research*. Edited by Harry Frank. Boston: Kluwer Academic Publishers, 1987.

Vilà, C., P. Savolainen, J. E. Maldonado, I. R. Amorim, J. E. Rice, R. L. Honeycutt, K. A. Crandal, J. Lundeberg, and R. K. Wayne. "Multiple and Ancient Origin of the Domestic Dog." *Science* 276 (1997): 1687–1689.

Wachtel, Hellmuth. "Breeding Dogs for the Next Millennium (1997)." *Lhasa-Apso Organization*. www.lhasa-apso.org/health/hellmuth.htm.

Walton, Marsha. "15,000 Years with Man's Best Friend." *CNN.com Science and Space*, 22 November 2002. www.cnn.com/2002/TECH/science/11/21/coolsc.dogorigin/.

Wayne, Robert, and S. M. Jenks. "Mitochondrial DNA Analysis Implying Extensive Hybridization of the Endangered Red Wolf *Canis rufus.*" *Nature* 351 (1991): 565–568.

Weiss, Harold B., Deborah I. Friedman, and Jeffrey H. Coben. "Incidence of Dog Bite Injuries Treated in Emergency Departments." *Journal of the American Medical Association* 279 (Jan. 1998): 51–53.

Wise, Steven. *Drawing the Line: Science and the Case for Animal Rights*. Cambridge, MA: Perseus Books, 2002.

Zeuner, Frederick. *A History of Domesticated Animals*. New York, Harper & Row, 1963.

Zimen, Erik. *The Wolf, a Species in Danger*. New York: Delacorte Press, 1981.

Further Reading

Bekoff, Marc. *Minding Animals.* New York: Oxford University Press, 2002.

Bekoff, Marc, ed. *The Smile of a Dolphin: Remarkable Accounts of Animal Emotions.* New York: Random House/Discovery Book, 2000.

Bradshaw, John W.S. and Helen M.R. "Social and Communication Behaviour of Companion Dogs." In *The Domestic Dog: Its Evolution, Behavior and Interactions with People.* Edited by James Serpell. Cambridge: Cambridge University Press. 1995.

Campbell, William E. *Behavior Problems in Dogs.* Third revised editon. Grants Pass, OR: Behavior Rx Systems, 1999.

Case, Linda P. *The Dog: Its Behavior, Nutrition and Health.* Ames, Iowa: Iowa State University Press, 1999.

Diamond, Jared. "Evolution, Consequences and Future of Plant and Animal Domestication." *Nature* 418 (8 August 2002).

Donaldson, Jean. *The Culture Clash.* Berkeley: James and Kenneth, 1996.

Fisher, John. *Think Dog! An Owner's Guide to Canine Psychology.* North Pomfret, VT: Trafalgar Square Publishing, 1991.

Hoffman, Matthew, Ed. *Dogspeak: How to Understand Your Dog and Help him Understand You.* Emmaus, PA: Rodale Press, Inc., 1999.

Lachman, Larry and Frank Mickadeit. *Dogs on the Couch: Behavior Therapy and Caring for Your Dog.* Woodstock, New York: Overlook Press. 1999.

Lopez, Barry Holstun. *Of Wolves and Men.* New York: Simon and Schuster, 1978.

McConnell, Patricia. *The Other End of the Leash.* New York: Ballantine Books, 1993.

Milani, Myrna. *The Body Language and Emotion of Dogs.* New York: William Morrow, 1986.

Pennisi, Elizabeth. "A Shaggy Dog History." *Science* 298 (22 November 2002).

Peters, Roger. *Dance of the Wolves: An Engaging Close Up Look at Wolves in the Wild.* New York: Ballantine Books, 1985.

Price, Edward O. *Animal Domestication and Behavior.* New York: CABI Publishing, 2003.

Weston, David and Ruth Ross. *Dog Problems: The Gentle Modern Cure.* New York: Howell Book House, 1992.

Willis, M.B. "Genetic Aspects of Dog Behaviour with Particular Reference to Working Ability." In *The Domestic Dog: Its Evolution, Behavior and Interactions with People.* Edited by James Serpell. Cambridge: Cambridge University Press. 1995.

Index